THE EROS OF PARENTHOOD

The

Eros

of

Parenthood

Explorations in Light and Dark

NOELLE OXENHANDLER

ST. MARTIN'S PRESS ⚏ NEW YORK

FOR ARIEL

. . . and in memory of Nancy

www.stmartins.com

"The Eros of Parenthood" first appeared as an essay in *The New Yorker*. That essay
has now been incorporated into this book's Introduction. "Buying Ladybugs"
originally appeared in *The New York Times Magazine*; "My Daughter's Dance" in
Family Life. "Noli Me Tangere: The Family Photographs of Sally Mann" has been
slightly altered since it first appeared in the on-line magazine *Nerve*.

Library of Congress Cataloging-in-Publication Data

Oxenhandler, Noelle.
    The eros of parenthood : explorations in light and dark / Noelle
Oxenhandler.
        p.   cm.
    ISBN 0-312-26976-5
    1. Parent and child.   2. Love, Maternal.   3. Love, Paternal.   I. Title.

HQ755.85.O94 2001
306.874—dc21   00-045763

First Edition: February 2001

10   9   8   7   6   5   4   3   2   1

Copyright Acknowledgments

CONTENTS

Acknowledgments   *ix*

A Note to Readers   *xi*

INTRODUCTION: *The Eros of Parenthood*   *1*

I. SOMEONE IN SKIN: *The Way We Love*   13

   1. Attunement   17
   2. Not One, Not Two   24
   3. Only You   34
   4. The Flesh Is Willing   45
   5. Cute   50
   6. Night Love   54
   7. Sleeping Babies   59

II. A NEST OF DREAMS: *Love and Imagination*   61

   1. Dreaming of Babies   64
   2. Thomas and Ann   69
   3. Worry   77
   4. The Son I Don't Have   82
   5. Ghosts   88
   6. The Flesh Is Sad   91

III. SCISSORS AND BUDS: *Separation and New Life*   99

   1. Strings   102
   2. Infidelities   108

3. Disgust   118

4. Seasons   124

5. Tempo   128

6. Buying Ladybugs   133

7. Last Things   137

IV. THE TEARS OF EROS: *Love's Dark Shadows*   145

1. The Bath   149

2. I Looked in Her Eyes   159

3. Play   167

4. Memories   175

5. Changelings   182

6. Who's at the Door?   189

7. *Noli Me Tangere:*
   The Family Photographs of Sally Mann   195

V. GOLDILOCKS'S JOY: *Finding the "Just Right"*   201

1. The Forbidden   205

2. Edges   210

3. Innocence   216

4. Peaks   225

5. Hot and Cold   228

6. Fathers and Daughters   240

7. My Daughter's Dance   247

VI. CONCLUSION: *Beneficent Boundary Loss*   251

1. Zones   254

2. Rapprochement   256

3. Ashes   261

4. Tending the Small   275

5. Dilation   284

6. Boundary Loss   289

7. Time Overflowing   293

8. The Hardest Thing   301

Notes   305

Bibliography   319

About the Author   322

ACKNOWLEDGMENTS

TO WRITE A book is to experience the reality of interdependence.

I am grateful to Lawrence Weschler: my longtime writing angel.

Laura Yorke, the book's first editor, brought her rare combination of human warmth and critical acumen to the task. Through her own qualities of warmth and meticulous attention, Lara Asher, the book's second editor, made a seamless transition. Kim Witherspoon, my agent, proved a guide to trust through all the unexpected twists of the journey.

While writing this book I had occasion to experience the life-sustaining value of true friendship. I am grateful beyond anything I can ever express or hope to repay to: Deborah Clarke Blome, Margaret Lee Braun, Dana Davies, Jane Kingston, Lynn Martin, and Deborah Young. I am grateful, too, for the wise and compassionate counsel of Carol H. McIntyre and Jack Kornfield.

Barbara Baer and Robin Beeman were the two who read, page by page, from start to finish: their encouragement and their criticism were an indispensable part of the process. Sarah Outten Brown, Alev Lytle Croutier, Virginia Hubbell, Fran Lerner, Jane Praeger, and Sarah Stone have lent the bright and steady glow of their support and companionship. Barbara Nuss opened her heart and her home to my daughter when I had to be away.

Thanks to Sonia Beck, Joseph Bobrow, Jane Kingston, and Jonathan Slavin, who, as practicing psychotherapists, were particularly discerning readers. Christina Barasch, Michael Basta, Mary Biggs,

Peter Levitt, Kathleen Murphy, and Stephanie Osier also contributed many valuable insights. Thanks to my mother, Jean Romano, for her tender translations from the Italian.

Thanks to all of the people who shared their stories with me, many of which were "hard to say."

Last—but this last is really first: without my family, how could I ever have written about family love? This includes Eliot Fintushel, the best father I could ever have dreamed of for my daughter, and her beloved grandmother, Rose.

A NOTE TO READERS

EACH OF THE following chapters consists of a collection of "explorations" that are thematically linked. These shorter pieces build on one another: certain premises in the early pieces lay the foundation for what follows, and much of what comes later refers back to the beginning. Yet they are also designed to stand alone, and to that end, there is occasionally some repetition or overlapping of material. My working metaphor has been a musical one: each piece may be thought of as its own melody, to be played by an unaccompanied piano or cello, or by a solo flute. Yet the whole has been composed so that the effect—both within each chapter and from chapter to chapter—could grow gradually deeper and more resonant.

In talking about the eros of parenthood, one is talking about origins, about patterns of interaction that lie at the very root of human behavior. For this reason, I have felt more drawn than ever as a writer to unravel the secrets that lie coiled in the origins of words. Even the most abstract words tend to have their roots in the earth, in the flesh, and so it makes sense, from time to time, to allow the ancient roots of a word to shed light on the most primal of all human bonds.

Because this book had a long incubation, some of the children I have written about appear on different pages at different ages.

As for gender: in referring to infants and children, I alternate between "he" and "she." Although fathers have a strong presence in this book, there are more references to mothers, and this is for two reasons: I draw from my own experience as a mother and as a close friend to more mothers than to fathers, and mothers still tend to be (or are assumed to be) the primary caretakers in our culture. Though this last is a very significant fact, it is nonetheless true that much of what I say about "the mother" could be applied to whoever is the principal care-giver in a child's life.

The names and certain identifying characteristics of some people who shared their stories with me have been changed.

IT'S NOT GOD I WANT, IT'S SOMEONE IN SKIN!

—*Child overheard in conversation with his mother*

INTRODUCTION

The Eros of Parenthood

WE CALL HIM "Folds," a friend once wrote, in a rapture over the voluptuous plumpness of his baby son. My own daughter was delicate—even a bit worrisomely so—but what I wrote again and again in her baby book was "She is too much." When I read those words now, I remember how palpably I experienced her too-muchness: it was a kind of shudder in my body, an energy I had to soften, rein in, lest I squeeze her too hard, startle her with too exuberant a kiss.

We call our children "honey" and "dumpling" and "pumpkin" and "sweetie pie." We tell them, "Oh, I could eat you!" And what this exclamation gives voice to is both the experience of being overwhelmed by their irresistibleness and the knowledge that we must resist, that we must respect their separateness from ourselves—a separateness made all the more poignant by their complete dependence.

This feeling lies at the heart of what I want to call *the eros of parenthood*. It is a feeling that operates like gravity or magnetism, drawing us near. In its intense physicality, it partakes of the essence of love between lovers—but it is different in some absolutely crucial ways. For healthy parental love is a sheltering, protective love. It is one that respects the radical inequality—in size, power, and maturity—between parent and child. Though it sometimes flares into wild playfulness, its

---

A note to the reader: Etymologies have been taken from *The American Heritage Dictionary*, Third Edition, Boston and New York: Houghton Mifflin Co., 1996.

predominant rhythm is serene and relaxed—quite different from the climactic movement of adult sexuality.

We know that this love is natural[1]—indeed, not only natural, but necessary.[2] Taking care of small children is hard work, exhausting and unceasing labor. Thus the physical appeal of the young is one of the keys to their survival, and not just because it quickens parental energy. Loving touch, in and of itself, is necessary to the development of the healthy human child. Fifty years have passed since it was discovered that orphaned and abandoned infants would fail to thrive, even if they were kept clean and safe and well fed, when they were not held and caressed. In hospital intensive-care nurseries, it is not unusual to come across signs that read "Please Touch Me!" attached to the clear-plastic boxes where premature infants lie. (These babies, their sticklike limbs surrounded by a welter of tubes and wires, don't easily elicit the desire to touch and hold.) The social biologist Ashley Montagu has written, "By being stroked and caressed, and carried, and cuddled, and cooed to, by being loved, [the child] learns to stroke and caress and cuddle, and coo and to love others. In this sense, love is sexual in the healthiest sense of that word. It implies involvement, concern, responsibility, tenderness, and awareness of the needs and vulnerabilities of the other."[3]

Yet as I write of these things, I am aware of a strange unease that makes me feel I musn't stray too far from words like "necessary" and "survival." It's as if a stern and frowning face were hovering over my shoulder. I feel this hint of censure when my daughter climbs into my bed in the morning to wake me, wrapping her muscley little arms around me. I feel it as I stand, at her command, outside the glass shower door and wait for the pink blur of her silhouette to turn into her perfect, dripping body. This unease makes it difficult to speak of the sheer pleasure that parents and children take in each other's bodies. It is difficult to admit, for example, that one finds the warm odor of one's sleeping child delicious.

Even to put the two words together, *eros* and *parenthood*, is to take a step into forbidden territory. "Can't you find another word?" more than one person has asked me, suggesting instead "affection," "tenderness," even "intimacy." But Eros, the god of love in Greek mythology, *is* the god who presides here. His mother is Aphrodite, the goddess of love and beauty. His father is Hermes, the messenger god, the god of interconnection, who—being playful and quite unreliable—likes to mix people up, even as he keeps them in touch with one another.

Eros exists as a force of attraction, bringing people together and enticing them, through the pleasure of mingling, to step out of their separate skins. Like his mother, he is quite irresistibly beautiful. Like his father, he is playful, a trickster in his own right, and he can be dangerous. As the Roman Cupid, he carries a quiver of arrows and pierces unsuspecting men and women with desire. Once pierced, they are altered. Prone to impulsive, unpredictable behavior, they are apt to change directions suddenly, to forsake old ties. Forgetting what is appropriate, what belongs to whom, an old man begins to act like a young person, another man covets his neighbor's wife, an ugly dwarf thinks that even the most beautiful maiden must have him, a god takes on the shape of a bird or a bull and makes love to a mortal girl. Indeed, in the most ancient myths, Eros is not Aphrodite's child, but rather, one of the primordial gods who springs directly from Chaos. Even in his late incarnation as Cupid, he is often pictured as blind, or blindfolded—not someone to be trusted with a quiver of arrows. Is it any wonder, then, that we shrink at the thought of Eros in the nursery?

And yet, he belongs. He belongs, first of all, for purely chemical reasons. Oxytocin, sometimes called "the cuddle chemical" or "the hormone of attachment," is linked to many forms of human love. It encourages the contractions of childbirth, the mother's let-down of milk, and her desire to draw close to her child in breast-feeding. As Diane Ackerman writes in *A Natural History of Love*: "Mothers have told me that during their baby's first year or so, they were surprised to find themselves 'in love' with it, 'turned on' by it, involved with it in 'the best romance ever.' Because the same hormone controls a woman's pleasure during orgasm, childbirth, cuddling, and nursing her baby, it makes perfect sense that she should feel this way. The brain may have an excess of gray matter, but in some things, it's economical. It likes to reuse convenient pathways and chemicals for many purposes. Why plow fresh paths through the snow of existence when old paths already lead part of the way there?"[4] For men, too, oxytocin is associated both with sexual pleasure and—though less dramatically than for women—in interaction with their babies.

The language of Eros is the language of touch, and we learn this language as infants, in the arms of those who first care for us. As we grow into adult sexuality, we alter this language, extending its range and our own fluency. But its deep structure, the grammar of how we experience touch, is absorbed in the context of our earliest relationships.

Between parent and small child, as between adult lovers, the primary medium of communication is the body, with its unique lexicon, its basic ABC's of:

TEXTURE: *rough/smooth*
LOCATION: *in/out, here/not there*
PRESSURE: *hard/soft*
RHYTHM: *quick/slow*
TEMPERATURE *warm/cool, wet/dry. . . .*

Making use of this basic alphabet, erotic love between adult lovers revolves around certain polarities: fusion and separateness, safety and danger, excitement and repose. . . . Each of these is a polarity that, even in its simplest physical expression, is charged with emotion. And each of these is present already in the physical relationship between parent and child. A mother cradles her baby against her body, she puts his mouth to her breast. She pulls his mouth from her breast, wipes his wet lips, holds him out for a moment at arm's length before nestling him against her shoulder. This is fusion and separateness. She tickles him under his chin and under his arms until his whole body wriggles with sensation; then she stops tickling and strokes his chin with firm, predictable, circular strokes until his body goes soft again. This is excitement and repose.

Who could deny that adult sexual love evokes the earliest feelings of childhood? Lying naked on a bed, spread out before the eyes of an admiring lover, one is not so far away from the naked baby, lying on his changing table, under his mother's gaze. The sense of exposure, surrender in nakedness, one's whole body held close against another's skin, the playfulness, the secret language, the giggles, the tickles, the litany of "favorite places"—*I love the curve between your waist and hip,* a lover says . . . *It's so soft under your chin,* a parent says—so much belongs to both worlds. If we've become afraid to admit this in our rational discourse, we still know it when we sing: "Oh baby, baby . . ." "Hold me tight . . ." "Rock me, mama . . ." "Don't ever let me go . . ." Even when we say, speaking of two adult lovers, "She dropped him," the phrase connotes a small bundle that she once held in her arms.

Isn't this the lion's share of the immense vulnerability that opens up in us when we open to another through the medium of the body? We become as little children when we enter the gates of this particular heaven—and this, in turn, is the lion's share of why this particular heaven can so easily turn to hell. For better and worse, our adult love relationships constellate our most primal feelings: of trust; blissful surrender; fear of surrender, abandonment, loss. . . .

But why, beyond a certain point, do we experience such profound unease at the comparison of these two forms of love? Where does it come from, that sense of a frowning gaze bearing down?

This unease does not come out of the blue. It is not a hallucination or a psychic projection. I have only to pick up the newspaper to realize just how suddenly this haunting presence can materialize into brute reality. There are so many stories. There are the parents arrested and separated from their families for having taken photographs of their naked children—even when these photographs, in their reverential and sometimes playful celebration of their children's bodies, were as far away from the realm of pornography as are the many paintings of naked children that hang enshrined in the world's great museums. Along with the true accusations of child abuse, there are the devastating false accusations. Among the most searing stories of recent years is that of a young mother outside Syracuse whose two-year-old daughter was taken away from her after she naively confided to an uninformed stranger that she had become aroused while breast-feeding. She had called a community volunteer center to find out how to contact the local chapter of the La Leche League support group. Anyone at La Leche could have assured her that such feelings were utterly normal. Instead, the community volunteer center referred her to a rape crisis center, which in turn reported her to a child-abuse hotline. She was arrested and subjected to a five-hour police interrogation, and was separated from her daughter for an entire year.[5]

It is understandable that after decades of secrecy and denial concerning the sexual abuse of children, there should now be an almost belligerent attitude of caution. As we have, at long last, acknowledged the reality of sexual abuse, it's as though our thick public hide has been replaced with a new skin. And while there is virtually nothing to be said in praise of the thick hide of the past, the new skin presents certain liabilities of its own. For having been formed in reaction to the often brutal disregard of the past, it is an extraordinarily sensitive skin—a skin that shudders at the mere suggestion of inappropriate contact between adults and children. Keeping ourselves vigilant, bristling with suspicion, it sometimes seems that we are trying to do a form of penance for our past failures by obsessively searching for hints of trouble.

And it is possible that this thin, twitchy skin makes us insensitive in other ways. It is possible that in our zeal to atone and to protect, we do another kind of damage—less spectacular, but not insignificant. For what does it mean when the atmosphere becomes so thoroughly saturated with anxiety that it begins to intrude on the most intimate and loving moments between parent and child? A nurse-midwife I know reports that almost every day she hears from mothers and fathers who feel troubled, ashamed, or fearful about the physical closeness between themselves and their children. One woman whose son had not been weaned until well after he became a toddler worried that something was terribly wrong with their relationship when, the night before he was to begin kindergarten, he expressed a longing to nurse again. And recently a friend of mine exclaimed with exasperation, "I can't even take pleasure in rubbing lotion on my baby's sweet bottom without feeling that the vice squad is going to break down my door!" Surely, when parents begin to feel this way, we are in danger of throwing out the baby with the bathwater.

And was a metaphor ever so apt? For, if we are honest, we can acknowledge that in the pleasure of giving a baby a bath—in the slippery softness of warm, soapy skin, the exchange of glances, the coos, the giggles—we find ourselves at one end of a continuum of human sensation and emotion that reaches to the place inhabited by adult lovers.

One has only to look at the great painters who have taken mother-child love as their theme to see the visual celebration of this continuum. In the paintings of Raphael, of Rubens, of Mary Cassatt, one sees a mutual absorption, a complete relaxation, an absence of self-consciousness, a melding of one body with the other. All these are qualities that one might find in a scene of lovers, lying in a tangle of limbs, resting in the peaceful lassitude that follows lovemaking. Indeed, as Freud wrote: "No one who has seen a baby sinking back satiated from the breast and falling asleep with flushed cheeks and a blissful smile can escape the reflection that this picture persists as a prototype of the expression of sexual satisfaction in later life."[6]

But such comparisons have again become as shocking as they were when Freud first made them. To feel the erotically charged nature of the parent-child relationship—the thousand small intimacies that weave parent and child together—is to feel that one is breaking a taboo. Some nights ago, my daughter reminded me, as she often does, of our secret sign. In case anyone were ever to try to substitute a double in her place, I must look for the freckle that lies between the third and fourth fingers of her left hand. She shows me every little changing and unchanging mark on her body and expects me to keep track—as a lover might.

And there I feel the gaze again—the gaze that cannot see that two things can share similarities without being identical. For this rigid mentality must have its boundaries in black and white; it cannot tolerate gradations or continuums. At the heart of it lies a sense of great moral fragility. Precisely because the soul is so likely to plummet to the abyss, it must be carefully protected by walls of prohibition.

Yet, as we will see in subsequent chapters, a climate of extremes is not the one that best protects our children. When we delve more deeply below the surface, it is hard to escape the conclusion that when the repertoire of touch is severely limited—so that touch is construed as always and only sexual—children are actually at greater risk of being touched in sexually explicit ways.

Recently a father told me, "My daughter is eleven, and I coach her soccer team. I'm an affectionate person, and I often have the impulse to reach out and tousle a child's hair or put my arm around her shoulder and encourage her. But I don't anymore." As he spoke, I thought of the other stories I've been hearing: about communities where child-care workers aren't allowed to hold children on their laps, and where crossing guards are prohibited from so much as laying a hand on a child's shoulder. To think that around the country, perhaps some thousands of times a day, these spontaneous impulses of human affection are being buried, stillborn, seems tragic to me.

I have known anorexic and bulimic women, and for them, there was no trust in a natural sense of balance or limits. Living in a terrible prison of self-imposed prohibitions, they kept their refrigerators empty or alternated between binges and purges. For the women I know who have recovered, part of the process of healing was to rediscover the simple pleasure of eating, to let go of the all-or-nothing approach, and to remember such magic words as "This is good. I will have some. Now I have had enough." In a similar way, we could seek to regain a certain spontaneous delight in our children as we pat them dry or twirl them in the air or gaze at them in their sleep.

This quest lies at the heart of *The Eros of Parenthood*. It is an exploration of the eros that exists between parents and children—both in its uniqueness and in its profound kinship to that which holds sway between adults. As the book unfolds, it moves up against the edge of some very controversial material—but it does not make a beeline for the sensational. To wrest this subject from the highly charged and polarized atmosphere into which it has fallen, is to embrace the full range of its territory. This includes material as subtle as the flutter of a baby's eyelids and as intangible as a pregnant mother's dreams. It includes the political—and ultimately, the spiritual implications of parent-child love.

And yes—though this is primarily a book of celebration, an evocation, an ode, it necessarily involves a degree of anxiety, a queasiness that is there already when we put the two words together: *eros* and *parenthood*. To bring a certain spontaneous delight into the light, it is necessary to bear a certain measure of darkness, to be willing to examine where we can go wrong, stray too far, or come too close. And that is why I've chosen a rather unlikely heroine—Goldilocks—as a companion for the journey. For as daffy, reckless, and ill-mannered as Goldilocks might seem, there's something brave and moving about her quest, something worthy of being appropriated:

> In a dark woods, in a place where animals live, a young girl has lost her way. At last she comes upon a house. When she knocks and no one answers, she turns the doorknob and enters. Feeling both ill at ease and irresistibly drawn, she moves through the house. It's a lovely house, in which nothing is lacking. The pantry is full, the table set, the porridge served, the beds made up. . . .
>
> The problem is, the girl doesn't seem to know who she is in this house, or what belongs to her. Disoriented, she can make her way only by sampling the extremes. Too hot, too cold, too hard, too soft. . . . What joy she feels each time when she lands upon "just right!"
>
> When the bears return, her bliss seems to dissolve in fright and flight—yet it remains a deeply satisfying story. Hearing it, we know that Goldilocks had to find her way to the house in the dark woods. She had to risk disorientation and to breach propriety—to open and enter, to taste and touch what was not hers—in order to discover who she was, where she belonged, and what belonged to her. At the end of the story, we feel that having come through the dark woods to

discover the "just right," she is ready to take that discovery back into her life.

This book offers itself as that house in the woods. In the darkness that surrounds its subject, the eros of parenthood, it stakes a clearing. In that clearing it provides a sequence of rooms, a banquet of bowls, in which it is possible to discover—between the poles of too hot and too cold, too much and too little, too hard and too soft—the relief of *the just right*. For those just brave enough to enter and find their way through the dark, it lights a path toward the true measure of a profoundly human[7]—and profoundly necessary—delight.

PART I

SOMEONE IN SKIN

The Way We Love

1. Attunement

2. Not One, Not Two

3. Only You

4. The Flesh Is Willing

5. Cute

6. Night Love

7. Sleeping Babies

"It's not God I want, it's someone in skin!" a child once cried out to his mother. With an almost unbearable honesty, he expressed the extravagant—and even sacrilegious—nature of parent-child love. "Thou shalt have no other gods before me," God boomed in the desert. But parents and children do have a way of filling the universe with each other.

At the same time that this child's words express the immensity of parent-child love, they also express its essential physicality. Feeding, rocking, washing, dressing: this is the first language of parent-child love. It is part of what makes the experience of parenting redemptive, for our children love us in and through our sheer physical presence and they re-root us in earthly existence. But this same physicality can also be relentless. It's possible for a woman to feel worshiped by her small son and utterly unseen by him—for what does he care about her dreams, her ideas, her plans for the future? It's the texture of her skin he loves, the way she wrinkles her nose when she laughs, and the sheltering curves of her body.

This chapter focuses on the early phase of parent-child love, and the ways in which this phase lays the ground for love in later life. It begins by appropriating the notion of attunement as the royal road through the eros of parenthood. Because attunement involves the mutual adjustment of two separate beings, it opens the way to an intimacy that is not fusion, but rather an intimacy that respects the boundaries between parent and child. Because attunement involves a fundamentally open, supple attitude, it is the antidote to the rigidly dogmatic attitude that threatens the eros of parenthood. An essentially dynamic notion (think how musicians have to pause and "attune" to one another several times in the course of a single concert), it can travel all the way through the life span of the parent-child relationship. For a parent to attune to an infant requires something quite different from attunement to an adolescent child.

This chapter explores parent-child love in its first incarnation: from the complex process of attunement to the sheer surprise of gazing, dumbstruck, at a sleeping child.

1

ATTUNEMENT

⌒

ONE DAY, WHEN I was seventeen, I went for a walk along the brown hill, lined with eucalyptus trees, beyond our house. Some months earlier, I'd found out that my mother was pregnant, and I was taking it hard. Underneath a layer of acute mortification at having a pregnant mother when I was a senior in high school, there were deeper, Oedipal swirls. Caught in my own dark emotions, I had not grasped the most obvious fact: that soon a baby would enter my life—a baby whom, the chances were good, I would love.

But on this particular day, walking along the brown hill, I heard a rustle of wind among the eucalyptus trees. I looked up into the shimmering leaves and suddenly grasped, for the first time, the reality of the single being—one leaf among the many—who would soon enter my life. "That was the moment I met you," I have said to my sister, more than once, ever since she was old enough to understand. It was as though in the rustle of leaves, I had caught the sound of her.

In East Africa, so I've heard, there is a tribe of people who actually make a practice of listening for the sound of their children before they are born. When a woman feels that she is ready to bear a child with her mate, she goes out to sit alone under a tree. She waits there, listening— through the sound of the wind in the leaves, of the birds, insects, and small animals in the branches—until she believes that she has heard the song of the child that she hopes to conceive. Returning to her hut in the village, she teaches the song to her mate and when they make love, they sing the song, inviting the baby to enter their lives.

Throughout her pregnancy, the mother sings this song to the child in her belly. When the child is born, the midwives welcome him with this song. As the child grows, he will hear this song again and again, at key moments of danger, initiation, celebration. The song will be a part of his wedding ceremony, as will the song of his bride. When he lies dying, his family will gather around him and sing the song one last time.[1]

Closer to home, and in a much simpler manner, this attitude is present on the part of those parents who, rather than deciding beforehand, wait to see who their child is before giving it a name. When their daughter was born, my friends Bob and Sarah waited almost two weeks—enduring the uncertainty, the advice and consternation of relatives, as well as the ever more imminent possibility that an unfortunate nickname would arise and stick—before they alighted upon "Amanda."

This period of "waiting to see" really did involve a period of listening, not unlike the East African mother who sits under the tree waiting to hear the song of her child. Names arose in Bob and Sarah's minds; they murmured them aloud to themselves and to each other, and it was as though they were sounding the name against the reality of who their baby—vigorous, blond, blue-eyed, with a piercing cry—had turned out to be. Before the birth, they had decided on the name "Danielle" for a girl. It was a name Sarah had always loved, but when their baby was born, they realized, in Sarah's words, that "The name was too soft for this powerful being."

It was as though in seeking a name, they were bringing two things into attunement—the sound of a name, with its history and connotations, and the *who* of this particular child. And, in fact, this process of sounding and listening until what begins as distance, disparity, even discord, is brought into alignment and harmony—this is the very essence of what is meant by attunement. One of the first ways that a mother attunes to her baby is by learning to interpret the sound of its crying. In order to match her responses to its needs, she has to differentiate the cry of hunger from the cry of pain or fatigue. Not all mothers learn to do this, but most do—sooner or later, through trial and error.

Trial and error: the attitude of attunement is the very opposite of a dogmatic attitude. For the latter begins in certainty, with beliefs that it imposes like a grid on what it encounters. *Children are by nature bad and willful* is an example, par excellence, of the dogmatic attitude that prevailed for some hundreds of years in much of Europe and the New World in the name of Christian parenting. Even into the early twentieth century, children were regularly flogged by their parents and schoolteachers without tangible evidence of their having done anything wrong, but simply out of a presumption of guilt. Needless to say, such presumption is a world away from the pliant, wondering quality of attunement. Such presumptions represent a form of fundamentalist thinking, in relation to which attunement is much closer to the *via negativa*, the *not this, not that* of the mystical approach, which itself has often been described as a form of listening. Unlike the fundamentalist, who starts off professing a set of preordained beliefs and who wills others to do the same, the mystic listens to "the still, small voice" that leads him—no, not this way, not that—to the state of divine union.

Do such comparisons seem highfalutin, far removed from the realm of parent and child?

Just look at a mother trying to comfort her fussing baby. She lifts him up against her shoulder, but he catches his breath and begins to cry again. She takes him down from her shoulder and holds him against her chest, rocking him. The cries get even louder. Finally, she stretches him belly-down on her knees and begins to stroke his back. The crying grows gradually quieter. . . .

With each change in position, the mother waits for a few moments, watching, listening, to see if she's getting it right. When orchestral musicians tune their instruments, they begin with a single note: the A at 445 vibrations per second, sounded by the flute. Between parent and child, there is no such single, preordained point of departure, but rather, an ever-changing series of states—hunger, repose, restlessness, excitement, delight—through which the two continually adjust to one another. Yet the process—if vastly more fluid and variable than its musical counterpart—is not willy-nilly.[2]

It is guided by many things—by a mother's protective urge, by her own visceral response to her child's discomfort, and also by the pleasure of mutuality. Doesn't our greatest pleasure, both as parent and child, tend to come from those moments when we feel ourselves to be *in sync*—another musical word—with one another? Among my own happiest memories from childhood are those hours that I spent leaning against my father, dictating a story as he typed it on his typewriter; or leaning with my mother over one of my father's shirt boxes, cutting out figures for a cardboard circus. Among my most satisfying memories as a parent are those moments when my daughter and I seem to vibrate on the same frequency. We lie on my bed sorting through our jewelry boxes together; we lose ourselves in making a sandcastle; we find ourselves laughing at the same slip of the tongue; or are suddenly seized, driving through evening light, by the same mood of melancholy that makes us begin to remember the people we miss, the places we've left behind. And certainly the hell of parenthood is made of those moments of utter discord: a small boy bangs his metal spoon on the radiator as his mother lies nearby with a headache; a jet-lagged father, who wants nothing so much as to stay deep under the eiderdown, wakes at the crack of dawn to the shouts of his daughter, her mouth pressed to his ear, "Eggs, make me eggs!"

Just as water takes on the shape of its container or a liquid takes on the temperature of the room around it, one might characterize a healthy parent-child relationship as one in which both parties have an inclination to adjust to one another. And here inclination seems the right word, as in *they incline toward each other, they lean into one another*, as my mother and I leaned over our cardboard circus, as I leaned against my father, my words turning into the movements of his fingers on the typewriter keys. . . .

The primal pleasure between parent and child of being *in sync* plants the seeds of a lifelong pleasure, one that lies at the heart of all forms of love.[3] Through hours of close observation, psychologists have learned that the degree to which people match one another—in posture, gesture, inflection—is an index of how much they like each other. This is true not only of romantic partners, but of friends, teachers and students, even of new acquaintances. When we are well-disposed toward another person, we have a tendency, for the most part unconscious, to bring ourselves physically into alignment with him, through our posture, our gestures, the rhythm and volume of our speech.[4]

Yet attunement, this bringing into alignment of two separate beings, is not the same as fusion, the merging of two identities. A mother who is attuning to her baby as he makes the first sounds and rhythms of human speech does not just parrot his sounds and facial expressions back to him. From the beginning, attunement has the quality not of call and echo, but of call and response. A mother who attunes herself to her baby's communication does not simply repeat his sounds and imitate his expressions; rather, she responds to him in a way that signals, "I see what sort of mood you're in right now, and I—in my own way—am letting you know that I see, I understand, and I participate."

This is the beauty of attunement: it permits us to embody the mystery of being one not two, two not one. It is an experience that we seek our whole lives long. As Daniel Goleman, author of *Emotional Intelligence*, has written: "Making love is perhaps the closest approximation in adult life to this intimate attunement between infant and mother."[5] And for the psychoanalyst Jessica Benjamin, it is the primal experience of attunement, defined as a process of "mutual recognition," that underlies the adult capacity for erotic love. In *The Bonds of Love*, she writes:

> The positive experience of attunement allows the individual to maintain a more permeable boundary and enter more readily into states in which there is a momentary suspension of felt boundaries between inside and outside. The capacity to enter into states in which distinctness and union are reconciled underlies the most intense experience of adult erotic life. In erotic union we can experience that form of mutual recognition in which both partners lose themselves in each other without loss of self . . . Thus early experiences of mutual recognition already prefigure the dynamics of erotic life.[6]

———

It is because attunement contains the reality of both separateness and mutuality that it is the key to understanding the eros of parenthood. The rewards of this love, in its healthy state, may be understood as a function of proper attunement. And its dark side may be seen as a failure of this attunement, in the form of a parent who remains too separate, unable to resonate empathically, or a parent who floods the boundaries of the child's self—through violence, sexual abuse, excessive neediness, or what has been called "emotional incest."

It's not God I want, it's someone in skin!
A real child called out those words, a child in skin. And what they mean is: *You, my mother, in this very body, with your particular smell, the color of your eyes, the sound of your voice, the texture of your hair, you are the supreme value in my universe, the source and sustainer of my being.* A mother, attuning to the passionate intensity of this request, consents to be that someone to her child, that god in skin. She does so knowing that the very destiny of such a god is that as her child grows, she will have to shed one role after another in relation to him, just as a snake sheds its skins. She will have to shed her child's various perceptions of her, including some that are most flattering, most gratifying, to her—for this is the essence of a healthy mother's attunement to her child: she takes her cue from him, she keeps his needs uppermost. Yet sometimes, in order to attune to his deepest needs, she—like the mother bird who pushes her chick from the warm nest of sticks and moss so that it may spread its wings—may need to frustrate his more immediate desires.

For though an infant may be perfectly content with a mother who is completely immersed in him, a growing child needs a parent who, while remaining empathically aligned, exists as a separate self, a self with its own needs, desires, gifts, griefs. Recently a friend told me about a young mother she knows who, though she is recovering from a serious back injury, will not let go of her intensely self-sacrificing style of mothering. Even when other caring adults are in the house and she is nearly immobilized with pain and fatigue, she cannot bear to leave her three young children long enough to take a nap in her bedroom. My friend described her lying collapsed on the sofa as her youngest boy ran a toy metal truck over her face. When her husband tried to rescue her, she protested, "Oh, let him be—he's just playing!" This is an example of a mother's self-abnegation, her disappearance into her child—not what I am calling attunement, which is the bringing into alignment of two separate beings.[7]

In the earliest phase of parenthood, the infant needs the parent to harmonize as closely as possible with him: to meet hunger with food, loneliness with presence, boredom with playfulness in a way that minimizes frustration. While the latter represents the orthodox definition of attunement, I am using the term in a much broader way as *a process of mutual adjustment that continues throughout the growing years of a child.* Thus I am asking it to encompass also those later stages during which the responsive parent must learn to frustrate the child's desires in an appropriate way, in order to confront both the reality of the external world ("No, that's hot!" "No, that will break!") and the subjectivity of others—including the parent herself. ("No, I can't play right now!" "No, I need to be alone!")

When attunement is defined in this broad and flexible way, it can become the prime navigational tool through the eros of parenthood. As such, it does not provide the comfort of ready-made certainty or of absolute safety. It cannot guarantee that we won't sometimes lose our bearings. But if we remember to pause and take a reading at regular intervals, the chances are good that we will not stray too far from the one sure note: the sound of our children's needs. These needs change over time—so that what we're listening for becomes a great deal more complex than the difference between a cry of hunger, pain, or fatigue, yet the basic process remains the same. Listening and responding, we chart our course. Attunement is not magic, like a wand. It does not even have the static reliability of a key. But it is the compass in Goldilocks' hand, and with its quivering needle, it guides us—*not this way, not that.*

2

NOT ONE, NOT TWO

⌒

WHEN MY DAUGHTER was quite small, I carried her in a red-and-white seersucker pouch against my chest. Taking a walk with her in this pouch felt like the perfect way to be out in the world with her. Perched on the little cloth seat inside and with the zipper closed, she was barely visible. Only a few wisps of her dark hair showed above the rim. After the blatant hugeness of my belly in the last weeks before she was born, when I went out with her in the pouch, I recovered some of the secret quality of early pregnancy. Then, of course, my secret had been that there was a child growing inside of me; I had no idea of who or how this child was. Now my child's hiddenness was without the anxiety of uncertainty for me, for I could peer inside the pouch at any time and see her whole and perfect, alive and breathing. She was a secret I could feast my eyes on.

One of the first times that I went out with her in the pouch, I walked (and here, twice now, I've stopped writing "I," then "we," then "I," then "we") to the International Festival, held in a small park a few blocks away. On a wooden stage, people in bright costumes—with ribbons, embroidered vests, satin kimonos—performed folk dances from China, Sweden, Ghana, Mexico. Underneath the trees tables were spread with dim sum, tapas, Greek olives, French cheeses, sweets from many lands. And in the midst of this celebration of difference, of multiplicity, I walked around with my secret cargo, the coil of my child on my belly, in a celebration that I felt to be intensely private and yet knew to be quite universal. For my rapture in the warm bundle on my belly sprang from the fundamental state of the human mother and her child: the state of being no longer in one body, yet still so connected that it is hard to express the number of it, except to say *not one, not two*. Of all the baby things I gave away as Ariel grew older, that pouch was the hardest to let go of. It felt almost like a part of my own body, and it belonged to the time when she, no longer held within my body, was still almost a part of it.

The mother-child dyad is another way to name this number of numbers, this *almost* that is the primal pair. And actually, the hyphen alone is powerfully expressive here, for it indicates two words that should be read as one: *mother-child*. It is such a small mark, this little umbilical of the hyphen, yet what it signifies is of vast consequence for human life. In the words of the distinguished child psychologist D.W. Winnicott, "A baby is not a person, but a person and someone."[8] So much is folded into the small word "and."

For it is quite literally true that the human infant is born physiologically incomplete. "Altricial" is the term, meaning relatively helpless, as opposed to most other animals which are "precocial"—all the way from bugs that, upon emerging from their chrysalis, spread their wings and fly, to colts that within moments after birth, stand on wobbly legs and walk.[9]

One day when a friend of mine was six-months pregnant, she began to experience cramps and then the leaking of fluid. When she went, frightened, to the nearby clinic, she learned that the fluid was amniotic. Clearly concerned, the doctor told her to go home and go immediately to bed. That night she dreamed that on her belly there was a pouch of skin. From this pouch, a tiny girl with black hair and big dark eyes was climbing out. Looking right into this dark little daughter's eyes, she spoke to her fiercely: "Get back inside that pouch! You're not ready to come out!" The cramping stopped. Three months later, a black-haired, black-eyed baby girl was born to my blond-haired, fair-skinned friend and her fair-skinned husband. The doctors and nurses joked: "Where did this Eskimo baby come from?"

It is only natural that we human mothers should be able to identify with kangaroos, with bandicoots, wombats, and opossums. For even when they are born full term, our babies, like theirs, are unready. Marsupial babies, whose mothers lack placentas, continue their gestation in the inside-out of their mothers' pouches. We human mothers may not have literal, anatomical pouches for our offspring once they are born, but our babies nonetheless demand that we function as if we did, keeping them safe and warm, and with the thinnest possible layer of distance between their bodies and ours.

And when we say that our babies, after birth, are not separate beings, this is quite literally true. We know now that the very breathing of an infant is designed to synchronize with the parent's. One of the reasons, it's believed, that sudden infant death occurs less frequently in cultures where infants sleep with their parents is that if the baby's breathing falters, the parent's breathing will "jump-start" the baby's.[10]

Yet even when a baby sleeps in its own crib in a separate room, there is an inescapable *not one, not two-ness* in the primal relationship. The most elemental rhythms of the mother's life will be transformed by her baby: her sleep patterns, what and when she eats and drinks, how she moves. Even as her body begins to return to itself after pregnancy, her locomotion will continue to be cumbersome for a long time. Holding a child, pushing a stroller or a carriage and a bag of gear, she will have to think about negotiating doorways, steps, curbs, and small bathrooms. Even if she experiences her child as a joyful burden, the fact is that her sense of being a body in space will be transformed almost as radically as if she had suddenly become handicapped. "The simplest thing isn't simple anymore," one new mother told me after explaining to me how it had taken her a while to figure out how to take a shower in the morning, given that her infant son didn't nap and couldn't bear to be apart from her.

The human baby, you might say, demands that its mother make a pouch of her very existence. And indeed, anthropologists sometimes refer to human infancy as a form of "external gestation."[11] Even for the modern woman who, a handful of weeks after her child's birth, returns full-time to work, her child is folded into her life; it accompanies her in her thoughts, her existence is now irrevocably doubled. One working mother told me that during the first week back in the office, her breasts leaked in response to the wailing phone.

Mother-child. It is such a small mark, the little umbilical of the hyphen, yet it contains the possibility of worlds of difference. For how the "and" is negotiated—the baby *and* someone—can vary tremendously from one pair to another, with tremendously different consequences.

Imagine two mothers, both of them very affectionate, physically expressive women, who each give birth to a rather uncuddly baby boy, the sort whose body tends to arch and tense rather than melting in response to touch, and who, as soon as he is strong enough, tends to wriggle out of close embrace. One mother experiences her child's behavior as rejecting. Without the reward of his physical affection, she tends to feel resentful of the labor of caring for him, and gradually she withdraws from him, both physically and emotionally. The other mother, despite her initial disappointment, takes her baby's temperament as an interesting challenge, a game even, in which—while respecting his need to feel unrestrained—she tries to see how much he'll let her get away with. "He doesn't like to be held against my chest, but he loves it when I stroke his back as he falls asleep in his crib" is the sort of thing she might say. It's not hard to imagine that two very different mother-son relationships might evolve out of a similar set of givens and that two rather different boys grow to manhood.

At first, of course, the *how* of the *not one, not two* is largely regulated by autonomic processes. A pregnant woman breathes, she drinks a glass of orange juice, and the oxygen, the vitamins and minerals that she takes in enter the bloodstream of her child. She might adjust her diet, her daily routine, her attitude in certain ways that affect both the child growing within her and her relationship to this child, but for the most part, the mutual adjusting is carried out without her conscious choice or intervention.

At this stage, when the baby is actually part of the mother's body, it is the placenta—the "flat cake"—that does the work of mediating. A protective barrier, it is both pillow and wall. A permeable barrier, it both supplies and withholds. A filter, it makes "decisions" as to what is pure or impure, nourishment or waste.

The truly momentous process of pairing—momentous both in its shaping of the parent-child relationship and of the person that child will turn out to be—occurs after the separation of birth. The umbilical cord is cut, the placenta expelled, and now the literal link that was the medium of mutual adjustment is replaced by an infinite number of largely intangible threads.

No—not intangible—for once the child is born, the primal relationship is constituted by the most tangible activities of feeding, holding, bathing, dressing. . . .

But what is so amazing about the thread of these connective activities that go on once the child is born is that it can be woven in so many ways. I feed my baby from my breast, I feed her from a bottle. I feed her on a schedule. I feed her every time she cries. I let her sleep in her own crib. I carry her against my body at all times . . .

How different this is from the Kung! woman who knows, simply, as her mother, as her grandmother, as her grandmother's grandmother knew: you put your baby in a sling *like this* and keep her fastened to you all day long. Or the Mayan mother in the Yucatan who knows: you put your baby in a hammock of woven string, you turn her around once, twice, three times, and she will be safely wrapped for hours.

Among traditional societies, the culture itself functions as a kind of placenta, regulating degrees of closeness and distance, filtering the noxious from the nourishing. We modern mothers have no such buffer—for our own society provides vastly more options. How close? How far? How much? How little? In the course of a single day, we face myriad possibilities, among which we are left to find our own way. We value this freedom, this openness, but it is also part of the anxiety that so strongly permeates parenthood in our time.

As a girl, I loved the story of *Katy No Pocket*, the kangaroo mother who had no pouch for her baby, Freddy.[12] Watching the other kanga-roos leaping about with their babies ensconced in their fur pockets, Katy and Freddy felt such longing. They began to look about at other mother-baby pairs: the lioness and her cub, the bird and her nestling. All the other creatures seemed to exist in a state of simple, natural choicelessness. "Why, on my back, of course!" Mrs. Crocodile says when Katy asks her, "How do you carry little Catherine Crocodile?" And when Katy asks Mrs. Monkey, "How do you carry Jocko?" the answer is: "Why, in my arms, of course! How else would any sensible animal carry anything?" In desperation, Katy makes her way at last to the city, and there, among all the people, the stores, the houses and automobiles, she comes upon a truly wondrous sight: a man covered with pockets. He is a handyman, and he wears a work apron with pock-ets in different sizes. He is also a kind man, and seeing Katy's amaze-ment, he takes off his apron, shakes all the tools out, and ties it around her neck. With Freddy tucked inside the biggest pocket, she bounds home faster than she has ever been able to go since he was born. Returning home triumphantly, she makes a further happy discovery: she has pockets to spare for other little animals—Leonard the Lion, Thomas the Tortoise, a baby skunk, a rabbit, a raccoon, a lizard, a pos-sum, and more. By the end of the story, Katy is beaming, with a beam-ing baby from every phylum in her pockets.

We human mothers, in our modern culture, are like Katy. At times, we'd love to have a pouch into which we could tuck our babies, resolv-ing in one fell swoop all the questions about how near, how far, how much, how little . . . a pouch that, while keeping them safe and snug, leaves us free to leap about, assuring just the proper measure of connec-tion and autonomy. Once our babies are born, we have no set of givens waiting to receive them, and so we must suffer a certain measure of anx-iety, uncertainty, a feeling of exile that keeps us searching through books, through magazines, questioning experts, asking other parents, "How is it done?"

It is painful not to have been issued a regulation pouch for our babies once they are born. In its own way, it is a form of exile from the

Garden of Eden, where everything is just as it should be and there is no
need to question, to doubt, or hesitate.

And yet, this very exile permits the possibility of creative solution.
Having borne the pain of exile from the simple and choiceless, Katy
and her baby are gifted with something quite splendid. In the midst of
the human city, and fashioned of human hands, the work apron that
the man ties around Katy's neck provides something that none of the
other animals have: flexibility, a wealth of possibility. Because the
pockets come in all different sizes, there is room for many different
creatures, and because of this, new combinations, new camaraderies,

come into being. A frog, a duck, and a kangaroo can bounce through the landscape together, making a new kind of music of croaks and quacks and squeaks, a music never heard before.

And now, many years since I first encountered Katy No Pocket, it seems to me significant that when she goes among the humans, it's a man who gives her what she seeks. For in our own era, one of the most creative solutions to the question of "How to parent?" comes with the deepening involvement of fathers. Katy, who was born without a pouch, is a kind of mother-father, and one moral of the story seems to be that love and a bit of ingenuity—love and a contraption or two—can more than make up for what biology has failed to supply. And suddenly, under the heading of "Love and Contraptions," I am touched by a parade of images passing by, images of the fathers I know or have known: one is listening with a stethoscope through the mountain of his wife's belly to hear the sound of his baby's heartbeat; another is pouring milk from the breast pump into the baby's bottle while his wife is at work. Only a few days ago, an envelope arrived in my mailbox with this offering from my friend, the poet Peter Levitt:

A DREAM OF HEAVEN

A few minutes ago my wife went out to buy groceries and left me alone with the monitor so I can hear the baby, who has a terrible cold, should he wake up alone in his room. I go into my studio, set the monitor beside me on the table, and begin to read the day's work. After only a minute I realize I am breathing hard, as if I had just run out to get some firewood at the beginning of a rain. But it is my son's breathing, coming through the monitor, that has entered my body and become my own. I lift the white, plastic voice box of my son and hold it to my ear. In, out. In, out. In, out. And I wonder, almost pleading, let me hear it just like this, after I die.

Not one, not two. A human father feels it, too. I think of my brother, who has recently become a father. Though he never carried

Jonah inside his belly, I know that as he walks through his neighborhood in San Francisco with Jonah in the canvas carrier on his back, he feels something very close to the doubled existence that I felt as I walked with my daughter Ariel in the red-and-white pouch. I think of my friend Sorrel telling me of how he used to take his little daughter rock-climbing when she was no more than four years old. "We were tied together by a length of rope, and I'd have her climb ahead of me, feeling for handholds, for places to balance the tips of her shoes. Sometimes I started to feel afraid for her, but what I learned is that if I could let go of my fear, then she wouldn't be afraid." His feelings hers. Not one, not two.

And only now, and for the first time, do I feel that I begin to understand what for a long time I have thought of as one of the happiest moments of my life. It occurred the morning after we had brought Ariel home from the hospital. We had spent our first night in the house together, with her asleep beside the bed in a wicker basket. I was up with her several times throughout the night, of course, and even several times when she didn't cry, I woke up and peeked at her to make sure she was still breathing. In the morning when she began to make her little sounds, her father picked her up, put her over his shoulder and walked out of the room with her. He was taking her to her room, and it was going to be his first time to change her and dress her in her tiny new clothes. Already, as the two of them went out the bedroom door and I saw her dark head nestled against his fair one, I knew that *This is a moment I will never forget.* They went out the door and down the long hallway, away from me, and it was as though I saw the cord that had linked her to me, and to me alone—the cord that had been cut the night before—suddenly restored, and yet lengthening, becoming supple enough to include another life-sustaining connection. It was as though I could see the not-one-not-two of mother-child expanding, opening up to make way for this new mystery: the unfolding of the lifelong link between a father and his daughter.

Pouchless parents, both mothers and fathers, we discover that there are all kinds of umbilicals that can still connect us to our children after birth, all kinds of ways to negotiate how long, how short, how taut, how loose, to play the ropes. This play, though it sometimes comes laced with anxiety, is inextricably linked with the eros of parenthood.

"Madonno and Child"

3

ONLY YOU

ONE DAY WHEN I was six and had just learned to write, I came upon a large stash of photographs that my mother kept bundled in an old chest of drawers in the living room. She was quite preoccupied with something that day and so left me undisturbed as—with the odd form of energy that sometimes takes over young children, quasi-demonic and yet highly methodical—I spent several hours, legs folded on the hard wooden floor, working my way through the bundle. On the back of each and every photograph of a woman who was not my mother, I wrote, "I like my mommy better than you."

This labor was intrinsically pleasurable for me, a true labor of love, so I had no interest in speeding it up. But if I'd been more sophisticated, I might have short-circuited the whole process by simply writing on the back of a single photograph of my mother, "You are the ground zero for me, the absolute term of comparison, the woman of all women."

I remember being younger still and taking a walk one bright spring morning with my nursery-school class. Being utterly without a sense of direction then, I had no idea that we were walking through the very neighborhood in which I lived. I happened to look across the street and there was my mother, crouched in the garden before our house, digging behind a row of flowers. I felt my heart pierced with love—and I felt something else as well. It was something I could not have expressed then, but the sensation was so vivid that I have no trouble in summoning it now as I try to translate it into adult words. I felt a sort of perceptual shimmer, as though the medium in which I was moving, or the lens through which I was seeing, had suddenly undergone a radical shift in dimension. Shuffling along with my classmates and two teachers, I had been content to be among the Many. But now I had seen the One, my One, my One and Only, and this shift was almost more than I could contain.

Remembering this sensation, I feel I understand a common scenario. "He was doing fine/She was doing just fine," the teacher says as the parent scoops up a wailing child from the playroom floor. It's as though when the parent entered the crowded room, the child had suddenly moved from a thinner atmosphere and suffered the bends. The parent's face appeared, and bubbles of suppressed longing dislodged and burst in the child's heart.

Or—on the flip side of this scenario—the child doesn't fall apart but becomes suddenly radiant. My cousin, musing on what she would miss most about her daughter's early childhood, told me, "It's that moment when I come to pick her up at school, or playgroup, or the baby-sitter's. No matter what she's doing, when she looks up and sees me, her face gets that glow." That glow. Who besides a lover in the first flush of love greets us like this, day after day, with what is not so much an expression on the face as a form of interior light?

I only have eyes for you . . . the song goes, and *You are my sunshine.* . .

These are songs that our children could sing to us as passionately as any lover could. And though it is impossible for children ever to be chronologically the first love of a parent's life, they can stake another, uniquely powerful, claim to firstness. For on their part, they have loved us from the absolute beginning, and their preference for us is more primal, more original than that of any lover, ever—for it begins in the womb. A newborn can recognize its mother's voice, having grown accustomed to its timbre and rhythm in utero. I know that one of the reasons I will always keep the plastic wristbands, with their matching numbers, that Ariel and I were given in the hospital is not only that they are souvenirs of her birth. It is also that from the beginning, I couldn't look at those numbers without seeing them as a kind of absurdist joke, a sort of Duchamp or Ionesco inversion of the obvious, or convergence of opposites. How could anyone possibly mix us up? (Rationally, of course, I knew that babies do sometimes get mixed up, but what I'm talking about is the feeling I had of absolute belonging.) How could a row of numbers, connoting anonymity, faceless bureaucracy, possibly be the means to keep us linked? We, who were made for each other?

They're made for each other, we sometimes say of couples—but of no pair is this as literally true as of mother and child. A mother's body is made over to accommodate the baby who is made inside of her; her body changes in ways that correspond exactly to what her baby needs. Her hip joints loosen to make way for him, her breasts fill with just the liquid that needs to meet his lips. . . .

Of course it could be said that many of these changes do not represent a specific transformation for a specific baby; they are generic to pregnant females of the human species. Where would the ancient tradition of the wet nurse be if it were not true that, speaking purely physiologically, any nursing human mother can nurse any human infant? A midtown Manhattan mother could put a Bushman baby to her breast; an Eskimo mother, wrapped in her furs, could suckle a tiny Berber from the hottest desert. How could adoption exist if the made-for-each-other of biological mother and child were absolute in its specificity? Just yesterday I received a letter from my friend Deborah in Seattle that included a color Xerox of the first photograph she's been sent of "Phu," the baby boy waiting for her in an orphanage outside Hanoi. "Isn't he adorable?" she wrote—and it was clear to me from the ecstasy in her letter that she already had the sense of "being meant for each other" about her soon-to-be-adopted child.

Clearly, there is a certain flexibility in the human infant's capacity for primal connection, yet it is equally clear that this flexibility is limited. Despite the rare cultural variation—such as the Efe tribe in Nigeria, whose babies spend much of their time being passed among a group of nursing mothers—it is safe to say that the human infant, the world over, is emphatically not a promiscuous creature.[13] Rather, the human infant is designed to single out, and to be singled out, in an intensely mutual connection.

This intensity can be spread out among a small handful of significant others—but beyond a certain point, too much dispersal of attention becomes damaging. We know that to produce a healthy human child, it is not enough that the generic tasks of child care—feeding, washing, dressing—be competently fulfilled. The listlessness and the resignation of babies reared in institutions are legendary. And who among us has not either experienced or witnessed the suffering of a child whose parents, for whatever reason—illness, crisis, ignorance, their own emotional deprivation—were unable to make their child feel special?

Special. The word has become so blandified, euphemized, as to take on the very opposite of its original meaning. How many millions of greeting cards carry the salutation, "To Someone Special"? Whenever I receive such a card, my heart sinks and I feel precisely unspecial, unseen in my specificity. But the word itself, which springs from the same root as "spectacle," derives from the Latin *to observe*. This fact restores richness to a word that has become pallid and reveals something profound about the nature of human love, suggesting that what is special to us is that which we closely observe and that what we closely observe becomes special to us: we learn its particular characteristics, can distinguish it as a particular kind. In a meditation on love, Stendhal writes,

> Even little facial blemishes on other women, such as a smallpox scar, touch the heart of a man in love and inspire a deep reverie; imagine the effect when they are on his mistress's face. The fact is, that pockmark means a thousand things to him, mostly delightful and all extremely interesting. He is forcibly reminded of all these things by the sight of a scar, even on another woman's face. Thus *ugliness* even begins to be loved and given preference, because in this case, it has become beauty.[14]

In love with a woman whom he has closely observed, a man finds that even her scar has become special to him and that he has discovered a new kind of woman, a woman-with-a-scar. In the act of making special, which comes first? The love or the gaze, the gaze or the love?

At the start of life, the very physiology of the human mother-child relationship seems designed to promote a lavish mutual attention. How different it would be if human babies were laid in eggs and took form in a nest outside the mother's body. But "intimate" means *inmost*, and our babies grow in utmost intimacy inside their mothers' bodies. Thus they observe us, they make a study of us, they become experts on us from the very beginning, and by the time they are born, we are already special to them. It's impressive to hear about those little Tibetans, destined to be lamas, who can pick out the brocade hat, the bell, the drum of the one whom they are believed to have reincarnated. But even the most ordinary human babies can pass tests that, in their own way, are small miracles: choosing the scent of their mother's brassiere from a pile of others, recognizing the specific inflections of their own mother's voice when they've been out in the world for only a few hours.[15]

The fact that a human mother normally gives birth to only one child at a time seems designed to foster an intense one-on-one relationship. In traditional cultures, where mothers tend to nurse almost continuously, the average interval between the birth of one child and the next is four years—a fact that, along with the prolonged helplessness of the human child, underlies the immense involvement of the human mother with her child.[16]

The way in which the human infant feeds also seems designed to foster close observation, the passion of being special to one another. On the basis of fossil evidence, anthropologists speculate that mammals evolved from small egg-laying animals with "specialized patches" on their chests that gave off heat and also secreted a protective liquid when they sat on their eggs. In her book *Our Babies Ourselves*, Meredith F. Small writes:

> When the eggs hatched, the new infants probably licked up some of that egg-coating ooze, which turned out to be immunologically protective once ingested. . . . In any case, those babies who licked up the fluid gained an advantage for their efforts in terms of survival—they either grew faster or bigger, or they were healthier than those who ignored the opportunity. Maternal ooze eventually evolved strong nutrient properties that could sustain a baby even when the mother was unable to bring back food to the nest or the infant was too weak to forage on its own. Thus lactation was born.[17]

From this "maternal ooze," the most distinctive feature of mammals, that which sets them apart from reptiles and birds, evolved. Small continues: "We know that breasts, and the liquid they manufacture, must have co-evolved with the infants' ability to find the nipple, suck, and digest what was ingested. Mothers must have already been adapted to stay close to their infants and engage in some sort of positive maternal care, and infants must have been selected to turn only to their mothers and what they offered. . . Thus began the evolutionary path of modern mammals, animals in which the female members invest highly in each offspring by manufacturing and secreting for days, weeks, or months a fluid that is the sole food of their young."[18] Drawing from both modern cross-cultural studies and archaeological evidence, Small reports that the "blueprint of the way babies were fed for 99 percent of human history indicates breast milk as the primary or sole food until two years of age or so, and nursing commonly continuing for several more years."[19]

In addition to the long duration of human lactation, the position in which the human mother suckles her child is extremely intimate and interactive. Women do have two breasts—a built-in accommodation to the possibility of twins. Even so, human babies born in batches remain human babies, in need of lavish attention, and this is the great challenge of the multiple birth. How different it would be if the norm were that the human mother gave birth to a litter of babies and fed them—as some four-legged mammals do—from a series of teats on the underside of her belly. The far-off gaze of the cat, as her kittens suckle, is a world away from the gaze of the human mother, who, holding her child at her breast, below her face, cannot help but pour her attention into her child as the milk pours into his mouth. The child is nourished by both: the milk and the light of her eyes—a light in which, if all is well, he feels himself to be the light of her life.

"I like my mommy better than you," I wrote on the back of all those photographs. I was doing a kind of taxonomy, and she was a species of one. To be so loved in our specificity is one of the great rewards of parenthood. We are special to our children in a way we are to no one else, for it is in the ground of our own specificity—the sound of our voices, the rhythm of our heartbeat, the surrounding warmth and smell of our bodies—that their very existence takes root. Our specificity is vital to them, necessary in a way it is to no one else. "I can't live without you," a lover might say—and indeed, grieving lovers do sometimes leap from bridges or succumb to illness. When they do this, however, we understand it as a reversion to a form of infantile attachment, as evidence of the failure to truly become an adult. For to be "adult" means, precisely, to have left behind such radical dependency on a single other.

Our children's radical dependency is absolute. It is not a reversion to anything, for it simply *is* from the very beginning. Their "I cannot live without you" is not a metaphor, a way of saying "I care about you intensely"—it is the literal truth. And we feel this as we lean over their cribs and see their eyes meet ours, as we lift them up into our arms and feel them inhale our presence through their pores, feel them drink in the sound of our voices as, with their whole bodies, they greet us in a way that sings *It had to be you. . . .*

We are as necessary to them as sun to a plant—but whereas it is the light of the same sun that fuels all the earth's plants, what fuels a human infant's life-energy is not the sun's brand of impartial, universal light, but the light of a love that shines for him alone.

This light is not without its shadow side. The need for this light constitutes an immense vulnerability on the part of the human child, one that throws him, naked and utterly helpless, into the arms of his own particular fate. For whereas the infant is biologically compelled to form a powerful and unique attachment to his primary caregiver, the caregiver's ability to respond may be limited and distorted by a great many factors. It is a matter of sheer survival for the infant to form a bond of special intensity to the one or ones on whom he is so radically dependent, but, alas—though one might say that there is strong biological encouragement—there is no guarantee that this special intensity will be requited.[20] In the words of anthropologist Sarah Blaffer Hrdy, "The same processes by which babies attach to and learn to love their caretakers impose a tremendous cost when such attachments never form, or when sequential attachments are ruptured. Below a certain level of nurturing, the developmental outcome is disastrous."[21]

From the parent's point of view: if it is one of the great rewards of parenthood to be so special to our children, it is also one of the great burdens. How maddening it can be when a small child insists that "only Mommy" or "only Daddy" can perform a certain task—wipe my nose, peel my apple, button my shirt—which, to an exhausted parent, would seem so readily doable by any number of other people. And who among us has not been in the slightly comic and yet uncomfortable situation of sneaking past or hiding from our children lest they lay their eyes on us and devour us with their desire? How dreadful it is, just when we think we've made it out the door, to hear them wailing behind us, "Don't go! Don't go!" As if we were Jack, trying to slip back down the beanstalk, while their giant love for us wails like the golden harp, foiling the deft getaway.

It is deeply flattering to be made to feel so irreplaceable, and it is binding, constricting. Our children can circumscribe our activities more drastically than any authoritarian parent proclaiming "You're grounded!" ever did in our youth. This is what the famous experiment of lugging a five-pound bag of sugar everywhere is supposed to impart to impulsive teens. But what the sugar bag can absolutely not convey is that it is not through any official authority or physical power that they bind us, constrict us, but through their need of us, their love— expressed as an absolute preference for us above all others. It is this love, this need, that make us feel so rooted, tethered, bound. Is there anything else, anyone else, to whom we matter quite so much?

Some children seem to understand the power of their preference all too well. They learn to dispense tasks as if granting royal privilege. "Only Mommy can wipe my bottom!" a small boy declares, as if bestowing an allotment of the king's honey. Children can become tyrannical in their love, like those hoary fairy-tale men who lock fair maidens in towers. Even the mild young boy in A. A. Milne's early verse regards himself as his mother's keeper: *James, James said to his mother, "Mother," he said, said he, "You must never go down to the end of the town, if you don't go down with me."*[21] Rereading this verse, I remember how, when my mother pushed me, age three, in my stroller, I felt that it was I who made the path for her; I was her avant-garde, and her task was to follow behind. On those occasions when I glimpsed that there were dimensions of her life that did not include me, I felt indignant, shocked—in fact, the shock was as great as when walking among the Many in nursery-school file, I glimpsed her—my One, my One and Only, my Mine of Mine's—crouched in the garden. And the shock was not only that version of the bends, the bubbles of longing bursting inside a thinner atmosphere, but the realization that when I was not around, she continued to exist as someone beyond my own suppressed longing, that she had a life without me; she could crouch in the garden behind a row of flowers, digging with some intention of her own that had nothing whatsoever to do with me. Folded inside my amazement there was, I know, a certain sense of betrayal.

"I'm going to make a tape of his screaming," my sister-in-law Dawn says, only half-joking, because she knows a side of her one-year-old Jonah that the rest of us never see. We know him as a radiant, red-headed, mostly mellow little person. But she tells us that though she spends nearly every waking hour with him, he simply cannot bear it when she tries to steal the briefest morning shower. She sets him gently on the bathroom rug, surrounded by his favorite toys, and he screams without letup in a paroxysm of pure fury.

They are jealous gods, our children—so much so that the most devoted parent cannot fail to fail them sometimes. Even the fullest full-time mother has had a life that preceded her child and that to one degree or another, continues to lay claim to her. At most, she has other intimate relationships, she has work in the world. At least, she has daily tasks about the house, she has her own bodily needs. Has anyone ever captured on film the particular look of a mother who has managed to seize a few seconds of pure solitude behind a closed bathroom door? The look on her face—of total, dreamy absorption and slightly desperate vigilance, which comes from knowing she might be interrupted at any moment—is like that of a teenager partaking of an intensely forbidden pleasure. Or is it rather like the look of an Anastasia, a once-princess returning, for these stolen seconds on the throne, to the memory of a privacy that though she took it quite for granted then, used to stretch out around her like a vast domain?

Along with the tyrannical love of the small child, there is the reality that in their passionate preference for us, they can actually make us feel neglected, overlooked. They love us in our specificity, yes—but the specificity they love us for has largely to do with certain inadvertent, unintentional givens of our existence. It is deeply comforting, fulfilling, even redemptive, to be loved in such a way, but it does leave certain other needs unanswered. It may be lovely to be loved for the smell of my bra, for the particular way my voice goes up and down—but what about my wit? My fluent French? My publications?

Nor are small children capable of loving us in a way that takes account of our own subjectivity, our own needs and desires as separate beings who have an existence apart from them. This blindness of the small child can manifest in such small, comically touching moments as a boy choosing a bright-red fire truck for his mother's birthday. It can also manifest as a paradox, a paradox so huge as to be felt at times as an acute physical strain, the strain of being pulled in two directions by one and the same small being. On the one hand, to be so passionately desired, to have one's presence so needed, cherished. And on the other, to feel so utterly used, spent, treated with such disregard. D.W. Winnicott has written eloquently about the way a mother's sense of being a person unto herself is destroyed by the young child, who hunts out her every secret place:

> For the mother who is right in it there is no past and no future. For her, there is only the present experience of having no unexplored area, no North or South Pole but some intrepid explorer finds it, and warms it up; no Everest but a climber reaches to the summit and eats it. The bottom of her ocean is bathyscoped, and should she have one mystery, the back of the moon, then even this is reached, and reduced from mystery to scientifically proved fact. Nothing of her is sacred."[23]

In its most horrible incarnation in adult life, the passionate intensity and the obsessive exclusivity of this form of love become the nightmare of stalking. Indeed, part of what is so horrifying about the figure of the stalker is that he combines an adult male's aggressiveness with the helpless infant's desperate need of the other and the small child's tyrannical, utterly self-centered possessiveness—a need, a possessiveness, that devour the other, incorporate the other into himself. This combination makes the stalker a kind of two-part monster, like a shark with a trailing umbilicus, or a bull with a gosling's head. And as in Winnicott's description of the mother, but in a way that carries real danger, the woman who is stalked feels wholly invaded and wholly disregarded. She feels the stalker's eyes on her wherever she goes, she loses all sense of privacy, and even when she goes to sleep at night behind locked doors, she feels watched. Yet she also feels utterly unseen in her own subjectivity, in her ordinariness, her human need to feel both safe and free.

Fortunately, in normal human development, this devouring claim on the other is a temporary phase. As Winnicott writes: "The on-looker can easily remember that it is only for a limited time that this mother is free-house to her children. She had her secrets once and she will have them again. And she will count herself lucky that for a while she was infinitely bothered by the infinite claims of her own children."[24]

Intensity. The human infant comes into the world with what might be called a fundamental expectation of intensity—so much so that the lack of intensity, as in neglect or abandonment, can itself be experienced intensely as something horribly, overwhelmingly, gone awry. The very nature of human gestation and lactation promotes thousands of hours of rapt, mutual observation from the closest possible range—a situation through which parent and child tend to become passionately special to one another.

This intensity, going back even before we were born, is the wellspring of human eros. Is it any wonder that our whole lives long, we remain susceptible to the power, fragility, and danger that are the very essence of intimate connection?

4

THE FLESH IS WILLING

FOR MOST OF my adult life, I have been a list maker. Every now and again I come across an old list, folded in the pocket of a jacket I haven't worn for years or pressed inside a book I read long ago, and all at once the elements of a past life begin to reassemble before my eyes. *Aristotle*, begins a list from graduate school, then

> *Hegel,*
> *swim,*
> *olive oil,*
> *shampoo,*
> *C.'s @ 6.*

In the months before my daughter was born, I tried to prepare myself for being blasted out of my list-making consciousness, that part of me that so longs to wrest order out of chaos, gathering in all the loose ends, granting the proper degree of urgency to each of the day's tasks. I expected to be overwhelmed by having a child, to have the rhythm of my days and nights blown apart, and the order in my life upturned: rows of things with rubber nipples drying by the sink along-side piles of unwashed dishes, laundry baskets hugely overflowing with tiny garments, errands undone, lifelong friendships left to languish, my garden neglected, my own grooming unkempt. . . .

This chaos arrived, to be sure, very much as I had imagined—albeit with a degree of fatigue and dishevelment so purely physical that the mind alone could never really grasp it beforehand. Within this chaos, however, there was a hidden surprise: a deep sense of peace, and of order, that I could never have foreseen.

For what I discovered was that in a way new to me, what I most wanted to do, and what gave me the most immediate pleasure, was not only generous and pleasure-giving, but actually necessary. I wanted to hold my baby close to me—and this was good, and what she required. I wanted to stroke her, to rock her, to kiss her and bathe her—and all these desires, acted upon, made me a good mother and my daughter a lucky child. In *A Natural History of the Senses*, Diane Ackerman quotes the neurologist Saul Schanberg, who told her, "If touch didn't feel good, there'd be no species, parenthood, or survival. A mother wouldn't touch her baby in the right way unless the mother felt pleasure doing it. If we didn't like the feel of touching and patting one another, we wouldn't have had sex. Those animals who did more touching instinctively produced offspring which survived, and their genes were passed on and the tendency to touch became even stronger. We forget that touch is not only basic to our species, but the key to it."[25]

There it is again: that link between adult sexual pleasure and the pleasure we take in touching our children. Does the link make us queasy? In *Mother Nature*, Sarah Blaffer Hrdy writes, "It might be helpful for all concerned to keep in mind that maternal sensations have clear priority in the pleasure sphere. Long before any woman found sexual foreplay or intercourse pleasurable, her ancestors were selected to respond positively to similar sensations produced by birth and suckling, because finding these activities pleasurable would help condition her in ways that kept her infant alive. It would be more nearly correct, then, to refer to the 'afterglow' from climax, as an ancient 'maternal' rather than sexual response."[26]

As good as it felt to take good care of Ariel, it was not an unceasing flow. There were plenty of times when what she needed—feeding in the middle of the night, a diaper change in a tiny airplane bathroom—was not at all what I felt like doing. Underneath, I was always aware of a certain fragility; I knew that with a single twist of fate—illness, an unsupportive husband, the wolf of poverty howling at the door—the task of mothering could easily take on a very different color. When my daughter was small this awareness actually intensified the profound concordance that I felt between what I desired and what was needed. I felt this more powerfully and continuously than at any other time of my life, before or since.

This in turn added layers of pleasure to the pleasure of caring for Ariel. There was the immediate physical pleasure of holding her next to me, of gazing at her, rocking her, and then there was a pleasure in this pleasure—which was itself multilayered. It began as a simple, very earthy sense of rightness, like the pleasure one feels when watering a parched garden or shaking a crusted layer of snow from a branch of spring blossoms. It's not that such moments hadn't been available to me before, but they were few and far between. Haven't most of us become accustomed to feeling that what we desire—to lie in the sun, to smoke a cigarette, to drive without being strapped into our seats, to make love impulsively, to drink another glass of wine or eat another slab of cheese—is not good for us?

As a new mother, I actually began to experience the exact reverse of what I had grown so used to; whereas normally I feel bombarded by negative and discouraging data, now the more data I absorbed about the benefits of touch, the more I felt encouraged to follow my natural inclinations.

From the classic study of "withered children" to the most recent research, the data were interesting in themselves, and it added another layer of pleasure to the experience of being a parent—as when one learns that the Mozart one already loves listening to is beneficial to one's house plants, or when a doctor prescribes the very vacation one longs for. And below this layer of validation, I discovered an even more profoundly pleasurable sense of rightness.

One summer, long before I became a parent, I shared a house with a young Orthodox Jewish woman, and the experience was at first quite strange to me. I had grown up with religion. My father was a Jew who had become a Catholic shortly before my birth, and we went regularly to Mass and to Confession; we observed the holidays and sacred seasons of the year. But through Ann, I observed what seemed to me a very different kind of devotion. The God of my universe was above all concerned with the state of my soul. He did not concern himself with such matters as whether I turned a light switch on or off, or removed a cake from the oven before or after sunset on a certain day of the week. Though the long list of sacred duties—*mitzvah*—seemed encumbering to me, and sometimes, I confess, quite maddeningly superficial, I also felt a certain beauty in the way they ran through Ann's daily life, and I felt how reassuring it must be to feel so sure that certain things at certain times—resting, eating fresh-baked bread, making love—could be so absolutely right.

Yet this rightness is precisely what I felt much of the time now that I had a baby daughter. I felt relieved of the burden of choice, of what the existentialists call "the anxiety of freedom." I have a friend Stephanie whose early experience of mothering was immensely difficult. Her marriage was dissolving, and her baby daughter was already manifesting the signs of a serious neurological disorder. Yet even Stephanie is not without nostalgia. "Surrender/control, surrender/control," she wrote to me in a letter. "Usually it's such a struggle for me to get the rhythm right in my life. But not when Marris was a baby. Then it wasn't a struggle. *Then my whole day was simply about the next thing.*"

"It is we who endow the alarm clock with urgency," Jean-Paul Sartre said—but he was not speaking as the parent of a small child.[27] When Ariel howled in the middle of the night, this was urgency, and her urgency was mine. More than anything, when my daughter was small, I felt released from the struggle between what I felt compelled to do and what was good and right.

"The spirit is willing, but the flesh is weak," wrote St. Paul, and "The good that I would I do not."[28] But now—for much of the time, anyway—the flesh was willing, and what the flesh willed, the spirit endorsed. And though I experienced the kind of rightness that I imagine my friend Ann did as she fulfilled her list of *mitzvah*, for me, it was quite wonderful that I didn't need a list. Ariel's cries, her coos, her hunger, her sleep, announced the day's priorities. I felt relieved of that deep anxiety that had always lain at the bottom of my list-making tendencies: the need to rank the day's tasks in order of their urgency, and—above all—the struggle between desire and necessity.

The wind bloweth where it listeth, it says in the New Testament, revealing another root of the word "list"—from the German *Lust,* which means "pleasure."[29] And here it all has a chance to come together: having one's cakes and eating them too, attending to what is most urgent and doing so with pleasure, out of the pleasure of giving pleasure.

5

CUTE

WE THINK OF cute as soft, warm, fuzzy, round. . . .

But the word "cute" actually derives from the word "acute," whose Latin roots go back to *acuere*, meaning "sharpen," from *acus*, which is Latin for "needle." Isn't it true that the cuteness of a small creature—a floppy puppy, a fuzzy kitten, a plump baby—pierces us? It is meant to. "It's so cute I can't stand it!" we say, testifying to the *de trop* of cuteness that contains an element of pain. And that element functions rather like the sharp sound of the automated teller that drives us to make some response: take out money, receive deposit slip, retrieve bankcard—now!

We see a cute, small creature, all softness and folds, and we are moved to do something: to touch it, pet it, hold it, feed it. "Shrewd," one of the meanings of "acute," is folded into the word "cute," and indeed, cuteness *is* the baby's shrewdness, the only shrewdness it has. Its cuteness pierces the armor of adult self-interest and draws us, irresistibly, into connection. The needle of cuteness extends and stitches us to the small creature that so desperately needs us.

There is a deadly earnestness at the heart of cuteness, a life-and-death urgency. Perhaps this is why some people claim an active aversion to cuteness, because they sense its double nature, the needle hidden in its soft folds. I've known people who insist that they have always resented Shirley Temple, that paragon of cuteness, with her round cheeks, her big bright eyes, her dimples and shiny coils of hair.

Her career began, so the story goes, when her milkman father left an irresistible photograph of her inside the empty milk bottle of a Hollywood producer. And in so many of the movies she starred in, the plot revolves around the power of her cuteness to penetrate a powerful adult—a rich old gentleman, a sea captain, a Broadway producer—and thereby obtain rescue from poverty, loneliness, despair.

Like the baby birds whose wide-open throats scream "Feed me!" at their parents, the baby's cuteness functions like a flag. Babies are exhausting to take care of, and they submerge us in much that is unappealing: they spit up, piss on us, shit in their clothes. . . . Cuteness is a matter of survival.

All this gives us another take on the world of advertising, which we think of as the very opposite of what is natural. "That's so commercial," we say, meaning synthetic, man-made, not of the earth. The function of a commercial is to present something as irresistible—a car, a refrigerator, a shaving cream. But flowers, with their glossy pistils, advertise themselves to bees. Male birds, with their shiny red bills at mating time, advertise themselves to females of their ilk. And our babies advertise themselves to us.

This is their utterly naive shrewdness, their innocent manipulativeness. For we are made to be lured, enticed by them with their big heads, wide eyes, protruding lips. The anthropological study of beauty has discovered that "myotiny"—youthfulness—is cross-culturally one of the universal criteria of attractiveness. Look again at the models in *Vogue*, *Glamour*, or *Elle*, at their big, blank foreheads, button noses, prominent wet lips—see how babylike they are? Their faces "attract us," which means "to pull toward;" they catch us, as the shiny stalk in the Venus's-flytrap draws the fly, as the yellow center of the rose pulls in the bee. In their faces, too, as in the babies', there is something that we cannot resist, something that contains its dose of pain, the *de trop* that rings like the sound at the bank machine and makes us want to *do* something: to buy a pair of shoes, a new red dress, a bottle of perfume.

It is a fact that children who are not so cute—the tiny, premature babies under their welter of tubes, children with physical anomalies, or children whose misfortune it is to resemble someone that a parent dis-likes—are actually at greater risk of becoming children who are abused.[30]

Fortunately, there is another layer of wisdom hidden in the word "cute." For the very evolution of the word, which went from being a property of the beholder ("acute," as in "discerning") to being a prop-erty of the beheld ("How cute!"), expresses the extraordinary mutual-ity of the parent-child gaze, the circularity of beholder and beheld. What may begin as simple programming—the way the baby bird's red throat commands a worm—becomes, between human baby and par-ent, a deeply creative act. For *There is a point at which I cannot help but care for you because you are irresistible to me* becomes *You are irresistible to me because I care for you: I bathe you, I feed you, I get up in the middle of the night to change your clothes. . . .*

Cuteness begins in the realm of typology—a baby, almost any baby, appeals to us because it possesses the general features of cuteness: soft-ness, roundness, a certain proportion of big and small, of clumsiness and delicacy. When we love a particular baby, however, our love is not only elicited by its cuteness, but endows this baby with cuteness, inten-sifies its cuteness. "A child only a mother could love!" we say. Even parents, with the detachment that a bit of distance brings, can be amazed at how ravishing they found their children when they were small. A friend, coming across the Christmas photograph she sent some years ago of her chunky baby in the bath, exclaimed to me not long ago, "God, I can't believe I actually sent that to people!" The baby who looked like a jewel in a foam of bubbles to her then, now looked like a lathered fatso in the tub.

Adults are programmed to respond to the cuteness of the young, and the young have an analogous sensitivity to type. Their attraction is even more generic than ours; infants are irresistibly drawn to even the simplest representation of a human face, a circle and two black dots for eyes. For them, simply that we possess a human face, and that it is the face that is there for them, is enough. This is their gift to us: they find us irresistible from the very beginning, whether or not we are cute. In his novel *Life Is Elsewhere*, Milan Kundera describes a new mother who has allowed herself to become totally absorbed in the physical happiness of caring for her baby boy:

> Unfortunately, with all the happiness that her body was giv-ing her, Maman was not paying sufficient attention to its needs. By the time she realized her neglect, it was already too late: the skin on her belly had become coarse and wrinkled, with the underlying ligaments showing through in whitish streaks; the skin did not look like a real part of the body, but rather resembled a loose sheet. Surprisingly, Maman was not unduly upset by this discovery. Wrinkled or not, her body was a happy one, because it existed for eyes which had perceived the world only in vague outline and which had not yet become aware (they were *paradisiac* eyes) that in the fallen, cruel world, bodies were divided into the beautiful and the ugly.[31]

Once, following fairly serious dental surgery, a friend of mine was awakened by her infant son in the middle of the night. Stumbling into the bathroom to throw some cold water on her face, she winced in hor-ror at her reflection in the mirror. She went to pick up her son, afraid of what his reaction to her might be, but when she leaned over his crib, he stopped howling and gazed up at her, eyes shining through tears. "I looked like a monster," she told me, "but he was just happy that it was me. No one else has ever loved me like that."

At such a moment, our children bring us a world away from cute-ness, to the love that lies below all showiness. "Show me your face before you were born!" is an old Zen koan: a challenge to reveal that about oneself which is utterly unconditioned, neither old, young, pretty, ugly, cute, not cute. Our children are mirrors reflecting that face back to us, again and again.

6

NIGHT LOVE

⌒

THE NIGHT BELONGS to lovers, it is often said. To thieves.

And to the parents of babies—?

No . . . the word "belongs" isn't quite right when applied to parents. For where lovers and thieves might be said to be at home in the night, in their element under cover of darkness, the parents of babies have a far more uneasy alliance. They get thrust into the night, forcefully ejected from sleep. "When should we set the alarm to wake up and feed him at night?" some neighbors of mine, the young parents of a brand-new baby boy, asked me the day they brought him back from the hospital. I laughed. Ask not when to set the alarm. For it will ring. And ring for thee. . . . The next morning, when I saw their haggard faces, I knew they would never need to ask again.

The night thief had been with them, the thief of sleep who comes in the form of a baby. Seeing the circles under their eyes, the rumpled clothes, the unkempt hair of the morning-after, it was as though I caught the whiff of something that—like any extreme physical sensation, whether heat, cold, pain—can't really be remembered. There's a sort of slot one holds in the memory; one can say, "It was so hot, our skin was melting into our seats," or, "It was so cold, I wanted to be in a warm hospital, having my feet amputated," but when the physical sensation is so powerfully raw and immediate, it seems to drain off like spring thaw, leaving only a surface impression. I do remember that when my daughter was a baby, I developed a longing for sleep so intense and so cellular that for the first time, I felt that I could really grasp what it must be like to be a junkie craving heroin. Other parents of babies have told me that they had moments of feeling sleep beckoning to them "like a mirage"—like a shimmering lake appearing to someone dying of thirst in a sea of sand, or that they saw a painting or photograph of someone sleeping and felt a rush that was almost sexual.

Sleep, the anthropologists and ethnopediatricians tell us, is among the major obsessions of the modern Western parent. A baby who sleeps through the night lies at the very core of our definition of "a good baby," and a baby who does not is both one of the chief laments that parents bring to doctors and one of the most heated topics of conversation among parents themselves. Sleep is not perceived as a problem, the scholars tell us, in those less-developed parts of the world, where it is the custom for babies to sleep with family members—with both parents most often, or with the mother alone.[32] Furthermore, within our own culture, it appears that the more education the parent has, the longer it takes their children to go to sleep![33]

Is such information really usable? I imagine a line of Ph.D.s, trading in their diplomas for a good night's sleep. Meanwhile, a friend of mine, going mad from sleep loss, tried instigating The Family Bed recently, only to discover that at eight months, her son was already " too old." "Too old?" I asked her, amused at the thought of little Gabe as somehow already irrevocably corrupted. "He thought it was a party and that we were jungle gyms," she explained. "All night."

Perhaps purely from the vantage point of a parent whose nights are no longer punctured by a baby's howls, I've arrived at a different take on the problems of sleep. I've come to believe that if, when my daughter was small, I had changed places with some other kind of parent, or some other kind of culture, I might indeed have solved the problems of sleep—but I would also have discovered a different obsession. I've seen those wooden angels that Indonesian parents hang above their babies to keep them from being stolen at night. I've heard about the Japanese parents who anxiously deflect any compliments to their children, lest a jealous spirit seek revenge; about Greek villagers who worry that "the evil eye" may fall upon an uncovered child; and of Italian peasants who desire, above all, that their children should be "good eaters."

I have nothing against The Family Bed, and if I had it to do all over again, it's probably what I would try from the very beginning. But for now—rather than seeking cultural escape or strategic relief for parental sleeplessness—how about plunging deeper *in*?

What does it mean that we fret so much about our babies' sleep? If the anthropologists are right—that we fret because we demand an unnatural, essentially un-human, autonomy from our babies, expecting them to sleep in separate beds, in separate rooms, from the very beginning, a practice apparently quite shocking to parents in other cultures—then a rather marvelous irony emerges. For the very parents who—placing a baby alone in its crib, tiptoeing back out the door to the privacy of the parental bed—declare that *You and I have our separate skins. You must learn to lie the whole night through with only the warmth of your own body, the rhythm of your own heartbeat*—these very parents find their own existence overtaken, invaded by their babies in the form of sleeplessness. There are few conditions as total as chronic fatigue. It affects the working of the muscles, their coordination and speed; if affects appearance, skin tone, the shine of the eyes; the working of the brain, speech, memory, alertness, mood, the quality of dreams.

In traditional societies around the world, sleep loss is a crucial ingredient of many initiation rites. Writes Mircea Eliade: "This initiatory ordeal is documented not only among non-literate cultures . . . but even in highly developed religions. Thus, the Mesopotamian hero Gilgamesh crosses the waters of death to find out from Utanapishtim how he can gain immortality. 'Try not to sleep for six days and seven nights!' is the answer."[34]

A woman I know wrote this about being up in the middle of the night with her baby boy:

My dreams are always cut short, a brittle breaking-off at the climax: a baby crying. That's when I hear our owl hoot at night. It's a sound I'd never heard before, a sound that thrills me, so deep, so mysterious. It's just like in the children's books: Owl is awake at night. Awake and waiting. My friend. He pulls me out of sleep into the night, still and sharp and out of my mind. It is then, in the darkest of nights, that I am truly quiet. My dreams trundle along without me. Stepping out of myself, I stumble into the room where my sturdy little baby wails, holding onto the crib, his fingers so small and strong around the rails.

I whisk him to bed almost violently. He attaches to my breast and only then do I stroke his fine hair, his scent coating my throat with the food I crave. This moment of dark love, of duty that is mine. He sucks from me my dreams, then yanks away, smiling to the digital *clock*, a distant sun, before he falls backward to a cocoon of sleep. I imagine my mother, every woman who has done this. How could we ever know what this would bring out in us?

What she describes has many of the elements of an initiatory ritual. Painfully roused from the familiar, from the warmth of her bed and the continuity of her dreams, her mind is open to an experience of great intensity; she hears sounds she has never heard before, feels a love she has never felt before, and through this, feels connected to generations of women before her.

For the modern parent, sleep loss virtually *is* the initiation into parenthood. It's the archetypal figure we see in the movies: the career-driven mother, the corporate father back in the office, struggling to swim with the sharks as valiantly as ever while melting to Jell-O from sleep loss. The actual experience of chronic sleep loss is rarely comic; one tends to feel irritated at best, overwhelmed, panicked, clinically depressed at worst. But the sleep-deprived parent is a staple of modern comedy. What makes us laugh? It's always funny to see people bumbling, especially if they're trying hard to appear powerful and in control. But perhaps there's something deeper. Perhaps, inside our modern body-mind, there's a primal human memory that stirs—a memory of all those centuries when babies were in virtually continuous bodily contact with their caregivers, day and night, night and day. After all, as Sarah Blaffer Hrdy writes, "For more than thirty-five million years, primate infants stayed safe by remaining close to their mothers day and night. To lose touch was death."[35] Perhaps inside each one of us there is some vestige of that ancient human baby who—upon seeing the postmodern mother and father melting with sleeplessness—laughs with a delight not entirely sweet . . . as if to say: *You thought from the very beginning that you could treat me as though I had a body separate from yours, one that could sit for long stretches at a time in little plastic seats, one that could sleep at night in a box with wooden bars, far away from the sound of your heart and the warmth of your breath. Ha! I'll show you. With sleeplessness, I will mark you as my own. I will brand your existence, through and through, as mine. See how you stumble, how you stutter and yawn? That's how I fold myself into your body and make you carry me everywhere, even when you leave me behind. . . .*

7

SLEEPING BABIES

TO COME UPON a sleeping child is like coming upon the inside of a shell. There is the same sense of peering into something that belongs to another realm, a secret life of sea bottom or childhood dreams. It is only for children that the Sandman comes. The sleep of grown-ups, being rarely such a pure departure, does not require his gritty, magical sealing.

The sleep of babies—bottoms up like small, archaeological mounds, on their backs with limbs flung out like the petals of an open flower, or curled on their sides like an inner ear—is emblematic of the absurd injustice of parenthood. The same babies who ravage the nights of their parents make it look as if sleep were the cheapest of luxuries, a bliss most easily come by. And they sleep in utter ignorance of this contradiction—an ignorance that is part of what we see when we look at them sleeping, their lips parted, the sweat in their hair, the almost imperceptible lift and fall of their chests. Seeing this ignorance, we forgive them with the same abandon with which they sleep. We do this again and again. Anyone who looked at *us* that way would have to be a god.

With slightly older children, what is most striking is the contrast between their intense waking busyness and the stillness with which they sleep. This stillness has an uncanny quality to it. They are arrested in *medias res*, as in Sleeping Beauty's kingdom: the cook frozen in sleep as one arm stirred the soup, the other arm held out to give the kitchen boy, his fingers closed around a stolen tart, a slap. Sleep overtakes children like lava flow, showing us—though with none of the horror—the same mix of eternity and the fleeting moment that we see in the figures of Pompei.

But the truly irresistible thing when we look upon a sleeping child is to see him surrendered to invisibility. Where does the relentless "Look at me!" go when he sleeps? If only children knew it is when they have relinquished their claim on our gaze that our gaze becomes most rapt. This is not a willed irony on our part—when they're awake, they are a blur of need and movement; the very intensity of their demand for us makes it difficult to *see* them. Still, to gaze at them sleeping is our nighttime secret as parents. Our sweet revenge.

PART II

A NEST OF DREAMS
Love and Imagination

1. Dreaming of Babies

2. Thomas and Ann

3. Worry

4. The Son I Don't Have

5. Ghosts

6. The Flesh Is Sad

Eros, which is so fully expressed in touch, in the now of presence, experiences absence as acute tension. Yet it is also lived through absence, sustained and amplified through imagination, anticipation, and remembering. This is so for lovers, and it is so for parents.

Long before a child comes into the world, a parent has imagined a child. This imaginary child may exist with the vividness and coherence of a fictional character; with the fleeting luminescence of a sudden thought or premonition; or in an altogether hazier, less determinate way. Whatever its quality, this pre-existence mingles with the existence of the actual child. Daydreams, night dreams, wishes, fears, predictions—with all these we build our nests, and the nests we build, however fantastic or ethereal, become, once a child is born, part of the real "stuff" of connection.

From the moment of birth, the dialectic of real and imagined child continues—sometimes for better in the form of hopes fulfilled, exceeded, or joyfully surrendered; sometimes for worse. This chapter explores the imaginative life of the parent-child bond, a life that precedes the birth of a child and that weaves itself through all the years that follow . . . and even beyond.

1

DREAMING OF BABIES

A SWIRL OF guppies, leaping frogs, a furry rodent, a puppy dog. When I was pregnant, I had creature dreams that as my belly grew, moved up the evolutionary ladder. The creatures that I dreamed of also went from small and plural to larger and more singular. Meanwhile, when I went to see the doctor, he described my womb to me in terms of ever-larger fruits: grape, apricot, lemon, grapefruit. Only in the last few weeks, when we had gone beyond the biggest melon, did he drop the imagery. Uterus was uterus—and in my dreams, the creature inside was human.

My friend Deborah, waiting to adopt a child from Vietnam, dreams, too. And in her dreams, as in mine, there has been an evolution. Even as the adoption process itself has proceeded from a far-off, open-ended possibility to an ever more imminent connection to a specific child—the baby boy named Phu—so the dream image has moved from multiple small animals, through larger animals, to an increasingly specific and singular human child.

Dreaming is one of the ways that we prepare for our babies. It is a form of nesting. A woman's body makes itself ready to bear a child, we make our houses ready, and our psyches make ready through a progression of images. Even before the child is born, this progression represents a form of getting-to-know, of deepening familiarity, belonging.

A thick lore surrounds the dreams of pregnant women.

There are things one hopes not to dream of—monsters, catastrophes—as if the quality of our dream life, like an amniotic fluid, might somehow seep through and affect the child. And also, of course, it's as if the things one dreamed of were omens. Even women who would ordinarily describe themselves as unsuperstitious find themselves susceptible in pregnancy and ascribe to their dreams a predictive power. These dreams have remarkable resiliency. After the child is born they continue to linger, like a scent or an aura—even when it might seem they had been rather unambiguously disproved. A close friend dreamed she would have a boy. A Tibetan lama confirmed this, adding that the boy would surely be a leader. She gave birth to a girl—but a powerful, strong-willed girl, which salvaged the prophecy. My neighbor dreamed of pink litmus paper and knew she would have a girl. She had a boy who is four now, and on his birthday, pink balloons came floating over my fence. "Of course, pink is his favorite color," she told me. "Of course," I said, and then I listened to her explain—as though her child had been born with a rare allergy—about the problems this posed : how do you find a pink tractor, pink high-top sneakers, for a boy?

It's no wonder that we ascribe such power to our dreams of unborn children. For though they live inside us, breathe the air we have breathed, ingest the food we have eaten, they are sealed off from us, veiled, mysterious. We are desperate for news of them, and dreams seem the right sort of news—a news from within—to receive from the creature within. Even the purely physical signs—a small foot moving, a somersault—are at first so subtle, so delicate, that they require dream-like images in order for us to perceive them. I really don't know if I would have been able to recognize my baby's movements in the fifth month of pregnancy if someone hadn't told me, "Wait for a butterfly's flutter."

There are other sorts of fore-news, too; there are cravings, and all manner of omens and ways of predicting. If you crave sweet foods, you'll have a girl; salty foods, a boy. In olden days, people said, *If nuts are plentiful in the orchard, children will be plentiful in the town. If apples abound, it's a good year for twins.*[1] Today in schoolyards, girls still jump rope to determine by the letter or number on which they stumble what their husband's name will be and how many children they will have.

A child does not come completely naked into the world, but emerges wrapped in a layer of images, and this process of wrapping can begin long before the child is even conceived. In pregnancy, the process takes on urgency; it might even be understood as part of the labor of pregnancy—a labor that demands time and energy, and to which we ascribe a certain causal power. Imagining certain things over and over, we feel as though we are helping to make them real, or to ward them off.

Pregnancy is not a passive form of waiting, neither in body nor mind. "To wait" and "to hope" are the same word in some languages, as in Spanish: *esperar*. While we wait for our children, we hope for them, and they emerge, for better or worse, as the fruit of our hopes. Our hopes and our fears: the hopes of a pregnant woman have fears inside of them, and the fears, hopes. A pregnant woman struggles to find what is for her the right balance of fear and hope. If she gives too much weight to the fears, will she make them come true? If she lets the hope grow too huge, will she tempt the sharp blade of fate?

In English, we say of a pregnant woman, "She's expecting," and to "expect" is another word related to *spectare*, like "special." Long before we can actually gaze at the spectacle of our children, we make them special to us through our expectations.

Of certain children, this is especially true. In legend, a powerful prophetic dream, or dreamlike visitation, often precedes the birth of a hero, a saint, a great spiritual leader. The Buddha's mother dreamed that a beautiful white elephant with six tusks entered her womb through her right side. When her husband, the king, summoned his brahmin advisers to interpret the dream, they told him that his wife would give birth to a son who had the thirty-two major marks and the eighty minor marks of a great being.[2] Christ's mother was visited by the angel Gabriel, who told her, "And behold, thou shalt conceive in thy womb, and bring forth a son . . . and he shall be great."[3] In these stories, the foreknowledge always comes absolutely true. There is no retroactive fudging over pink sneakers, or over a boy who turns out to be an unusually strong-willed girl.

Our heroes, our prophets, and saints must come to us under the sign of Necessity, and as far as the story of their lives is concerned, a slight miss is as good as a mile. Does there exist a universe in which Jesus might have become an average carpenter, or the Prince Siddhartha just any old king? Perhaps—but it is not the universe we live in. We want to know that extraordinary persons were extraordinary from the very beginning, that there has never been anything accidental, haphazard, or makeshift about them, and that even before they were born, they had to be who they turned out to be.

And now—not through dream, but science—a measure of Necessity attends the foreknowledge of even our most ordinary children.

The first time those photographs of the unborn appeared, the camera lens having found its way through the womb to the living embryo within, there was something deeply shocking about them. Like the first human foot on the moon, or the first shaft of light breaking into Tutankhamen's tomb, they were instances of a kind of trespass both huge and sacred.

But now the glimpse inside the womb is commonplace. We have the sonogram. We have amniocentesis. And if these technologies still provide momentous occasions for parents-to-be, they have nonetheless become part of the ordinary tackle and gear of pregnancy. It's easy to imagine that soon not just doctors, but parents too, will be able to read the genes of their unborn child as one might read the stocks or the baseball score on the ticker tape.

Will the dreams, then, lose their privileged status?

Perhaps.

In their book *The Earliest Relationship*, Drs. T. Berry Brazelton and Bertrand G. Cramer write, "One might expect attachment to, and early personification of, the newborn baby to be enhanced by foreknowledge of the baby's sex. Not at all." Based on a comparison of parents who were told the sex of their baby after amniocentesis or ultrasound with those who didn't know the sex until after the baby's birth, they report, "The parents who knew the baby's sex took longer to personify and recognize the individuality of the baby after birth. It seems there may be a protective system at work—protecting the parents and the baby from a too-early attachment. The work of attachment to an individual baby takes time, and early attempts to consolidate it may be rejected."[4] Those parents who had "trespassed" into the secret cave of the womb to gain their information seemed to compensate for it by remaining more resolutely vague about their unborn babies.

An ancient story of the Buddha's birth begins like this:

> One night during the midsummer festival in Kapilavastu, Queen Mahamaya had a dream. In the dream she ascended a height, and a large and beautiful white elephant with six tusks entered her womb through her right side. Then a great multitude bowed down to her. When she awoke, she had a feeling of great well-being and knew she was with child. Indeed, she thought she could already see the child completely and perfectly formed within her womb, as one sees the colored thread running through a clear bead.[5]

As one sees the colored thread running through a clear bead. . . . Centuries ago, there was already a dream of a see-through womb. Now, as the womb becomes increasingly transparent in reality, it seems that we still have a need to get to know our children slowly, and through a glass darkly. Even as our tools enable us to probe and peer and map and gauge with ever more certainty, we cling to the ancient human way and first meet our children through layers of dreams, long before we hold them in our arms.

2

THOMAS AND ANN

LONG BEFORE I ever imagined a husband or lover for myself, I imagined my children.

My mother and I spent my fifth summer in northern Michigan, in the same place where she had spent her childhood summers. It was a place of dark-green pines and paper birches surrounding a lake of clear turquoise water. In the evening, there were hot-pink-and-orange sunsets that gave way to warm black nights full of stars. But I must not forget to say that there were leeches that floated like white Kleenex in the turquoise water.

My mother gave me a green sketchbook at the start of this summer. Over and over, I drew my children. There were two of them. That was the perfect number, like the two-by-two's that boarded Noah's Ark. They were a boy and a girl. The perfect pair: *for male and female made He them.* Their names were Thomas and Ann. These, I believed, were perfect names.

Thomas and Ann were prototypical children, ur-children. I still have the green sketchbook, and now when I look at the drawings, they seem funny to me; the children have large, wobbly heads balanced on very small, spindly bodies. But to me back then, they were beautiful.

They were beautiful, and they were mine. I had no doubt that they would be mine. In fact, "would be" is not right. They were mine already. For *would be* and *already* were folded into each other, like God saying, "Let there be light," and there was light. As in *Harold and the Purple Crayon*, one of my favorite stories from childhood.[6] "Pies," thinks Harold with his purple crayon in hand, and there are purple pies. "Moose" to eat them, and there are purple moose. I drew Thomas and Ann and they were mine.

Along with the portraits of Thomas and Ann, there was another kind of drawing I did in the green sketchbook. That fifth summer of mine was the first time in my life that I experienced the world as "beautiful." It happened one evening as I was walking back from the edge of the turquoise lake, where I'd been trying to skip stones. Suddenly I was seized by a violently orange-and-pink sunset. I ran home, grabbed my crayons and drew this blaze of color. Over the course of the summer, I drew other things—clouds, pines, Queen Anne's lace, and Black-eyed Susans—that suddenly struck me as beautiful.

As different as the two kinds of drawings were—the children in methodical pencil and the others in an ecstatic scribble of crayon—they were linked. For at this time in my life, the beauty of the world and my belief in the reality of Thomas and Ann were one. In this world where the sunsets were a fiery pink-orange and the water was turquoise-blue, to imagine one's children was to know they existed. For the world was good. *Kitov*, God said in Hebrew when He spoke the world into existence, meaning *It was good*.

There were the leeches, of course. They floated in the clear turquoise water, and they were the one blotch, the snake in the garden. What did the leeches have to do with my future children? I didn't pose such a question then, during my fifth summer, in northern Michigan. But as I grew older, though the children I did not yet have continued to exist for me, I became less able to picture them, and there was a bit less certainty about them. Some gap between what I imagined and what might actually be had arisen.

Even into my twenties and thirties, I would look forward into my life through a very long, imaginary telescope. Through the lens, in a sandbox or playground, was a group of small children. I would pose myself this question: could I pick my own child out? The question had the quality of a test—like the girl doomed to spin straw forever into gold unless she guessed the name, "Rumplestiltskin!" If I couldn't guess correctly, I might forfeit my child. Though there was always some anxiety as I scanned the faces, in the end, I invariably found my son or daughter—for he or she had dark, curly hair just like mine.

Perhaps for each of us, there is one physical characteristic with which we feel most closely identified. For me, it is my hair. I'm not sure why, except that because my hair is unruly, I have often felt ruled by it. How surprised I would have been if I'd looked through the lens and seen the actual daughter who was destined for me. For Ariel has her father's light, straight hair, which I never once imagined.

Isn't that how it goes? The actual child replaces the dreamed-of child. We take that first look into our newborn baby's eyes, and—for most of us, as long as the child is healthy—the miracle of its real presence overwhelms any possible gap between the child we dreamed of and the child who has arrived.

It isn't long, however, before the dream child and the actual child begin their dance. And just as the dance between dream and reality exists between lovers, so it is part of the eros of parenthood. I bathe my baby, and the immediate pleasure of soaping her skin is intensified by all the times that I imagined bathing my baby, the times that I bathed my dolls, times that I saw my mother bathing my baby brother and sister, and that I saw other mothers bathing their children, whether real mothers bathing real children or mothers seen in paintings, in glossy magazines, or on TV.

Sometimes the pleasure is that there's such a perfect match between dream and reality. Bathing my real child, I have a moment of realizing *This is just as I imagined,* and such a realization can infuse the tiniest moment—lifting a child from the crib, wiping a grubby chin, untying the bow of a bib—with an almost numinous sense of rightness.

Sometimes the reality is better than anything imagined. A mother is awake in the middle of the night, nursing her baby boy in the dark. The owl hoots outside her window, her son pulls away from her breast for a moment and smiles at the face of the digital clock, "that distant sun." *How could we ever know what this would bring out in us?* she asks. The reality of the present moment, experienced so intensely through her body, her child's body, overwhelms anything she might have been able to conjure beforehand. "This may sound funny to you," my brother writes to me of his one-year-old Jonah, "but I never imagined a child could be so loving." What we could not have imagined, what surpasses our imagination, blows in like a provident wind and sets our ships to sail to places for which we had no map.

At other times, it's not so much about the reality being "better" than what we imagined, surpassing what we imagined, as that the miracle of real presence, however humble, ordinary, even difficult, seizes us, claims us, tells us in its own way: *Thou shalt have no other gods before me*. When this happens, it's as though the utter particularity of being with *this* child, in *this* moment, suddenly fills the whole universe. One morning when Ariel was three weeks old, I was changing her diaper when her eyes met mine and—quite unexpectedly, for I was immersed in lotion and cotton and pins—I felt us fall through to a new level of connection. I felt as if she had suddenly understood something, that I was not only the envelope of flesh that she had been born from and born to, but that *I was the one who tended to her.* If it is possible that there is something like the bare root of gratitude on the part of an infant, I felt it flare like a color in her eyes for a second. I felt thanked by her, and despite all the intensity of pregnancy, birth, the first few weeks of interaction, in some way I felt that our relationship truly began in that moment.

Whatever form it takes, the dialectic of dream and reality remains central to the parent-child relationship. And if it is often a source of pleasure, it can also be a danger zone. For here is where the leeches float, the white Kleenex in the perfect turquoise water. Here is where we find the children who don't match their parents' dreams. The longed-for boys who are born girls, like my great-great-grandmother, whose very name—Wilhelmina Henrietta Georgianna, for her three uncles—was testimony her whole life long to her father's disappointment. There is the musical prodigy who arrives with a tin ear, the beauty queen who didn't inherit her mother's high forehead, the perfect little sports fan who loves nothing so much as to read in bed. This is where the eros of parenthood, that powerful force of attraction, is powerfully challenged.

As a force that is fed by dreams, amplified through imagination—can it let go of its dream images when they threaten to come between an actual parent-and-child pair?

One afternoon when I was in my twenties and went for a walk in the city where I lived, I glimpsed a living tableau of mother and child that I instantly recognized as my future self with my future child. They were sitting on the front steps of their brightly painted row house, the mother on the top step, her little boy on the bottom step. She had set him up with a bowl of soapy water and a range of wands, and he was utterly absorbed in an ecstasy of bubbles. Big ones, small ones, long-lasting, brief, filled with rainbows and floating off into the sky or down the street. His mother was there behind him, exclaiming as he exclaimed, and though it was clearly she who had created and sustained his ecstasy, he seemed quite self-contained, this child of four or five, as he dipped his various wands and blew bubbles of various sizes. *That's the sort of mother I'll be*, I said to myself. *The quietly sustaining-in-the-background sort*, I thought. I was so sure.

But Ariel, almost from the beginning, was a child who wanted constant interaction with me. If she touched something, I had to touch it; if she saw something, I had to see it; if she said something, I had to hear it and respond. I could not be the supportive background presence that was my paradigm of the good mother. She positively forced me to be intrusive. Not only did this go against my grain, but it exhausted me. At times, though she was never prone to loud fits or prolonged tantrums, I was tempted to think of her as "difficult." Other mothers could put their children in a playpen for more than two minutes at a time. Why couldn't I?

Yet, in that exhaustion, in the surprise of her straight, light-brown hair, in the very places where she fails to match my image, where I am startled by her otherness—these are the very places, I have found, and continue to find, that when we find our way through them, can actually deepen the bond between us. Just the other night, she and I were in the car, heading home on a dark country road. It was a clear night, and she was gazing out the window at a sky full of stars. "Do you know that ninety percent of our universe is unknown?" she suddenly asked me. I didn't know that. Astronomy has always been too big and far away for me, and the things I wonder at are close at hand, like mothers and daughters driving in a car. "If it's unknown, how could we know that it's ninety percent of the universe?" I asked her. But really, I just wanted to hear the sound of her voice as her thoughts traveled to a place that my own almost never get to, without her. There is a special kind of closeness in such distance.

Yet because I am aware that I haven't been faced with a very large gap between dream and reality, I wanted to talk with my friend Stephanie. Her eight-year-old daughter is autistic—only "mildly" so, according to the official diagnosis, but her development and behavior have been strikingly different from those of her peers, and her condition has consumed an extraordinary amount of her mother's energy and devotion. I felt a little shy about broaching the subject with Stephanie, as if I were prompting her to tell me how her child had disappointed her. But the forthrightness of her answer made clear just what familiar ground this was for her. This was the territory in which she had been initiated into parenting, and for her, the very core of that initiation had involved the continual surrendering of any prior images as to the sort of child she would have, the sort of parent she would be.

Stephanie told me, "There are things you don't even allow yourself to imagine—all the coming-of-age experiences: the first slumber party, the first dance, going off to summer camp, to college. You stop yourself from dreaming, because it's too painful." Among the hardest things to let go of, she told me, were the conversations she had imagined having with her daughter. "I was going to do it so differently from my mother," she said. "When Marris got to the stage when girls start to hate their bodies, I was going to make sure she didn't fall into that. You know, I was going to give her a good feminist grounding! But I don't think I'll ever be having those kinds of conversations with her. I tell her how pretty she is, and it doesn't seem to mean anything to her. She just doesn't relate to her body that way, as an object for the eyes of others. So all of my years of planning to help a daughter through that passage aren't even relevant." All the years, she might have added, of imagining how in being a mother she would make up for the wounds of her own girlhood aren't even relevant. As a friend of hers, who also has a "special needs" child, said to her once, "We don't get to be the parents we want to be. We get to be the parents our children need."

Now that Stephanie has a second child, a little boy whose development is proceeding right "on track," it's this experience that's amazing, and even slightly freakish, to her. What surprises her, she says, is the way that her son's development seems to go of itself. "It's so easy with Gabe," she said. "He just pulls from me what he needs in order to take the next step. With Marris, she didn't initiate the next step, so I had to. To keep her from withdrawing into the privacy of her own experience, I had to continually enter her world and pull her forward."

Yet in the very surrender of preconceptions, in the necessity of entering the uniqueness of her daughter's world, Stephanie has found an extraordinary intimacy with Marris. "It's an intimacy that I don't think other mothers have with their daughters," she told me, "because it takes place in another universe, a parallel universe." At the very level of perception—in the way that Marris experiences sounds, colors, and smells—she lives in a different world from the rest of us. And she doesn't speak the way other children do. Stephanie told me, "She has her own way of talking: we call it Marris-speak. I've always been a bird to her. She tells me, 'You're half-bird, half-Mama.' She calls me 'Sparrow,' and she loves the space under my arm; it's a nest to her."

When I look up the word "tender," I see that it comes from the Latin *tendere*, "to stretch," and listening to Stephanie, the word rings true to its root. There, in the very places where the mind wants to cling to its own narrow version of how things should be—a daughter who goes off to slumber parties, a daughter eager to receive a good feminist grounding—there, where the heart might start to constrict and go hard around the sharp pangs of disappointment, there she has to stretch again and again. And there, it seems, is where she—bird-mother, with a small girl in the nest of her arm—has discovered a tenderness beyond anything she ever knew.

As for our children, they have no need for such stretching. They may be familiar at birth with the sound of our voices and the beat of our hearts, but beyond that, they arrive without images, without plans. They love us simply because we are there, and we are theirs. So long as we fulfill those primal conditions, they are ready to offer their unconditional love.

It's awesome, really.

For no one else has ever loved us that way. Not even our parents.

3

WORRY

WHEN I FIRST took Ariel out into the world, carrying her in my arms or in the red-and-white seersucker pouch, I found myself accosted by elderly ladies. "She needs a sweater on in weather like this!" "Where is her hat?" "Don't you have another blanket for her?" It was as though in bringing a baby into the world, I had come under the sway of the crones. They claimed me immediately, shaking their heads and wagging their fingers without so much as an "Excuse me," or "Do you mind if I say—"

Ariel was born in May, when the lilacs were in bloom and warm breezes blew through the windows even late at night, and I didn't worry too much about the temperature. I worried about other things. Even before she was born, I knew that to have a child is to have one's nerve endings multiplied by a factor of millions and to discover that even the softest bed could be a source of danger. When we first brought Ariel home from the hospital, I worried that she might suddenly stop breathing in her little wicker basket in the middle of the night, or smother in the blankets when she lay next to us, or that I might drop her as I went up or down the stairs. When she grew older and began eating bits of apples and biscuits and carrots and cheese, I worried that she would choke. As she grew mobile and more exploratory, I worried about sharp edges, falls, outlets, and poisons. During pregnancy, my dreams had moved up the evolutionary ladder and now that she was born, my worries had their own evolution.

Except for the fragility of early infancy, which managed to retain its privileged status, each stage of worry seemed dwarfed by the next. When she began to walk, I wondered how I could ever have worried when she was only crawling. When she stepped onto the school bus and waved good-bye, I wondered how I could ever have worried when, wherever she went, she was *en famille*. Parents of older children, even only slightly older children, still manage to make whatever I am presently worrying about seem quaint, even cute. Now that my daughter is thirteen, the parents of fourteen-year-olds shake their heads and tell me, "Just wait till she's fourteen. That was the terrible year for us." The parents of sixteen-year-olds tell me, "Just wait till she's driving." "Just wait till she has her first real boyfriend," says one mother. "Just wait till she leaves home," says another, whose daughter just recently e-mailed from Barcelona that she had fallen in love with an older man named Alfonso.

No one would call worrying a pleasant activity, yet it can feel as compelling as the most pleasurable addiction, as necessary as eating one more square of chocolate, lighting the tenth cigarette, reaching for another glass of wine. The fantasies spun from the worries that parents have—drownings, abductions, illnesses—can be as vivid as sexual fantasies. Sometimes I find myself panting with anxiety and realize that I have been completely absorbed in pulling my daughter from a tangle of car parts or rushing her to the emergency room that is open twenty-four hours a day, inside my mind.

If pleasure is not the motor that drives this spinning—what then?

In part, it seems a kind of magical thinking—oddly enough, very much like the sort of magical thinking that children engage in. "If I shut my eyes, no one can see me," a small boy thinks, crouching behind a blade of grass. He believes that what happens inside his mind spreads through the world. When parents worry, there's often a similar sense of agency—but in reverse. *If I imagine this disaster carefully, in vivid detail, it will not happen,* a mother believes. . . . *for the terrible things that happen are those that come out of the blue.* In their book *The First Relationship,* Drs. Brazelton and Cramer describe the pregnant mother's worry about her baby as a form of "work." If something should go wrong with the pregnancy or the birth, or if the child should turn out to be defective in some way, the mother will feel betrayed that her work was for naught.[7] And if something bad happens that she neglected to worry about, she is apt to feel that this neglect had a causal power, that if only she had been thorough enough in her worrying, she could have kept the misfortune at bay.

Worrying, then, is a form of vigilance, a parent's way of keeping sentries posted at the gates, on the mountaintops, to make sure no secret enemy advances. A parent's worry, you might say, functions as a kind of gargoyle—an unpleasant, unattractive creature that serves as conduit to keep both rain and evil spirits from entering and doing damage to the inner sanctum, to the sacred treasure of a child's life.

Worrying has another *raison d'être*. And like the first, it is a *raison sans raison*, an unreasonable reason, a reason for the heart, not for the mind. For worrying is simply an expression of caring; it is one of the ways—however useless, absurd, and even irritating to its object— that affection expresses itself. Chimps groom each other, and humans fuss over each other. Mothers brush and braid their daughters' hair; villagers share gossip at the well; if a son or a husband has gone off on a journey, he will be worried about—and it is all a form of braiding, bonding, of staying in connection. "Close-knit," we say of families and communities that maintain strong ties, and worrying is a form of knitting. One of the ways I know that I've fallen in love with someone is when I start to worry. I find myself thinking "His car is too small" or "The way home is too dark" or "That beach where he swims is too wild," and then I realize, "Oh—this is someone I really care about."

Couvade (from a French word meaning "to hatch") is the term for the sympathetic symptoms of pregnancy that expectant fathers sometimes develop: nausea, food cravings, weight gain. "Sympathy," meaning "affected by like feelings," seems indeed the right notion here. For one way of understanding couvade is that in intensifying a husband's involvement in his wife's experience, it deepens his connection to his not-yet-born child. And if couvade isn't exactly the same as worrying, it seems to belong to the same family of phenomena that while utterly useless from a certain perspective, can be seen from another to have an important role in strengthening the ties that bind. As the anthropologist Bratislaw Malinowski wrote in 1927:

> Even the apparently absurd idea of couvade presents to us a deep meaning and a necessary function. It is of high biological value for the human family to consist of both father and mother; if the traditional customs and rules are there to establish a situation of close moral proximity between father and child, if all such customs aim at drawing a man's attention to his offspring, then the couvade which makes men simulate the birth-pangs and illness of maternity is of great value and provides the necessary stimulus and expression for paternal tendencies. The couvade and all the customs of its type serve to accentuate the principal of legitimacy, the child's need of a father.[8]

Worrying, then, like couvade, is a form of "attention to [one's] offspring." Sometimes when Ariel has gone off on her own for more than a few hours, I suddenly catch myself *not* worrying. It's like being jolted awake by the sound of someone who has stopped snoring, or like being startled into awareness that a painful wound has stopped its throbbing. And the feeling then—though part of me says that I should experience it as coming to my senses, as being restored to reason—is that something is wrong, something is off. It's as though I've dropped a stitch, allowed a gap to occur, a gap in our connectedness through which only God knows what might slip: an accident, a sudden illness, an evil stranger. Discovering this gap, I pick up the thread and begin spinning again. . . .

These images of thread are apt. The word "worry" is linked to "strangle" through the root *wer,*which is found in "wrap." The etymology captures something about the double nature of worrying. To wrap one's arms around someone can be a gesture of caring, but if the pressure is too intense for too long, the gesture becomes strangling.

In the past, had I been asked about worrying, it's the negatives I would have emphasized. Such an inherently fruitless activity, I would have said, not even pleasurable in itself; boring, irritating, constricting to others.

But now, beyond the knitting of connection, I see that there is still another way to take the link between worrying and wrapping, threading, binding, weaving. For there is something about its very uselessness that—if I squint in a certain light—I begin to see as a kind of extravagant marvel, something carefully made, unmade, and remade each day by some sort of Penelope for the sake of the creature she loves. And so it is that even as my daughter enters her teenage years and the worries I have for her grow more highly charged, the fantasy-dangers more dangerous as we move from apple chunks and cupboard edges to fast cars and wild boys, I find that there is something new that I have begun to appreciate about worry, something I conjure in the following scene:

It's late at night, and a daughter is trying to slip unnoticed through the door—but she can't. Her mother has been lying in wait at her post on the sofa and at the first squeak of a hinge, she sits up and exclaims, "Where were you? I've been up for hours!"

What comes through to me now in those words is that the mother wants the daughter to see the labor of those hours, to appreciate them, as if they had produced not just a bundle of nerves but something truly valuable, as elaborate and intricate as a lace gown. It's as though the mother is exclaiming, "But look what I made for you while you were gone!"

And though the mother throws up her hands in a gesture acknowledging that she is indeed empty-handed, I want to shout "No!" In a reverse ending of "The Emperor's New Clothes," I want to insist on her behalf that she has indeed made something. It is something that a child could never appreciate—this garment that a mother knits, unknits, and reknits, and that can never be seen or worn.

4

THE SON I DON'T HAVE

EVERY NOW AND again I see him: the son I don't have. I've had sightings of him for a long time now. Unlike Thomas and Ann, the children I dreamed into existence when I was five, this son—who was not imagined but actually glimpsed, in different but very real incarnations—began appearing intermittently from the time I was thirteen.

Now I think it is no accident that he arrived just at that time. My first period came on my thirteenth birthday, and there is a link between puberty and this son. For a son is so clearly the fruit of sexual reproduction, the mingling of oneself with an-other, giving rise to still an-other. How else could a small penis emerge from a woman's body? Even when a grownup mother has an actual daughter, it is possible to imagine that the child emerged through a kind of mitosis—which is how small girls tend to imagine their children, and how I had imagined Thomas and Ann, as emerging wholly from my own existence and without intercession of male. Now that I was actually capable of sexual reproduction, the son began to appear.

He was a Christopher Robin-like boy, with bangs in his eyes and rubber galoshes. I spotted him from time to time at the beach in Santa Monica, wading through the channel that flowed out into the sea, or gathering driftwood and stones in a manner both dreamy and purposeful. He was a slightly odd child: always alone, he never appeared lonely, but rather as if he were accompanied by an entourage. Content, self-contained, he always looked as though he were fulfilling some urgent, yet mysterious, errand, or was about to happen onto another. He was exactly the right sort of not very labor-intensive boy for a thirteen-year-old mother like me.

The following year, my family lived in Paris, and now when I spotted my son, he looked more like Pascal in *The Red Balloon,* with a round French head and large eyes, shorts, knee socks, and a leather satchel. Though still quite engaged in his own world, he was less self-contained than the Christopher Robin boy. Sometimes, if you caught him in off moments, he had a lonely, somewhat anxious look, like the boy Pascal when his balloon is endangered. At other times, he rushed about with a quality of exuberant energy that when it wasn't intensely focused, could get wild and slightly manic. I often saw him at the Luxembourg Gardens. Running with a long wooden stick in his hand, he would give his rented sailboat a shove from the edge of the great fountain basin that sits under the Palais. Or, holding another wooden stick, he would ride the merry-go-round, thrusting his stick through a metal ring each time his horse came around. Small girls did these things, too, of course—but for me, at this time between girl and woman, at the critical moment when girls tend to subdue themselves, to tighten the reins, there was something quite compensatory about these small sons rushing about with their sticks, impelling their wooden boats across the water, accumulating the maximum number of metal rings on the carousel.

As I've gotten older, this son has gotten older, too.

I seem, conveniently, to have skipped his troubled teenage years—the years when he might have been skulking around with a buzz of green hair and a ring in his nose, or wanting a motorcycle or a set of drums—because he's in his early twenties now. I see him once or twice a week, behind the counter of the coffeehouse where I go sometimes to write or to meet friends and where he works, making steamed-coffee drinks. He has dark curly hair like mine and a Chagall-like profile. I try not to betray any undue interest or emotion as he hands me my double latte, and so far, nothing seems to have leaked out. We are friendly, in a pleasant, cordial way. I imagine that when he is not at the coffeehouse, he is an artist of some sort, a sculptor perhaps, or a dancer. I do not know his name.

―――――

There's another difference, too, now that I am older. In my early sightings of this boy, he represented *the son I might one day have*. Over the past few years—imperceptibly, and yet quite radically—his status has changed. One day, as the young Chagall man asked whether I wanted cinnamon or chocolate sprinkled on my milk foam, I realized that he was *the son I would never have*. And this realization has given way to a deeper and more intricate understanding of what it is that "son" has meant to me.

For though over the years I've glimpsed him in actual real boys, this son has always been an abstract son, an essence of son. And now, seeing him through the deepening intimation of my own mortality, I realize more clearly what it is that I will never have: the miracle that a small penis might actually emerge from my own body. Aside from what seems like the sheer physical marvel of it, not unlike pulling a rabbit from a hat, what this has meant to me is the possibility of an *other* that belongs to me as no other ever has. I imagine that this is what a friend means when she tells me, speaking of her young son's love for her, "It fulfills me in a way that a man never could." And when I think of a father's counterpart, I imagine a man who, taking his baby daughter in his arms, feels both her startling otherness and a startling permission. For this is a female body that, utterly helpless and having been made from him, "belongs" to him in a way that even her mother's body does not.

I imagine, too, that this dynamic is somehow part of an amazing dream that a therapist told me of. A woman he knew was intensely grieving the death of her teenage son. One night in the midst of her grief, she dreamed that her son had come back to life. He was lying beside her, naked, and she had her hand lightly resting on his penis. The feeling-tone of the dream was very peaceful, and it was only as her waking consciousness returned that she felt somewhat disturbed by the image, and wondered why it had brought her such comfort. Hearing of the dream, I wondered, too; in touching her son's penis, did she make contact, once again, with his vitality? Did she feel that once again he belonged to her in the miracle of his otherness? Had he returned to her with the physical intimacy that exists between a mother and her baby boy? What made me gasp when I first heard the dream was that both transgressions (for to "transgress" means to travel beyond, to cross a boundary) were equally radical: a son returns from death, a mother lays her hand on her grown son's penis. Yet both, in the dream world, were so powerfully right, and together, they made a powerful medicine for her grief.

When mothers dream of the daughter they don't have, when fathers dream of the son they don't have, it's a seamless familiarity, a pure reduplication of themselves they long for. The first time I put Ariel in the pink-and-white-checked dress—no bigger than a handkerchief—that I had worn as an infant, I felt a moment's absolute fulfillment of my hope for a daughter. And a woman I know wrote this description of her daughter: "I watch her one day in the bath while she is draining the tub, her pink, fleshy buttocks partly rising, like half-moons, out of the dirty water, the distinct brown freckle along the crack, and am taken back by the sensuousness of the scene. Is it just me seeing her that way? A kind of autoeroticism, as I see her body turning into mine, in a younger, more beautiful, incarnation? It is almost as though in writing this, I am transformed, as though my own exhibitionist self can rise up and show itself, finally, like the hidden jewels in a display case in a dream I once had."[9]

But to long for a child of the opposite sex is to long for a marvel of difference, not for sameness. A friend whose first child was a daughter told me of how different the quality of intimacy is with her little son. She said, "He'll be sitting, facing me on my lap, and I'll find myself picturing him as a young man. And I'm wondering, 'What sort of driver are you going to be? What sort of lover will you be? Will you be a good lover?' And then, it's so strange, there's this baby sitting on my lap, and all of a sudden, I feel shy."

It's a shyness she never felt when her daughter was a baby, she told me, for in her femaleness, her daughter was so familiar to her that to touch her was like touching herself, to look at her was to look into the eyes of her own earlier self. No space for shyness there. And not the same parade of questions for the future—for such questions imply a recognition of "otherness" that was not yet apparent. "Shyness" seems a beautiful word in this context, one that balances on the rim between the awesome intimacy that is granted a parent and the deference that holds between the sexes.

———————

When I dream of a son as *the other who belongs to me*, I imagine a host of potentially healing benefits. Healing, that is, to precisely those wounds of difference, distance, and disappointment that can so easily arise between the sexes. Among these benefits, there is the thought that I could actually have a hand in shaping someone of the opposite sex. "A hand"—as in "the hand that rocks the cradle," the hand that lifts the breast to his mouth, wipes the applesauce from his chin, zips up his small pants. To think that with one's actual hands, the hands of a woman, one could have a hand in shaping a male self. He would grow up to be strong, my son. I can see him doing portage in the wilderness, carrying a canoe and all his supplies, building a fire at night, rising at dawn to paddle out over dark waters. But he would be gentle, my son, and—having been so close to his mother—deeply empathetic, a man who knows how to talk to women.

Whenever my dream-boy thoughts begin to float too high, my friends who are actually raising boys have a way of bringing me back to ground. One such friend is the poet Peter Levitt, who has a twenty-eight-year-old daughter and a three-year-old son. He told me, "When my daughter was small and I imagined her growing up, I had fears for her. I worried about the life of a girl in a world that is so hard on girls. Now that I have a son, I have worries for him, too—worries I never imagined having. He's a very gentle boy, and I want him to be gentle, but I want him to be able to hold his own in the world of boys, too— and it's not a simple thing. I call him 'Honey,' 'Sweetheart,' 'Darling,' *and I hear myself saying those words to a boy*. I will not withhold love words from my son, but I hear them in a way that I didn't with my daughter. And I can feel that it's the culture, coming between me and my son. Fathers don't want their sons to grow up and be some guy's sweetheart, right? I've talked with other parents about this, mothers and fathers both, and they agree. There's a way that we parents abdicate to the culture. We let the culture determine the level of eros between us and our sons. Everyone wants gentle boys—but no one wants to raise them."

As Peter talks, I make myself listen intently, as if through his words I could absorb something of the actual texture of what it is to have a son. But almost as soon as the conversation ends, I can feel my thoughts floating back up in the air like balloons. I could try to pull them back down—but why? Since I'll never have a son, why not let myself go and dream of the boy I have raised, without worry, to be as gentle as he is strong?

He has a lean but very muscled, manly body, my dark-haired Chagall boy, but he is sensitive and refined. He reads the poems of Rilke and Mandelstam, he remembers birthdays, grows a bank of sweet peas in his garden; his *yin* and his *yang* are in balance. With him, I can experience the most delightful combination of difference and sameness. I can take pleasure in our resemblance—our dark, curly hair, the high angle of our noses (redeemed by him; I always knew it would be handsome on a boy)—but he does not get under my skin as a daughter does, riffling through my nightgowns, borrowing my combs, losing my earrings.

In his boy-body, man-body, he is different enough that there is the magnetism of opposites, a certain flirtation even, for he knows how to charm me, cajole me, wheedle a favor—yet he is flesh of my flesh. Through him, I have an entrée into another world from the very beginning, all the way through to his young manhood and that vision of him carrying a canoe into the wilderness. Yet I am reassured that he won't take me too far into his world, for I am his mother, and a young man has a need to strike out on his own. At the same time, I know that he won't ever leave me completely behind. For this is not a lover, this man I don't have. This is my son.

5

GHOSTS

A FRIEND TOLD me, "One day when I was twenty-seven and lived in the country, I was taking the long walk that I took every day. All of a sudden, I felt inhabited. I knew there was a girl inside of me. In an instant, I fast-forwarded to her at age ten. I could see her so clearly, a dark-haired girl. I began to talk to her. I said, 'I'm not ready for you now. I'm very sorry. Will you come back to me?' "

My friend was indeed pregnant, and only a few days after that walk, she miscarried. She has a daughter who is twelve now, and she told me: "It's fourteen years since I had that experience, but I've never forgotten that little being who inhabited me for such a brief time. I look at my dark-haired daughter today, and she looks so much like the girl I saw on that walk. Sometimes I can't help but wonder: *did* she come back to me?"

Every family has its ghosts, its children who, once conceived, never fully took root in earthly existence. Through miscarriage, abortion, or stillbirth, they transited quickly, like shooting stars. Yet there is a way in which they do remain in the family. Sometimes, it appears, they have left more physical evidence of themselves than we have known how to interpret. Not long ago, I read that left-handedness may be the vestige of having begun life face-to-face in symmetry with a now-vanished right-handed twin. Another theory is that those strange hair balls, (called *teratoma*) that sometimes grow deep inside, containing bits of bones and teeth, are the remains of one's own double.[10]

For the most part, however, the traces we find are less substantial, coming to us in the form of a fleeting thought, a *what-if*, a *might-have-been*, a chosen name that remains forever attached to the child who didn't stay.

One night when I was five, my mother was tucking me in bed when a worried look came over her. She rushed to the bathroom and I heard the toilet flush, and flush again. The next morning, my parents came into my room, sat on my bed and told me in what I thought of as pale voices that there had been a little boy in my mother's belly who had died and that his name would have been *Jordan*. That's all I ever knew of him: my mother's kiss, her worried look, the *whoosh* of water, my parents' pale voices, the name *Jordan*. Yet this brother does have some form of existence for me. Once or twice a year, he wafts into my consciousness, and whenever I hear the name *Jordan*, I feel as though a little electrical shock is passing through my body.

My friend Lynn Martin was forty-one when she became pregnant for the first and only time in her life. She miscarried this child, and she is still acutely aware of him, so much so that the absence is in its own way a kind of presence. Lynn is a poet, and in a recent poem, she wrote,

> *Outside the window, the apple tree*
> *holds everything it has ever held*
> *within its branches. Who will see*
> *its radiance? House guests rise early,*
> *one a boy the age my child*
> *would have been*, ten years.
> This could be my son.

This conditional tense, the son who *would have been, could have been*, is one mode in which these children exist, with a subtlety that surpasses even that brush of "butterfly wings" that—if they stayed that long—is how their mothers first felt their movement in the womb. And sometimes, in their very subtlety, they press quite heavily, these almost-children. I know more than one woman who twenty years later still grieves or feels guilt over an aborted child. I know a couple whose stillborn child, their first, made a revolution in their lives. After her death, they sold their home in Montana and moved a thousand miles away to live outside a monastery in northern California. They have a grown daughter now, a beautiful girl in her twenties. The course of her life—the place of her birth, her unusual upbringing as a child among monks—was shaped by the sister she never met and who never saw the light of day.

In Japan, there are small temples and statues everywhere to honor Jizo, a bodhisattva, one whose compassion for others has been fully awakened. Jizo's compassion is especially directed to those who have died, and above all, to children who have died. He is usually depicted as a monk holding a staff with jingling bells in one hand and a jewel in the other. Mothers who have lost a child—whether through miscarriage, abortion, stillbirth, illness, or accident—pray to Jizo and place a child's bib around the neck of his image.[11]

We have no such symbol that represents, for all of us, the connection to those who never came all the way into our lives. Some of us believe in angels, some do not; there is no single custom or ritual to help us make the sense of ongoing connection tangible. For the most part, we simply go along, experiencing this connection in a private, inarticulate way—whether as the dull ache of a grief or a guilt that never completely vanishes, or as a presence that suddenly flares at the sound of a name, at the thought of a *would-have-been*.

Imagine a being endowed with an extraordinary form of vision such that he was able to see the ghost children that hover around each and every one of us: the daughters, the sons, the brothers, the sisters that *might have been*. What might this being tell us about what he sees? That the smallest family, indeed the least one of us, is a crowd? I like the way my friend said it:

> *Outside the window, the apple tree*
> *holds everything it has ever held*
> *within its branches. Who will see*
> *its radiance?*

6

THE FLESH IS SAD

NOT LONG AGO, in an old jewelry box, I found these words, written in purple ink on a small piece of paper:

> *Ariel missis papa*
> *She wants him now*
> *The fown isn't good*
> *A ledr isn't good*
> *And a memure is woors*
> *All I need is you*

What lover couldn't identify with this lament? Of course a fown isn't good, a ledr isn't good, and a memure is woors. For when a love is intensely physical in its nature, anything short of physical presence does not simply fall short, it leaves an abyss. A memory is even worse than the phone or a letter, for while the phone and the letter disappoint us in the thinness of actual presence they offer—the sound of a voice, a scrawl of words—memory torments us with the guise of full presence. To the one who thirsts, it offers not a drop of water, not a damp cloth pressed to the lips, but the mirage of a full and shimmering lake.

Adult lovers can sometimes make a kind of delicacy of their long-ing, turning the very torment of imagined presence, of acutely felt absence, into a kind of ecstatic absorption, a prolonged tension that heightens the anticipation of reunion, of consummation. Small chil-dren who miss their parents do not have this option. And their parents

suffer separation much as they do. Even people who miss their animals—their dogs, their cats, and their horses—can know the sharp
pain, the raw ache, that arise in the absence of one loved in and
through the body. It's a pain that permits of no sublimation and can be
remedied by one thing only: presence. *All I need is you.* . . . .

What *memure* could my daughter, at age five, have found so tor-
menting when her father went away for a few days? She had a habit of
falling asleep on his lap at night, her head nestled against his shoulder
as he sat before the computer screen; was it this particular scene that
came back to her, or one like it? Or was it a more diffuse, yet still
intensely vivid, sense of his presence, a kind of blur of face/voice/smell
that the moment she conjured it, made her with longing? Or was it,
rather, the ache that arose first and then gave rise to the memories that
intensified the ache: the ache giving rise to the memories giving rise to
the ache giving rise to the memories?

Ariel is thirteen now, and recently we were separated for a month
when I went across the country to teach. The first ten days or so, we
did just fine through phone, letter, and e-mail. *After all,* I said to myself,
*lately when we're together, she mostly ignores me; it's not the way it was when
she was little and her body was like an extension of mine. We've moved into
another mode of relationship, one more like close friends: you miss them when
they're gone, but you don't feel it in your body.* Then the ache set in. I felt
it first as a hollowness in my chest, a kind of ringing emptiness, and
then the ache seemed to give off images of her. It was much the way
the ache of hunger beyond a certain point generates images of food, but
without the degree of specificity with which hunger—with its meatloaf
and mashed potatoes, its fried eggs and slices of rye bread with butter—
seeking to satisfy itself, torments itself. Rather, it was that I felt the
ache, and around the ache there hovered a kind of general sense of her,
a sort of cloud of her, like a mist of fine particles that I could almost
breathe in before they vanished into absence and the ache again.

To breathe in. Isn't that what it's about, those relationships that
are inextricably linked to breathing the sheer physical presence of the
other, a presence that has the distinctness of the cloud that surrounds
one planet and not another, whether red or yellow, cool or warm, com-

posed of sulfur, ether, or oxygen, a fine yet utterly identifiable particulate mist for which no substitutes, no look-alikes, no runners-up, no *fown*, no *ledr*, no *memure*, will do?

In his novel *Oscar and Lucinda*, the Australian writer Peter Carey describes the way in a which a son's love is inextricably linked to the experience of his father—a scientist who carried with him the scent of certain chemicals—as a kind of atmosphere. "His father was close and familiar, so familiar he could not have described his face to anyone. He was a shape, a feeling, that thing the child names 'Pa.' He was serge, formaldehyde, a safe place."[12] When father and son are separated, Carey conveys the physicality of the son's grief in a way that is all the more striking because its expression, in this Protestant English household, has been so restrained. "He wished to be home by the fire in the clean, lime-cold cottage where his father and he frightened Mrs. Williams [the servant] by discussing famous murders in calm and adult detail. They were closest then. Afterwards his father would give him a sharp hug and rub his beard across his cheek, making him giggle and squirm. This was called 'a dry shave.' It was an expression of love."[13]

I have friends to whom I am devoted, whose loss I would grieve acutely—but I don't need to inhale them. In these other relationships—between lovers, between parents and children—absence engenders a kind of cellular grief, a grief that is deaf and blind to all but its need to breathe in, breathe out, to smell, to touch the body of the other. In Jane Hamilton's novel, *A Map of the World*, a mother who has been in prison for several months is reunited with her family. As the father drives them all home in the car, he turns around to look at his wife: "She was holding both girls in her lap in the back seat. She was resting her head against them, breathing heavily as if their dirty hair and clothes, and the forced air of the heater was fresh."[14]

In the same jewelry box in which I found my daughter's note to her papa, I found several torn pages from a journal I had kept long ago, before my marriage, at the time of a tormented love. Rereading them, I see how close they are: the adult's grief, the child's sensation of abandonment. From these journal pages, written in a kind of shorthand as both a daily log and a reflection on absence, I reconstruct this painful passage in my life. It was a time when even though I saw quite clearly through the mind's eye what it was I had to do, the clarity brought cold comfort:

February 20: . . . I've made it through the first week of separation. It's an elaborate regimen. As I go through each day, I recite, just under my breath, a list of phrases regarding M's untrustworthiness, his paranoia, his chaotic mode of life. As if fingering beads on a rosary, I recount for myself the various milestones of his wounding behavior. In the morning upon rising and at night before bed, I do my cognitive therapy exercises. On one side of a sheet of paper, I write down one of my operative myths, such as: My *happiness is dependent on being in connection to this man.* On the other side I counter it with what I know to be true: *No one I have ever known has caused me such pain.*

But my body aches for him. I've been unable to sleep and have great difficulty swallowing. I'm growing thinner and thinner, and as I move about the world, I feel small and painfully singular. Above all, I have the sensation that there is too much air on and around my skin. The entire surface of my body feels exposed.

Exposed. Like a baby left on a mountaintop. Oedipus. All of a sudden, it hits me. Isn't it strange that Oedipus, who was destined to enter the most devastatingly proximate of relationships—incest with his mother—began life lying utterly alone, on a bed of rock under a huge sky?

But perhaps it's not so strange. Perhaps it is the very memory, or imagined fear, of such bare aloneness that propel us into our own dangerously too-close relationships. . . .

As a child, I slept with my father's handkerchiefs. At the start of each week, I picked a clean one from his mahogany drawer: its fresh, thin-cotton smell, mixed with the odor of dark wood, was him to me. I couldn't fall asleep unless I held one under my nose. I didn't suck it or twist it or stroke it the way some children do with their fetish cloths. I just had to breathe through it. If I didn't, I had a sensation of too much air—and too much cool air—against my nostrils. And that minute, almost microscopic, sensation was the portal to an immense anxiety.

Exposure. Oedipus lying on the mountaintop. Too much cold air bearing down. What one wants is muffled air, air breathed through a loved one's skin.

February 24: Yesterday was Day 10 of the separation. Unbearably restless in my house all morning long, I drove through a drizzle of rain to the bookstore. I walked up and down the aisles, completely unable to focus. Fiction? Religion? Psychology? Self-Help? I might as well have been in a cigar store or a bait-and-tackle shop, so remotely did the shelved objects seem to have anything to do with me. I found myself murmuring the words of a Mallarmé poem: *La chair est triste, helas, et j'ai lu tous les livres.* "The flesh is sad, alas, and I have read all the books."[15]

Yes, the flesh is sad. And not just sad; it is utterly ungrounded, uncentered. I flee the bookstore, with no book in my hand. How can I settle on a book when my very being is unsettled, dispersed?

I get into my car, turn the key in the ignition, pull out into the street—but where is there to go? Now, without the body in relation to which my body has known where it was—near to him, far away from him—my being floats. Here is panic again, with its root *pan*, meaning *all*, *everywhere*. Everywhere and in all places, he is nowhere. Without being in relation to his body, whether near or far, there is no near or far anymore. There is no there anywhere.

I drive past his house. My car pulls in his driveway. This is so unlike me. I don't do things like this. Hang up calls. Sudden stops. Where did the clarity go?

I go up to the door.

I knock and he comes.

The greeting is awkward. All the habits are changing. Do we still embrace when we say hello? How close do we sit on the living-room sofa?

Still—what have I got to lose? We make chitchat for a while, and then I tell him, *I need you to hold me*. We go into the bedroom and lie down on the bed. He puts his arms around me. It's clear to me that he's not in good shape. There is something dark and slack in his face—a deeply self-estranged look in his eyes that has grown all too familiar.

Hold me harder, I say.

In my mind, I'm berating myself. *Backslider,* I say. If the one or two people I've confided in could see me, they'd be aghast. They know the oracle has spoken clearly to me: would Oedipus, having grasped the truth, slip back into bed with his impossible love? Yet, here I am, back in the lair with the beast. He begins to rant, in a particular way that he rants in his paranoid states. "The dogs . . ." he begins. "They're at my heels. The spears. They throw spears at me when I'm down. . . ."

I used to try to reason with him, but I won't anymore. *Let him rant,* I say to myself, pressing even closer to him, my face against his neck, the top of my head under his chin.

He smells right.

He smells right.

His is the only skin in the world through which I want to breathe.

Now, here I am.

Here I am, where he is.

There is a here here.

Driving home, my mind is confused. Have I made a terrible error?

Back in my house, I put on my nightgown, brush my teeth.

Somehow I know, deep down, that in the morning—Day 12—I will wake up and resume the labor of separation.

For now, I will climb into bed, close my eyes, and sleep like a baby.

PART III

SCISSORS AND BUDS
Separation and New Life

1. Strings

2. Infidelities

3. Disgust

4. Seasons

5. Tempo

6. Buying Ladybugs

7. Last Things

The umbilical cord is cut and a baby is folded into its mother's arms. From the very beginning, the dialectic between fusion and separation is present in the parent-child relationship, and it intensifies as our children grow. Sometimes it takes dramatic form, but often it is more subtle, requiring of the parent a complex movement of both receding and staying in place. On the brink of adolescence, my daughter is clearly beginning to snip at certain threads of familial connection—at the same time that she requires them to hold steady. Nearly every day presents me with at least one moment in which I have to discover whether to step forward or to blend into the background of her life.

Lacking the powerful initiation rituals of traditional cultures, our own children's attempts to separate from us often take place through the mechanism of aversion. How I hated the sound of my parents' eating when I was a teenager! And now, as a parent, I sometimes feel the same sort of disgust emanating from my daughter, and I feel something close to the pang of a jilted lover. You, who used to gaze at me with such adoration! Now if the cut of my pants is wrong, or if I hum too loudly in a public place, you look at me as if you wished I'd disappear into the ground.

This chapter explores the paradox at the heart of the parent-child relationship. For though it is called the greatest of all human ties, it has betrayal built into its core. Our children must abandon us, and we—without abandoning them—must allow ourselves to be abandoned. Between lovers, separation carries tragic implications, but between parent and child, it represents fulfillment—the telos of the relationship. As such, it is an essential feature of the eros of parenthood.

1

STRINGS

*

"NO STRINGS ATTACHED," we say—meaning that it's genuine, without special interest, with no entangling possessiveness or ulterior motive.

Yet there is string from the very start, at the very nexus of mother-child love: there is that cord in the womb. (And *nexus*, meaning "center" or "core," comes from *ned*, "to bind.") We begin life in the core of our mothers, bound by a cord.

At birth, the cord is cut. Sometimes there are other cuttings, too: the string beneath the tongue in some cultures, the foreskin of a baby boy. And sometimes the mother, having been torn in the violence of birth, is sewn with thread so her body can reknit itself into a separate whole.

Strings tied and strings cut: a play of strings attends us all life long. The original string, the umbilical string, is cut, but new strings await the human child.

Babies are tied in slings to their mothers, rocked asleep in the woven strings of hammocks, bound in cummerbunds, wound in bands of cloth, nestled in packs that tie around a parent's waist . . . and what are a parent's arms if not for fastening?

In times past, European children wore "leading strings," with which adults could guide them like puppets, and though it has grown unfashionable, one can still sometimes see toddlers toddling in a kind of halter.[1] We speak of a child as tied to its mother's "apron strings," and we speak of "heartstrings"—which my dictionary defines as "the deepest feelings or affection."

And so it seems that there are strings, and there are strings. When we speak of "pulling strings" or "strings attached," these are the tight strings of self-interest. What characterizes the strings of real love?

One summer many years ago, I went to visit my mother's friend Amalia, an anthropologist doing fieldwork in Asturias, the part of northern Spain that looks like Ireland, with mountains, intensely green fields, mists. Amalia had three children, and the youngest was a little boy named Max. By the time he had come along, Amalia thought she knew what sort of mother she was—but Max demanded a whole new set of responses. An intense little boy, and very bright, he was less verbal than his brother and sister, tending to express his desires and aversions through vigorous gesture and movement, and by emphatic grunts, whoops, and growls. He was less cuddly than his siblings, the sort of child whose body tends to tense when touched and who wriggles out of embraces.

Yet Max had a sort of chant at that time, four words that held considerable power for him and that he repeated at different times throughout the day, sometimes belting them out at the top of his lungs. *belly-button-piggy-boy*. I don't know what the "piggy" might have meant to him, but the belly button seemed clear. Over and over, he drew two creatures, one big, one small, connected by a line. And every morning after our breakfast of fresh coffee (ground by Max himself by turning the long brass handle on the wooden coffee box) and a round loaf of bread from the bakery, Max had a ritual. We would go outside with a length of string and he would tie things, one to another: a stone to a tree, a tree to a fence, himself to a tree . . .

Writing this down now, in black on white, it seems obvious to me that Max was passionately concerned with the thread of connection. Yet for a mother living in the thick of it, it wasn't so obvious. What Max expressed directly to his mother was often a form of resistance. Amalia would have loved to have a more physically affectionate relationship with him, but she learned to wait for those rare moments—of illness, forgetfulness, or on the brink of sleep—when he relaxed in her arms or nuzzled against her face. Gradually she learned that he was a child who needed his mother to be there, in the background, as he manipulated the strings that bind. He was like a little kite that, flying off into the sky, wants to reel its own string—yet also wants the steadfast presence of the human it belongs to, standing on the grass below.

And she consented. Living among them that summer in Asturias, I witnessed it again and again. I could see the moments when Amalia's patience snapped, when she felt close to tears. And then she would reel in her own desires. Every now and then she would erupt and grab a hug from him or chide him for his brusqueness—but then she'd let him go again.

Taut, slack. Short, long. Thick, thin. Visible and invisible. The strings of real love are mutable, flexible, allowing themselves to be shed, cut, tied and retied, to appear in different forms. Isn't this play of ropes at the very heart of parenting—and indeed, the very thing that makes of parenting an art and not a science?

It begins in small moments. A friend told me about the morning her son wandered into the kitchen and she noticed that his shoes were tied. Somehow he had mastered this skill without her even knowing it. Those two small bows held something huge for her: the reality of her child's growing separateness. *Partir, c'est mourir un peu*, the French say. "To leave is to die a little." Such moments are leave-takings; they are little deaths.

If we learn to die in the little moments, and to die well, will the big moments be easier when they come? And what would it mean to "die well"? I imagine it is like that moment in body-surfing when you drown your fear by diving under the wave. You consent, surrender to the big thing that threatens to overwhelm you, and in doing so, you don't feel quite so overwhelmed. *Rather than resisting wave, I become wave, and only then can I discover that secret place inside the wave, below the turbulence, where my human body floats.* A mother is standing at the kitchen stove when her small boy wanders in. She notices that his shoes are tied—they were tied by him alone—and for one moment, the aloneness pierces her; for one moment, she knows that in this tiny leave-taking, the giant leave-taking is already coiled. "You tied your shoes!" she exclaims, and turns back to stir the oatmeal. In that moment, she has died a little, she has surrendered to the wave.

Once I saw a television documentary about a certain kind of bear. When the cubs are small, they are trained to wait patiently in treetops while their mothers look for food. If they climb down before their mothers return, they are punished with fierce growls and an occasional rough slap or nip. The threat of this punishment, you might say, hangs like a kind of rope that keeps the little one fastened in the tree. But the day comes when a mother, indicating that it is time for the cub to climb up into the tree, goes off to forage—and she does not come back. Hours go by, the young bear gets hungry. His mother has left him in a place where he must either disobey—or starve.

It's as though the mother had given her cub the knife with which to cut the rope that bound them. Isn't this what is asked of a human parent, over and over? You let your toddler toddle farther and farther away from you. You learn to bite your lip, to refrain from shouting "Careful!" as many times as you feel wont to. You put your child on the school bus and watch the bus drive off, your child's face one small, disappearing oval among others in the long yellow streak. You hand your daughter the car keys and go back inside the house, trying to suppress the terrible *what-if's* that start to drum in your mind. You drive your son to college and leave him there, in the place where he abandons you. You "give away" your daughter to her groom.

I don't imagine that the bear mother struggles or grieves in the same way that a human parent does. Rather, I imagine that she simply wakes one morning and knows, in some deep cellular sort of way (who knows, perhaps it's the young one's changing pheromones that signal to her?) that the time has come.

It is rarely as clear or as simple for us human parents—and the stakes can be so high. When my friend Deborah was sixteen, she announced to her father that she was leaving home. Her mother had died a few years earlier; her father had remarried and had a new little daughter, and what Deborah wanted desperately was for her father to say, "No. Don't leave. You belong with us." But he didn't. He let her go. She traveled by herself all the way from Taiwan, where her family lived, to California. She made her way. It is more than two decades later, and her father has been dead for several years now. Though Deborah was with him in his last illness and the final parting was tender, it is still hard for her to talk about that first parting. He let her go too easily. A father broke the heart of his motherless daughter.

Yet if we try to extract the lesson from this story and apply it to the next, we falter. We become like the fairy-tale figure Silly Jack, who began his misbegotten step-and-fetch-it role by carrying a stick of butter on his head under the summer sun. "You foolish boy!" cried his mother when he arrived home with butter dripping down his face. "You should have wrapped it in cold, wet leaves and carried it under your hat." The next thing he was given to lug was a tiny puppy, and after he wrapped it in cold, wet leaves, he arrived home to find it dead. "You foolish boy!" his mother cried. "You should have. . . ."

When my friend Sorrel's daughter, Lisa, was fifteen, she announced that she wanted to move out of state to live with her mother. Because her mother was seriously manic-depressive and did not reliably take her medication, Sorrel did his best to dissuade Lisa, but she was determined. He saw that if he didn't let her go, they would be locked in endless struggle. Because the school year had already begun, and he didn't want her to go in and out of schools, he made her promise that she would finish out the year with her mother. She promised. He drove her the long ten hours to the city where her mother lived. All the way, he tried to keep the lid on his emotion. Not until he had dropped her off at her mother's house did he allow himself to feel the grief of losing her, the fear for her, the sense of being abandoned by her, of abandoning her. In his words, "I drove to the nearest motel and threw up all night." Yet two months later when she called him, begging him to take her back again, he felt he had to hold her to her promise. Now, in hindsight, he feels clearly that he made the best decision (she moved in with a friend's family in the city where her mother lived, finished out the school year, and then came back to him). But at the time, his decision—to pull hard? to let go?—arose from pure anguish.

Bertolt Brecht's play *The Caucasian Chalk Circle* makes use of an old Chinese parable about a boy and the two women who lay claim to him.[2] One is the governor's wife, who gave birth to the boy. The other is Grusche, the servant girl who rescued him in the midst of political upheaval. Years pass, the governor comes to power again, and his wife demands her child back. Grusche protests, for she has raised the child as her own. A chalk circle is drawn and the boy placed in the middle. Each woman grasps one of his arms and is told to pull with all her might. They pull and pull. Grusche lets go: she can't bear to see the boy in pain. It is she who is rewarded with the child, for she has shown the greater love.

Perhaps we all have these two mothers inside of us: the one who wants to hold on at any cost. And the one who, dying to her own desire, lets go. Perhaps we all have these two fathers inside of us: the one who lets go of the string too easily, and the one who, swallowing his grief, says, "Cut."

2

INFIDELITIES

TWO YEARS OLD, I stood in my crib and mimicked her every move as she stood before her mirror. She brushed her hair, powdered her cheeks, colored her lips, and I did the same with an imaginary brush, puff, and lipstick. Then my mother kissed me good-bye and left the room to join my father for an evening out.

I howled.

Left in the company of an Italian baby-sitter, a young man named Dante, I had a traumatic evening—as did he. When my parents returned, they found me collapsed in a disheveled heap in my crib, my fingers tightly closed around the one shred of comfort that remained to me: the frayed bit of blanket that was my beloved Noserubber. The baby-sitter looked exhausted, and he was very apologetic. "I struggled hard for much of the evening to get *questo straccio* away from her," he said. *That rag.*

I don't remember any of this, of course, having been only two when it occurred. But the sense of betrayal—as my mother went out the door with my father, leaving me with imaginary powder on my cheeks and a baby-sitter who didn't even know the difference between a *straccio* and a Noserubber—is not something I have any difficulty summoning.

For betrayal is sewn into the very fabric of the parent-child relationship, and even the most beloved and hovered-over child is not immune from its pain. Perhaps there is a very brief period, in earliest infancy, that is without a rift. In his book *Monogamy*, the British child analyst Adam Phillips writes:

In the beginning every child is an only child. The child is not possessive of the mother because he already possesses her; he behaves—in fact, lives—as if he is entitled. Our first inklings, that is to say, are monogamous ones: of privilege and privacy, of ownership and belonging. The stuff of which monogamy will be made.[3]

Others would argue—and when I hear the sound of a newborn wailing, or the sight of its small limbs flailing when it is set down or held out away from the sheltering warmth of another body, I have to concur—that the shock of separateness pierces even the earliest phase of infancy. But why quibble about timing? No one could argue that at the very dawn of consciousness, the human child begins to experience what Phillips calls the "dismemberment" of independence. As he acknowledges:

But if monogamy is where we start from, our first knowledge is of infidelity; that is what knowledge is about. Temporarily the mother can be everything to the child, but the child cannot possibly be everything to the mother. He can't feed her or sexually satisfy her, or have adult conversations with her. From the child's point of view the mother is—as the father will soon be—a model of promiscuity. She has a thousand things to do. She knows other people. Small children, like uxorious husbands, are the most devoted of partners to their parents (they like coming with us to the toilet). Their parents, however, libertine if only in their responsibilities, have other commitments.[4]

Even before there is any awareness of a parent's "other commitments," the small child suffers from a parent's multiple desertions . . . for there is that great gateway to pass through: the concept of object permanence. It takes thousands of appearances and reappearances before a child begins to grasp that when a mother's face disappears behind a corner, she continues to exist and will most probably return. In the meantime, each of these disappearances is—no, not "a small death," but a death, pure and simple, for the child. Sometimes I think there's nothing quite so wrenching as to witness, in the form of a small child howling before a closed door, that particularly human combination of intelligence and ignorance. It's a combination that so quintessentially defines us as a species—a species capable of anticipating its own death, yet unable ever to know with complete certainty the *when*, the *how*, or the *what-happens-after* of this death.

Similarly, it is the intelligence of the human child that makes it able to anticipate danger, loss, grief; yet until the brain has mastered the concept of object-permanence, it does not know that the teddy bear is behind the pillow, the ball will come back from the bush, Daddy will return from the office, and Mommy will be back in her car. Thus during the most formative years of existence, the human child suffers countless betrayals. These betrayals take the form of disappearances that seem like "forever" on the part of those whom the child loves most and on whom it is most radically dependent. I remember how relieved I was when Ariel was old enough to understand the words, "I'll be back soon." Only then did I feel some respite from the heartbreak I had inflicted on her so many times.

As if the myriad daily betrayals aren't enough, there are other big ones. There is the big one of the parental couple, from which the child is excluded from the very beginning. Among my earliest memories is that of crying "Sandwich! Sandwich!" whenever I saw my parents embrace, and rushing in to wedge myself between them as the filling. As Phillips describes it, this exclusion is a particularly ambiguous zone to inhabit—because where would the child be if he were *not* excluded? "It may be purgatory to be left out," he writes, and then he continues, but it is hell to be left in.

> As every child knows who has watched his parents kiss—or indeed, who has suffered the consummate betrayal of their sleeping together—when you are excluded you can do something (you can imagine what it would be like if you weren't). But if they invited you in where would you start? How could you participate? It's a terrible deprivation for the adults to exclude

the children from feeling left out; but it is a terrible deception to pretend it is possible to protect them from feeling left out.[5]

Perhaps this helps to explain why, for many small children, the most terrible blow of all to their passionately monogamous love is the existence of siblings. For within the family there is the natural expectation that the connection between parents is unique. Even as I cried "Sandwich!" and rushed to interpose myself as peanut butter or Swiss cheese between my parents, there was the tacit recognition that they, both being slices of bread, shared something that differentiated them from me. It is much harder for a young child to grasp that the same kind of love his mother has for him could be equally available to another child. "Why did you have a boy before me?" a young man I know asked his mother when he was small. His question expresses so perfectly the child's sense of entitlement to the one and only throne. It wouldn't have occurred to him to ask, "Why did you want me when you already had a son?" For, primogenitur be damned, in his mind, the brother existed only in relation to him, as the one his mother had before the one she *really* had, the one who really counted—himself.

It's this very sense of entitlement that makes the human child so vulnerable to feelings of betrayal. To help parents grasp how radically unseated children feel upon the arrival of a sibling, the British child psychologist Penelope Leach translates it into a language that adults can understand: the language of a faithful wife being asked to welcome her husband's new lover.

PARENT TO CHILD	HUSBAND TO WIFE
"We're going to have a new baby, darling, because we thought it would be so nice for you to have a little brother or sister to play with."	"I'm going to take a second wife, darling, because I thought it would be so nice for you to have some company to play with."
"We like you so much we just can't wait to have another gorgeous boy or girl."	"I like you so much I just can't wait to have another gorgeous wife."

"It'll be our baby; it'll belong to all three of us and we'll all look after it together."

"I shall really need my big boy/girl now, to help me look after the tiny new baby."

"Of course I shan't love you any less, we'll all love each other."

"It'll be our wife. It'll belong to both of us and we'll both look after her together."

"I shall really need my reliable old wife now, to help me look after this young new one."

"Of course I shan't love you any less, we'll all love each other."

Having made her case, Leach asks, "Don't you think that you might be just as liable to hit first your husband and then that dear little wife over their heads with a frying pan as your toddler is to hit first you and then that baby with the nearest block?"[6]

When I first saw her table of correspondences, I thought her analogy brilliant and witty—but a bit far-fetched. I don't anymore. For now I see the primal experience of love and betrayal as quite literally the matrix of all future experiences. As Phillips writes of the child's experience of exclusion, "Where we go is where we go from there. Our life will be what we can make of feeling left out. That experience, which takes so many forms, is the raw material."[7]

"Which takes so many forms" . . . indeed. For the tables can very readily turn and a parent become the one left out. The father who feels excluded from the passionate intensity of the mother-infant bond is a classic figure, and the triangling-out of one parent by the intense connection of the other parent with the child is a classic pattern in family life.

In Milan Kundera's novel *Life Is Elsewhere*, a mother finds a form of physical intimacy with her young son, Jaromil, that creates a distance between her and her husband:

No, no, she would never forget that the excitement her husband made her feel was full of risk and uncertainty, whereas her son gave her a tranquillity full of happiness . . . At one point the child became gravely ill, and for fourteen days Maman hardly closed her eyes; she ministered to his little body which was hot and writhing in pain. This period, too, was one of ecstasy; when the illness faded, it seemed to her that she had walked through the realm of the dead carrying her son's body in her arms, and that after this experience nothing could ever separate the two of them again.

Her husband's body, robed in a suit or in pajamas, discretely self-enclosed, was moving away from her, day by day losing more of its intimacy, while her son's body continued to depend on her; she was no longer suckling but she was teaching her son to use the toilet, she dressed and undressed him, fixed his hair and chose his clothes, and was in daily touch with his insides through the food which she lovingly prepared for him . . . Ah—her son's body, her paradise and home, her kingdom.[8]

Even the parent to whom the child is most passionately attached will experience—if all goes well—some degree of being left behind when the child enters the stage known as *rapprochement*. This is the process whereby a child moves out to explore his world in ever-widening circles around the safe hub of a parent or other attachment figure. Intermittently, and in one form or another, the child checks back in with the "hub" as if to say, "You're still there, right? And I'm going to be okay, right?" Though this process continues throughout a child's development, and in our culture, even well into young adult-hood, it has classically been identified with its first manifestation in toddlerhood at roughly fifteen months to three years.[9]

If the seeds of betrayal are already present in this very early phase of life, it is when children enter adolescence that they ripen in earnest. It is not uncommon for a parent in this phase to have moments of feeling like a discarded lover. In Iris Murdoch's novel *The Sacred and Profane Love Machine*, she writes of her heroine Harriet:

She was thinking about her son. Every mother has to endure it, I suppose, she thought. The marvelous intimacy could not last. . . . He had become untouchable; and Harriet, with her long habit of touching was suddenly in a dilemma, in an anguish. She was visited by alarmingly precise ghostly yearnings. Feelings very like the torments of an unrequited love made her blush and tremble. It was indeed dreadfully like being in love. She wanted to hold him in her arms again, to cover him with kisses, to untangle with caressing fingers that untidy and now absurdly long golden hair. But nothing was less possible.[10]

The torments of an unrequited love. There is something unequal, isn't there? For a child is the flower, the fruit, of a parent's life in the way a parent never is for the child. Our children represent a crucial part of the completion of our lives, but for them, we are the point of departure. Offspring, they spring off from us. They leave us behind—if not in the dust, then in our gradual progression toward dust, for from dust we came and to dust we shall return, and in the normal course of things, it is they who will see us return to that dust.

Some time ago, I was with a group of women who were talking about hair—how long, how light or dark, curly or straight our hair had been when we were young. One woman, whose hair was now chin-length and brown, said that she had had a long blond braid when she was a girl and that her mother had recently sent it to her, in a scented box. "Yuk!" the women cried. And the woman whose braid it had been agreed. Several other women described how their mothers had kept a hank of their daughter's hair, a tooth, or a bit of blanket in a special album or drawer, and it was generally agreed that this was a disgusting motherly fetish. *There it is*, I thought, *that unrequited love, that inequality*. A mother might keep a lock of her child's hair as a sacred relic, but it's hard to imagine a daughter keeping her mother's hair. A small child worships his mother's body, but as children grow, it is the mother who remains faithful; it's her reverence for the child's body that endures. The child's imperative is to move beyond the parental body.

But here, perhaps, in the being left behind, it is possible for a parent to discover something that is in its own way a fullness of presence, an abundance. For from the very beginning, rapprochement is not simply something that a child does—it is something that a parent permits and sustains. The British psychologist D.W. Winnicott devoted a great deal of thought to the way that a healthy parent makes it possible for her child to depart from her, to leave her alone, to be left alone. She does this by attuning herself to her child's constantly varying need for her closeness and distance. If she is always "in his face," interacting with him, fulfilling his every desire, resolving his every frustration, he will not be able to develop his own independent relation to the world. On the other hand, if she withdraws too far, too long, his anxiety will interfere with both his ability to explore the world and to tolerate solitude. In his book *Going to Pieces Without Falling Apart*, Mark Epstein, a contemporary American psychiatrist who draws from the work of Winnicott, provides a lovely example from his own life of what can happen for a child when the right balance is struck. He describes a moment that occurred during a summer visit with his family in Maine:

> I came upstairs one evening to find my seven-year-old son alone in his darkening room with his nose pressed against the screen of the open window in his bedroom. "The air smells so sweet here," he said dreamily. Alone in his room, he was having a new, and unexpected, experience. His senses were expanding his reality . . . With too much interference from parents, or too much absence, a child is forced to spend her mental energy coping with her parent's intrusiveness or unavailability instead of exploring herself . . . If my son had been worried over where I was, or how I was doing, he could not have smelled the air.[11]

What Epstein doesn't discuss with regard to this incident is his own response. To have been so struck by his son's exclamation—"The air smells so sweet here!"—and to have remembered the moment, give testimony to a particular kind of parental pleasure that not all parents are capable of. For it requires that a parent be able to take pleasure, and perhaps even a certain pride, in the fact that his child can forget about him, ignore him, float free of him—at least for certain long, and gradually for longer and longer, moments. This is a very complex and subtle movement on the part of a parent. It involves the ability to take pleasure in one's child as other than oneself, and to recognize that as a parent, one fulfills one's role by becoming, as it were, increasingly obsolete. How far this is from the narcissistic need to keep the child forever tethered to oneself, as in Kundera's further description of Jaromil's Maman:

> And what about her son's soul? Was that not part of her kingdom too? Oh yes, yes! When Jaromil uttered his first word and that word was "mama," she was deliriously happy. She told herself that her son's mind—now still consisting of only a single concept—was completely filled by her, and that even later on when his mind would begin to grow, branch out, and flower, she would continue to remain its root.

For a parent to be able to leave her child alone, she must be able to be alone herself, and she must have a basic trust in the dance of near-and-far that is so fundamental to the eros of parenthood. If she cannot bear this aloneness, if she does not have this basic trust, she will, like Murdoch's Harriet, be prone as her child gets older to "feelings very like the torment of unrequited love." If she can find her way through these torments, there is the possibility—even as she grieves—of discovering a fullness within herself, an ability to reside in her own life, and a trust in this ability that permits her to be in the world in new ways.

A friend whose grown daughter first left home to be an exchange student in Europe told me, "I had so much anxiety and anticipatory grief before she left. But then, when she really was gone and I found myself alone in a way I hadn't been alone for seventeen years, I felt almost giddy. The feeling was very much the same as I had the first time I went out on my own when she was an infant. I remember that day so well. I went to have a cup of coffee, and it seemed like the most extraordinary thing. I felt as though I'd pulled off an escape, like a creature who at any moment might be caught and sent back to the zoo! On that day, I had only an hour, but now my life is made of such hours. I can get very wistful about my daughter's absence, but it's really quite amazing to be nobody but myself."

And when the grown daughter returns to her mother, there will be more of her to return. Her head will be full of stories, her suitcases full of the booty—chocolates from Belgium, a clump of unspun Irish wool, a photograph of herself dunking in a fountain in Italy—that belong to her own new life. One friend said to me about her twenty-four-year-old son, "When Michael comes back to visit me now, it really does feel like a lover coming back. He's growing more and more distant, and yet now when he gives me a hug, it's somehow more of a hug. It's not over . . . ."

A kind of giddy freedom, an amazement at "being nobody but myself," a daughter who returns with her souvenirs and her stories, a wandering son more present than ever in his hug: these are among the treasures that it is possible to find, where once there were eggs, in the empty nest.

3

DISGUST

"I'D HAD SEVERAL big teeth pulled from the back of my mouth," my friend Marysia told me, revisiting a scene from her son Alex's babyhood. Marysia's English is fluent, but her Polish accent is still so heavy that everything she says—no matter how urgent and even, at times, horrific—comes out sounding dreamy and languorous to me, as though she was lying back in a drifting rowboat, describing a slowly changing pattern of clouds. "I fell into a heavy sleep that night, from the pain and the painkillers. I don't know how long Alex was crying for me in the middle of the night, but when I finally woke up, he was howling. I got up and stumbled into the bathroom to throw some cold water on my face. When I saw myself in the mirror, I gasped. My face was green and purple; my eyes were almost swollen shut. I was afraid to go in to Alex, afraid I'd terrify him, but he was crying so desperately for me that I had no choice. I went in and bent over his crib, and he stopped his crying immediately. I lifted him up in my arms, and it didn't seem to matter to him how horrible I looked. . . ."

Our children's love for us begins with the most extravagant forgiveness—if one can use the word "forgiveness" for a love that recognizes no breach in the first place. Small children are utterly indiscriminate in their love for their parents—to a degree that can at times become pitiable, as in the stories of bruised children who cling to the necks of their abusing parents as a kind nurse tries to carry them away to safety.

Why did you climb the mountain? Sir Edmond Hillary was asked. "Because it was there," came the famous reply, and this is the way our children love us—simply because, because we are there, because we are theirs—even as we lean over them in their cribs with our faces green and yellow, our eyes swollen shut.

When they are small, they not only forgive our great flaws, but they love the least things about us: the smell of our sweat, the particular sounds we make, the way a father clears his throat, a mother's way of yawning. A woman I know who is horrified by her own plumpness, and especially by her "flabby" arms, wrote a poem in which she described her daughter's "favorite place" as the cool softness under those very arms.

As the Tibetans say, "Who looks not with the eyes of compassion sees not what the eyes of compassion see." Each of us has a body that exists only for those who love it. It's as though we went through several incarnations in a single lifetime, for we have a different body for each of those who love us. A daughter's "favorite place" may be underneath her mother's cool, plump arms, while her father's favorite place is the warm nape of his wife's neck—a place that doesn't even exist for the daughter. Of these many love-bodies that we acquire and shed throughout a lifetime, the one our small children endow us with is the most wondrous. For the body they love can do no wrong. In *Life Is Elsewhere*, Milan Kundera describes a new mother's experience of being physically redeemed through her infant son:

> Ever since her childhood Maman had felt an intense aversion toward all physicality, including her own . . . Now, the elevation of her son's physicality beyond any taint of ugliness had a peculiarly cleansing effect on her, and served to legitimize her own body as well. The dribble of milk which occasionally appeared on the wrinkled skin of the nipple seemed as poetic as a droplet of dew. She would often reach for her breast and squeeze it slightly in order to produce the magic droplet. She wet the tip of her little finger with the white liquid and tasted it: she told herself that she was doing so in order to learn more about the fluid that nourished her son, but actually she was curious about the taste of her own body, and the sweet taste of

the milk reconciled her to all the body's other juices and excretions. She began to think of herself as tasty; her body had become as agreeable and legitimate as any other object of nature—a tree, a bush, a lake.[13]

How cruel, then, that as they grow, these same children whose eyes transformed our flaws into their treasures, our flabby arms into their favorite places, begin to give us exactly the reverse. They whose faces lit up at the sight of us even as we bent over them looking like monsters, now find us monstrous in the least and most innocent of our habits.

"You're not going out of the house with your hair like *that*!" my friend's daughter calls after her mother, who's flying out the door to go jogging on a virtually empty country road, her hair in a sloppy ponytail.

"Stop humming!" my daughter will hiss at me when we are walking together if anyone seems to be approaching within a mile of earshot.

Can't bounce a quarter on that bunk! When my father was a young soldier in training, the sergeant would march through the barracks each morning with a quarter in his fist to see how well the men had made their beds. If the quarter didn't bounce, the bed had to be made again, tighter, tighter. Increasingly, as my daughter gets older, I have moments of feeling that I am living under a strict military regime. "Mo-om," she says, and when she draws the two syllables out like that, I know I have committed another infraction: worn colors that are too bright, been overly friendly at the checkout stand. . . .

Where do they come from, these small, glowering dictators who—usurping the most adoring, uncritical fans we've ever had—take up residence in our midst?

A young Navajo girl who has just begun menstruating participates in a ceremony that lasts four nights and five days. Central to this ceremony is a form of massage that the girl receives at the hands of certain respected older women. Known as "molding," its goal is the reshaping of the girl's physical form and moral character; for it is believed that at puberty, her body has become as soft and her character as pliable as it was at birth. After four days spent largely in seclusion, the girl's new status will be celebrated in an all-night sing.[14]

Among the aborigines of Australia, writes the anthropologist Ruth Benedict, puberty ceremonies for young men involve "elaborate and symbolic repudiations of the bonds with the female sex; the men are symbolically made self-sufficient. . . . To attain this end, they use drastic sexual rites and bestow supernatural guaranties."[15]

In traditional societies around the world, young men and women have participated in some form of ritual—often involving a combination of seclusion, suffering, and celebration—that distinctly marks the passage to adulthood. In the absence of such powerful cultural tools to aid in the process of separating from their parents and leaving behind their childhood selves, what means do our children have at their disposal?

Disgust.

How well I remember, beginning from around age twelve and lasting well into my teenage years, how unbearable I found the sound of my parents eating. There were quite particular things I fastened on, of course: the way my father rinsed Jell-o through his teeth, the way my mother could worry a bone. . . .

But now I think that no matter how exquisitely, how soundlessly, the two of them had managed to eat, they were doomed in my presence. What had begun to horrify me was an acute awareness of them as bodies, a fact that was particularly apparent when they were eating. And now, from a distance of many years and miles, and with my own daughter beginning to train her critical gaze on me, I understand that my distaste for the sound and the sight of my parents eating was a young girl's way of trying to distance herself from her parents' bodies.

Distance through distaste, disgust. The very words *dis-taste* and *disgust* imply that one has lost the taste for that which one once savored. When once I drank from my mother's body, now suddenly I could not bear the sound of her drinking, the way the liquid gurgled in her throat, the way her tongue slipped out from behind her teeth for a fraction of a second to wipe her lips.

Breast milk is sweet. Wormwood is a bitter substance, derived from plants of the genus *artemesia*, once used in making the potent drink absinthe and in flavoring certain wines. In olden days, women smeared it on their nipples when it was time to wean their babies. They turned the sweet to bitter; they brought about distaste for that which was formerly delicious before all else.

It is bitter for parents when their children, who once loved them in their bodies as no one else ever has, begin to curl their lips in disgust at the mere fact of their parents having bodies. And given that many parents are entering middle age as their children are entering adolescence, the timing can seem exquisitely cruel. Just as they look into the mirror and see their own faces frowning back at them with hair turning thinner and grayer and with a gathering crisscross of lines, their children seem to confirm their own most negative judgment. "No one should have to go through adolescence and menopause at the same time!" a friend said to me recently. But in fact, our children's distaste for us at this juncture has very little to do with our own growing older and a great deal to do with theirs.

A friend told me that until her husband was thirteen, he had thought that his mother—a very graceful, aristocratic woman—was "perfect." And then one day as he walked into the living room, he saw his mother's skirt fall open in a way that revealed to him "her jiggly, white thighs." As insignificant as such a glimpse might seem, it was a crucial moment for him, an initiatory moment—not unlike the moment when Dorothy, stepping behind the screen, sees the little bald man behind the Wizard.

The age of the boy was significant, too: thirteen, the traditional age for the rite-of-passage. The heroes and heroines of fairy tales are often boys and girls of twelve or thirteen—and for girls in particular, some form of disgust is often the medium of their transformation. A demure maiden must kiss the slimy green mouth of a frog or allow that slimy green mouth to eat from her plate of food, and when she consents, something momentous happens. The frog becomes a beautiful prince and she, having gone beyond the threshold of a young girl's disgust, is ready to partake of sexual pleasure.

The young girl's disgust is a gate that she must pass through in order to fully become a woman. But this passage also involves a disenchantment with the parental world. The famous story of the frog prince begins in the king's garden, when his daughter loses the beautiful golden ball that has been her favorite plaything. The radiant roundness of her childhood world, within her father's kingdom, has been broken open. And it is through that opening that the slimy frog—her next great love—can enter.[16]

These things don't happen only in fairy tales. A young boy walks into the living room and upon seeing his mother's jiggling white thighs, falls out of the perfection of her world. Without this fall, he would never be free to fully fall into the arms of another woman. What is different in real life, of course, is that the movement from old life to new is rarely total or instantaneous. The jiggling white thighs don't immediately give way to the firm, youthful flesh of his golden girl. The young boy has miles to go before he finds her and before he becomes fully able to love her, but through that fall in the living room, he finds the trapdoor that opens the way.

And isn't there something like disgust that we feel when we encounter the grown men and women who never moved through this passage, who never withdrew from their parents the bodily intimacy they shared in childhood? Proust in his thirties, writing to his mother about his bowel movements; the classic figure of the unmarried daughter stirring her father's soups, trimming his whiskers.[17] Such ministrations feel unseemly somehow, a breach of taste. *I would never want to be one of those parents*, one thinks.

It isn't easy for us to suffer our children's disenchantment, to see the faces that once lit up for us now grimace with disapproval. But perhaps we can learn to think of our children's disgust as a kind of wormwood that they themselves—through an inner necessity whose origin and significance are often completely hidden from them—must smear on that which has been too sweet for too long.

4

SEASONS

WHEN PERSEPHONE, THE daughter of Demeter, falls down into the underworld, it's a kind of backward birth. Through Hades' dark hole, she is sucked off the face of the earth and into a hidden, interior world, a shadow existence.[18]

It's a horrible fate for a beautiful young girl who had been happily playing in her mother's realm, in the light of day. And yet there's a way in which her situation calls out for just such a fall, for just such a tearing away. For when your mother is Goddess of Grains, she covers all bases. You run to the hills, you run to the valleys, you can't get away from her. She loves you, she loves you, but her body is so big and sheltering, it leaves you no room to find your own way and make your own mark.

When Persephone disappears, Demeter's grief is vast, as only Demeter's grief could be. It covers the whole earth, for she withdraws her power to make things grow. Nothing is green anymore. The world goes cold. And down below, Persephone turns her own grief inward and she is wasting away. Finally, Zeus intervenes and Hades relents. He gives Persephone leave to return to her mother each year for a visit, and when she does, Demeter celebrates and there is spring on earth.

It's not a tragic ending, but it's not a happy-ever-after ending either, for each year, Demeter and Persephone must face the anguish of separation. Persephone must return to the darkness of the Underworld, while the darkness of winter reigns on earth. Nonetheless, it is through Hades' terrible intervention that Persephone attains a measure of existence that is not completely under her mother's sway. And it is through the pain of rupture and separation that the alternation of seasons comes about, and with it, the possibility that Persephone can help to bring about new life in the form of spring.

To say that Hades "rescues" Persephone from her mother's love may be startling, for Demeter's love is fundamentally benevolent. She wishes her daughter to be healthy and happy. Persephone does not languish in her mother's realm, as she does in Hades', so the two figures who compete for her presence are usually presented as opposites. Yet, seen from a different perspective, they represent two sides of one coin, two poles of excessive love, a love that comes close to obsession. They both want the beautiful object of their love to be with them forever, belonging to them and to no other, in the seasonless realm over which they preside.

Love without seasons is problematic. A woman I know is quite a bit younger than her husband, who is in his sixties. They have two beautiful little boys. She told me, "Recently we went to Florida to visit my mother-in-law, who's in her eighties. We found her where we knew she would be: sitting in the beauty parlor, having her hair pouffed and her nails polished. She hadn't seen her two little grandsons in months, but she really had eyes only for her son. She said to the other women in the beauty parlor, 'This is my son! This is my son!' Afterward, she told my husband, 'You know, the boys are cute—but you, Bill, you're the one!' " Another woman I know told me that she had been married for some forty years when, with a mix of triumph and indignation, her mother-in-law declared: "You know, when my son was with *me*, his hair wasn't gray!"

Such love, in its very lavishness, reduces the beloved, insisting that he remain a static object for his mother's consumption. The sixty-year-old man must forever be his mother's golden boy, and Demeter would have her golden girl with her forever. Such love is faithful, yes; devoted, yes. But it is faithful and devoted in a way that insists others remain faithful to a particular version of themselves, and thus narrows the scope of what they are permitted to be. In a poem called "The Blossom" by Eavan Boland, a mother asks, *How much longer will I see girl-hood in my daughter?* The daughter appears as a white spring blossom and says to her,

> *Imagine if I stayed here*
> *Even for the sake of your love*
> *What would happen to the summer? To the fruit?*[19]

D.W. Winnicott writes, "Some mothers operate in two layers. At one layer (Shall I call it the top layer), they only want one thing, they want their child to grow up, to get out of enclosure, to go to school, to meet the world. At another layer, deeper, I suppose, and not really conscious, they cannot conceive of letting their child go. In this deeper layer where logic is not very important, the mother cannot give up this precious thing, her maternal function . . ."[20]

It is not only mothers who are capable of clinging to the "most precious thing." Fathers, too, can cling to the perfection of a certain phase of the parent-child relationship. And children, too, can cling. I knew a girl, Sophie, who loved her father so much that when she once overheard some of his students talking about him, she ran into the woods at the edge of the campus and wept. It wasn't even that they had been saying anything particularly negative about him; it was that she couldn't bear to hear them saying "he." She lived in an "I–Thou" relationship with him, a perfect I–Thou that eventually had to be shattered in order for her to be released. It was, and the shattering was terrible—but if it had never taken place, where would she be? Skulking around in her father's world with her fingers clamped over her ears?

The writer Barbara Baer told me that her mother was "an almost perfect mother." She was loving and encouraging—"and she wasn't even suffocating." Yet, in her very perfection, in her delicate refusal to be smothering, she became oppressive. "It makes it so hard to leave," Barbara told me. "A child has to be able to find a fault, a fault that opens up and provides a way into the world."

In myths, in fairy tales, it is when the perfection of the parent-child connection has been shattered that something that needs to happen can happen: a great adventure, the discovery of a precious treasure, the blossoming of a new love. When parent or child try to keep their love for the other safe from the ravages of time and change, they make themselves vulnerable—in some form or another—to the ravisher who comes from without. I try to remind myself of this in those moments of falling-out that occur between my daughter and myself. "You don't want to read *To Kill A Mockingbird?*" I heard myself exclaim to her the other day. "But that was my favorite book when I was your age!" And then I saw that look in her face that reminds me, "Oh, right, you are different from me. There are places where we do not connect."

Such moments—small cracks in a certain image of perfection—happen over and over again in the course of a single day. I tell myself that when I open to them, Hades is appeased, and I keep him and the giant crack he makes through parent-child love at bay.

5

TEMPO

MY DAUGHTER IS growing up too fast.

Already, when she was nine years old, she crammed her vast collection of stuffed animals into black-plastic Hefty garbage bags and hauled them into the garage.

It was an awful scene to me. Through narrowed eyes, I watched her as if she were the Auctioneer, presiding so efficiently over the dismantling of my life. I begged her to keep at least one animal in her room—the moth-eaten black-and-white panda that I bought for myself the day John Lennon was shot, that I named for my favorite Beatle, and that I bequeathed to Ariel when she was born. She sighed and fished him out of one of the black-plastic bags.

Now she is eleven—only eleven—yet she worries that her face, to her mother's eyes a perfect oval, is too plump, that her large, blue-green eyes are too narrow, that her lithe, muscular body has secret deposits of—"What's that stuff that sounds like celery?" she asks me. "Cellulite?" "Yes." I snort—which is not the comfort she desires of me.

It is hard for me to give the proper kind and dosage of comfort when what I want is for the whole realm that we have suddenly entered simply not to exist. *Pouf!* A loud noise, a cloud of smoke—and there is my small girl again, surrounded by a throng of a hundred twenty-two stuffed animals, and not even capable of breaking her body into separate parts—"my face," "my thighs," "my stomach"—let alone finding fault with them. When she was small, to be pretty meant to wear a dress and have her hair brushed and tied with a ribbon.

I find myself wanting to slow the tempo, to play the scenes backward, to hold her girlhood in an eternal pause, as lovely as an Impressionist's painting. But she is rushing forward, reckless with readiness to be done with her own childhood. Her walls are hung with large color posters of teenage boy stars, slumped in baggy clothes and managing to look, in equal parts, utterly fresh-faced and irrevocably jaded. In the morning, under the gaze of these boys, Ariel puts on white lipstick that makes her look like an Ice Queen and that reminds me of the mean girls who frightened me in the junior high-school bathrooms of my youth. She and her friends can spend whole evenings on the phone talking about who is "going with" whom and who has "dumped" whom—both of which, as far as I can discern, are more virtual than actual activities. (No one seems to actually go anywhere with the person they are "going with"—which would seem to make "dumping" an equally abstract, if nonetheless quite dramatic, activity.)

Perhaps even more painful than to see her so giddily heading into the swirling water of adolescence is to hear, more and more often, a new tone in her voice when she talks to me—an impatient tone that tries to disguise itself with exaggerated patience. As if I were doddering. And this is an "as if" to which, in this particular moment of my life—when friends all around me are complaining of memory lapses and a certain midlife spaciness—I actually feel quite vulnerable. "Mo-om," she says, and the single syllable drawn out into two is always a sign of some infraction on my part. It is hard enough to have gone, in such a short time, the vast distance from "Mama" to "Mom."

Frequently I find myself cringing in my own home, like a child perpetually about to be scolded by a strict, perfectionistic mother whose standards are always changing in new and more exacting ways. And the house itself, where the two of us live together, begins to feel ever more like a hallway, an antechamber, a room you wait in or pass through. Is it any wonder, then, that I am sometimes tempted to rush past her, to outdo her, in the hurtling forward? More and more I catch myself living in a mode of anticipatory grief, mourning the empty nest even before it is empty.

Yet if I can pull myself back from this threshold at which I have not yet truly arrived, if I can press the pause button on my own tendency to try to outfox, or to foreshorten, grief by grieving what I have not yet lost, there is something I notice.

What I notice is not, in fact, an unremitting forward rush, but an irregular movement, a kind of arrhythmic pulsing or alternation of expansion and contraction. It's as if I were watching a slow-motion film of a flower pushing up from a seed, or a butterfly emerging from a cocoon, and I watch so carefully that I begin to see a movement between the frames, a movement in which I catch the green shoot folding itself back into the seed case, the butterfly curling its wings back into the cocoon.

One day Ariel suddenly asks me, "What would you think if I brought the dollhouse in from the garage and we made a sort of cabinet for it, so from the outside you couldn't tell there was a dollhouse inside, but I could just pull it out sometimes, on wheels . . ."

I see what she means. This is precisely the relation she is trying to construct toward her childhood right now—to have it hidden from view, yet close at hand, so that every now and again, free of self-consciousness and safe from any critical gaze, she can throw open the doors and play.

But the impulse itself is like that dollhouse-on-wheels. Her yearning flashes into view; then, finding a host of reasons why not, she pushes it back behind closed doors. I could easily have missed the moment, it happened so fast. And I find myself wondering *How many such moments have I missed?*

I discover that it's like dreams. At first you think you "never dream." Then, as you begin to attend—reminding yourself when you first wake up to lie in place for a few moments, reclaiming the dreams before you jump out of bed, or making the effort to jot them down—you remember them more clearly.

Now, almost every day, I catch one of these moments. Suddenly she asks my permission for something so minimal—"Is it okay for me to have these strawberries?"—that I realize she still savors the feeling that her experience is somehow granted or blessed by me, by my "Yes."

Then I notice that she is craving my company—I turn in the hallway, and she is dogging my footsteps; I'm brushing my hair in front of the bathroom mirror, and suddenly there are two faces in the mirror and I see that she has crowded into the small room behind me. Out of the blue, she wants to know something about me—"What sort of birthday party did you have when you were twelve?" "Did you like breakfast?"— as if this small fact had become indispensable, the template for her own mysteriously evolving existence.

Does remembering dreams make you not only remember more dreams, but actually dream more? I've always thought so. And now it seems as though attending to these moments with my daughter is making more of them occur, like a kind of observer effect that actually alters the thing it observes. And why shouldn't it, when the observer is a mother and the observed is the child whose very sense of self has been formed, to a great degree, by her sense of how her mother has observed her?

How else can I account for an incident like the following, which, given what I've been looking for, seems positively made to order— almost—almost as though I'd hired an overly accomplished writer to invent the script of our interactions?

We only recently got on the Internet, and the first night as I was looking over Ariel's shoulder, I was really quite disturbed at the offers of pornography, the low-level chat in the rooms. The next morning, I voiced my distress to Ariel. "You've always been so creative," I told her. "You get up in the morning and you write stories. I'm worried that with the Internet—"

"Mo-om—" she said to me.

That voice again, and something in me clenches.

"What?" I said, waiting to hear how impossibly doddering and obsolete I was.

But what she said took me completely by surprise.

"Look."

"What?"

"I'm sewing a teddy bear."

And she was.

A small, blue teddy-bear, the size of her hand, made from an old cushion of mine, the fabric so worn it was almost see-through. Sewn in black, wobbly stitches, and with the fabric cut so that the cushion seams ran across the back of his head and the front of his stomach.

It was all I could do to keep from laughing.

"What's his name?"

"Ritardando," she told me, remembering a word from her piano book.

She meant that he looked simpleminded, with his crooked face and seamy body. But I thought once again, as I had with the dollhouse-on-wheels: what perfect images she provides for the process of her own growth. She's like a conductor who, in the middle of conducting the fast movement—*allegro*—suddenly remembers the words *ma non troppo*—not too much—and, dropping her hands in a gesture of subduing, mouths *ritardando*—slow down—to the musicians so feverishly playing.

6

BUYING LADYBUGS

⁂

LAST WEEK I bought ladybugs. I bought them at the nursery to eat the aphids that have been eating my roses. "There's a thousand of them in there!" the woman told me as she handed them to me. It seemed like a kind of miracle: a thousand ladybugs in a bag. It seemed like something one shouldn't be able to buy.

I wanted to exclaim. But the lady behind the counter was used to selling ladybugs; she was already in the midst of selling garden gloves and fertilizer sticks to someone else. I walked back through the parking lot, got into my car and set the ladybugs beside me, the whole time feeling a strange mix of elation and emptiness. The ladybugs were silent, but so busy in their net bag—wiggling their legs, climbing over each other, opening and shutting their wings—that they looked as though they should be making a deafening noise. I wanted to exclaim again, and that's when I realized what was missing.

My daughter.

It's a well-known fact that young children require the gaze of their parents in order to feel that whatever is happening—whether they are jumping from a rock, throwing leaves in the air, or sprinkling sequins in their hair—is indeed happening. "Look at me!" they call out—and not until the parent looks are they indeed jumping, throwing, sprinkling. What is less often acknowledged are the ways that parents use their children to make their own experience of the world more real.

Not long ago, a friend of mine told me, "I witnessed an extraordinary thing today! The filling of the lake at the park! One moment there was nothing but a dry lake bed, and then there was a loud, exploding sound. A jet of water came shooting up like a geyser, and all the children went running into the spray."

What I heard in his voice was the child as intensifier, exclamation point. But even more fundamental is the child as lens, as window to an otherwise invisible world. Without the children, I wondered, would he even have seen the filling of the lake? When Ariel was born, it was as though certain dimensions of the world that had been lost to me since childhood rose up out of oblivion. "Cow!" "Horse!" "Train!" I would hear myself exclaiming as I drove past green and gold summer fields with my daughter swaddled in her little seat beside me. Where had they been hiding for the past thirty years, those cows, horses, and trains that the world was now suddenly so full of?

Along with the numinous, elemental things that rose up—the animals, mailmen, airplanes—as my daughter grew older, she led me back to another realm that lay in my past: the realm of the ecstatic errand. Without a child, could one even dream of putting those two words, "ecstatic" and "errand," together? I had memories, of course. Memories of going with my father to the cleaner's to see the circle of clothes spinning and then—how did the clothes know?—coming to a halt at his brilliant white shirt. Virtually any errand was proof of a generous universe, for most transactions yielded not only the thing you went for—a clean shirt—but something else: the sight of the clothes spinning, the smell of the starch, the pieces of cardboard that fit into the shirt's collar and that I saved because they reminded me of the paper-thin coils made out of sand that some mysterious tidal creature made at my favorite beach. Sandcollars.

If there was ever an ecstatic errand par excellence, surely it is the buying of ladybugs. How could you beat the sense of abundance? A thousand in a bag! And the very idea of selling ladybugs is part and parcel with the child's game of playing store, with a world in which one has only to scribble a cardboard sign in order to open for business with a handful of gravel, inedible berries, or butterfly wings.

But Ariel was not with me when I went to buy the ladybugs, because she was buying CD's at the mall. She was buying them with the gift certificates she got for her eleventh birthday—which is almost all she got from her friends, along with a bottle of cologne, nail polish in blue and black, and a subscription to a magazine called *Teen Life*. She's in a nether zone now, somewhere between girl and woman, and as her mother, I'm in a nether zone, too—one even less well defined than hers. Should I just accept that the world that opened, or reopened, to me when she was born is closing up again, that my ticket has expired?

The day after I bought the ladybugs, I picked up Ariel at the friend's house where she had spent the night. She was sullen as she sometimes is when she's been away from me for a stretch of time; it's as if the strings of our connection go off pitch and need to be slowly retuned. When she began to speak, she drifted immediately to my two unfavorite topics: exactly what brand of shoe or shampoo she wished she had, and a complicated ranking of friends.

"Look at the yellow cactus flower!" I almost called out. We had just passed an immense cactus by the side of the road that blooms only once every other year or so, and it really is quite spectacular. But I could feel the aggressive edge in my impulse, and so I refrained.

We drove in silence again for a while. Then she asked me, "Would you like to hear the song I made up?"

"Of course," I said.

She began to sing. "You will never know, you will never know—" was the refrain. It was a melancholy song, about love and loss—emotions that I knew she hadn't yet actually experienced. It made me remember the sad songs that I loved as a young girl—about freight trains going around the bend, about empty rooms and narrow beds. Isn't it curious, I found myself thinking, that the "not yet" of the young girl is experienced as something lost?

Ariel went on singing, in a thin, rather plaintive voice that I had never heard her use before. As I listened, I could feel something opening—a door, a window—through which I saw . . . something delicate and uncertain. It had the shape of a melody projecting itself into the air, floating for a few moments, and then dissolving again. It was the arc of a young girl's voice listening for itself, a line cast out, then pulled back again. I drove and listened, and if there were cows in the fields, if there were horses or trains, I didn't see them.

7

LAST THINGS

LATELY I AM on the lookout for last things:

The last time she'll take my hand when we cross the street—

The last time I'll tuck her in bed—

When I gather with other parents who have children at this threshold, between childhood and adolescence, we find ourselves exchanging a litany of *he still/she still*'s:

She still sits in my lap sometimes—

He still likes me to stroke his back as he's falling asleep—

We would never say these things within earshot of our children, and even when our children aren't present, we speak in lowered voices. We realize that nothing would make them feel more betrayed, more exposed, than to know that we had shared such news about them. And even when we're alone with them and they suddenly take our hands or lean their heads against our shoulders, there's a particular way that we have to receive such offerings—as if they weren't really happening, or as if they were happening in some secret, invisible dimension. To give "positive reinforcement" at such a time, to say something like "It makes me happy when you take my hand," would be not just a faux pas, but a broken, if unspoken, taboo. As our children get older, their affectionate gestures become more like shy, wild, and even magical creatures. A quick embrace is the gazelle drinking at the water hole that will turn on its hooves and gallop off if its eyes meet yours. Or the unicorn that suddenly materializes in the woods and then—the moment you gasp "unicorn"—it vanishes.

There is a certain order to the disappearances. The gestures of affection vanish first from the public sphere. Your child won't take your hand as you cross the street. She won't let you kiss her good-bye at the door of her friend's house. You must act nonchalant when greeting her after a week of camp.

Without ever having been articulated, a new and quite elaborate set of rules comes into play. When out and about with your children, you must walk ten paces behind. Upon entering a store, you must immediately separate, allowing them to appear as if they were there entirely on their own recognizance.

For a while, certain interactions linger in the private sphere, like rare fish or birds in a natural preserve. Then these, too, begin to vanish—or to fall under ever more stringent restriction. Several parents told me that they were no longer permitted to initiate a tender gesture, but that their children could. "It's not that they don't want affection," one friend explained, "but that they want it on their terms." The night before, her daughter, cheeks smeared with some kind of green ointment, had told her, "You can hug me—but don't touch the face." My friend laughed when she recounted the incident, but I could hear an edge in her voice. All around her house there are framed photographs of this daughter's face. From babyhood through early girlhood, it's a face that brims with a mirth that seems just about to burst out of its skin. Round, ruddy, shining: it's a face that even through glass seems to offer itself like a bowl of cherries. But now this face that once beamed from the "I–Thou" of parent-child love takes on the aspect of "It," becoming *the face*, a kind of rare object in the house to which a mother, carefully and from a certain regulated distance, may pay homage under its layer of protective goo.

When was it that I stopped calling my mother "Mommy?" I don't remember exactly—only that I went through an excruciating period when I had no name for her. "Mommy" had become too vulnerably childish, but I hadn't yet grown into "Mom," which seemed abrupt, and even slightly tough. For months, I couldn't call out to my mother. If the phone rang for her, I'd have to run all the way out to the garden or to her studio and tell her, "It's for you." With my father, too, I got stranded in a limbo between "Daddy" and "Dad," and I remember the pain in his voice when he told me, "You don't have a name for me anymore."

At the time, I couldn't really understand that pain. I can now. It's the pain of a gathering distance, of something coming in between the I and Thou of parent and child, of a beloved, irresistibly touchable face receding behind *the face*, of suddenly becoming, to one's own child, anonymous.

I remember, too, how around the same age—twelve or thirteen— as I lost my childhood names for my parents, I began to have moments when I seemed to fall completely out of connection with them. They were odd, metaphysical moments, having nothing to do with conflict or emotional upset; in fact, usually they came in the midst of calm, very ordinary activities. Riding in the car, staring forward over the front seat at the backs of my parents' heads, I would suddenly find myself wondering, "What am I doing, shooting through space with these two dark-haired people?" Sitting at the dinner table, sometimes in the very midst of conversation or while lifting a fork from my plate, I might suddenly freeze, seeing my parents' faces, their mouths moving, as though they were alien beings. For a moment, often the briefest second, it was as though I'd fallen out of the circle of my family altogether, or had suddenly shot up into outer space and was now looking down from a vast distance. The experience wasn't painful for me—just strange, deeply strange. Realizing that my daughter may already be undergoing such brief but intense defections, however, is oddly painful.

What I uncover in myself is a double standard: the belief that I had no choice but to make tears in the fabric of my connection to my parents in order to spin the life that eventually led to my daughter's birth. But that she should now make tears in that life, the life out of which I made her, that the life I prepared for her should have turned out to be, as my parents' was for me, provisional, a platform, a passageway—it's dizzying.

And we live in a culture that doesn't give us much help with the dizziness, the gathering distance, the children who begin to recede behind a complicated and, for the most part an unspoken net of rules, children whose faces we are no longer allowed to touch, who may suddenly have no name for us. At haphazard moments, parents may find themselves exchanging a litany of *he still/she still*'s with one another, but overall, we are quite alone with the sense of loss.

Some elements of childhood do expire with a certain fanfare, becoming their own kind of ceremony. There are the milestone events: giving up the bottle, the highchair, the crib. A neighbor told me that when her son Jeremy turned three, they promised him a backhoe—a toy backhoe, that is—if he would give up his pacifier. Though sorely tempted, for there was almost nothing in the world that he loved more than backhoes, the power of the binky persisted, and for several months after his birthday, he was unable to kick the habit. Then one day, hearing a great, grinding commotion in the street outside, he ran to the window. There was a giant backhoe in the vacant lot right next to his house. Racing out the front door, in one joyful, triumphant gesture, he flung his pacifier into the newly heaved dirt.

When a child, in St. Paul's words, "puts away childish things," a parent's pain at what is lost is sometimes mixed with delight at what, for the child, is a leap forward, a spreading of wings. At other times, the sense of loss is all there is—as on that day when my daughter gathered up her huge collection of stuffed animals, thrust them into black-plastic garbage bags and hauled them into the garage. Watching her, I felt overcome by an emotion that I didn't feel entitled to. After all, they were her animals . . . but she was my child. She was my child doing away with my child—that's what was complicated. Dragging the heavy bags into the garage with a strange look on her face—both determined and slightly ashen—she was both the executioner and the one I mourned.

As difficult as such milestone moments can be, at least they permit a certain recognition and catharsis. The things that vanish imperceptibly are more difficult to mourn. A mother told me, "The other day my eight-year-old son had just gotten out of the shower. Passing me in the hall on his way to his room, he suddenly took the towel that was flung around his neck, wrapped it around his body, and I realized—oh, he won't let me see him naked anymore."

Suddenly you notice that something no longer happens, that it hasn't happened for a long time, and you didn't even see it go. How do you absorb such a loss? "If I'd known you were coming, I would have baked a cake," we say. "If I'd known you were going, I would have—" What would we have done? Is there a cake to bake for the things we didn't even know were leaving?

When I look up the word "savor," I see that it is related to the Latin word for "wisdom," and this make me happy. I love the thought of wisdom as the art of savoring, I love seeing the word "savor" tucked into the sage, and thinking of the sage as one who knows how to taste fully.

When I become aware of all that has vanished from my life without its having been fully tasted, I feel a sharp ache in my chest, but this ache intensifies my desire to savor the present. A teenage daughter rushes out the door to catch her ride to high school, and her mother, not yet fully awake, stumbles into the bathroom and discovers— among the eye-shadow pots, the crumpled Kleenex, mascara-smudged—a cup of coffee, still steaming, on top of the toilet tank. *I will miss this*, she thinks. Later that same day, she may once again find herself cursing her daughter's disorder, but the curse does not invalidate the moment of savoring that happened earlier.

I arrive home at the end of a dark winter day with my arms full of grocery bags, feeling tired, dispersed, aware of the errands undone, the phone calls unanswered. I have barely had time to set the grocery bags down in the kitchen, let alone begin to unpack them, when my daughter wanders in from the bathroom and asks, "Would you like a footbath? I made a potion."

I can't think of anything I'd like less at this moment than to soak my feet in warm, cloudy water in my salad bowl. *My salad bowl? You're using my salad bowl to wash feet in? And what did you put in that potion? My lavender bath oil? But it's so expensive, it was a friend's gift on my birthday and I've hardly even used it.* Whatever that sac, that gland is in my brain that secretes pure, unadulterated irritation, it's bursting. Close to the brink of saying something that stings, I take a sharp breath.

Wasn't it just the other day that I walked into a friend's living room and saw on the floor a circle of plastic horses, lying on their sides under lettuce leaves? My heart constricted. His daughter is eight, not twelve like mine, and at home, I come across such mixtures—small sleeping horses, lettuce leaves—less and less frequently. I allow myself to hear the word "potion" again, and remember how much I love the unlikely concoctions of childhood. I look down. There is my daughter, crouched on the floor below me. It will be a Mary Cassatt painting in reverse, a daughter washing her mother's feet. I sit down on the kitchen floor and allow my feet to be lifted into a salad bowl filled with warm, cloudy, lavender-scented water.

So this is one way to bake the cake. I take the pain of the moments that slipped through my fingers and bring it into the present. As hunger is a spice, we say, so this pain intensifies the taste of the present moment: the coffee cup on the toilet tank, the horses sleeping under their leaves, the feet in a salad bowl. . . .

But what about those moments that slipped away? Is there a way to savor backwards? A naked boy steps out of the shower, unabashed before his mother, and though she may for a moment savor his beauty, his unabashedness, the moment rises like steam in the damp, cluttered bathroom where she stands with the showerhead still dripping, the cat clawing at the door, the phone ringing in a far room, and the soup, she remembers, about to boil over on the kitchen stove.

Some days—weeks? months?—later, it will hit her: *I didn't realize the last time was the last time.* How could she?

But there *is* something being baked, something that rises in the heart like bread in that moment when a mother—nearly colliding with her boy, who darts, still dripping from the shower—realizes as he urgently wraps the towel around: *he's stopped letting me see him naked.* That moment has its own savor.

The wine taster doesn't drink a bottle of wine, he doesn't swim in it. But parents get immersed in their children's lives, they get flooded. And for this reason, there are some things that can only be savored backwards.

"Youth is such a wonderful thing. Too bad it is wasted on the young," said George Bernard Shaw. What I have always found espe-cially delightful about that quote is its implicit, ironic acknowledg-ment that the wonderful thing about youth is precisely that it spends itself so freely, it takes itself for granted. A youth that recollected itself in tranquillity by the glow of the evening fire would not, properly speaking, be what we mean by "youth." And, to a great degree, the young are wasted on their parents, because to be a parent is to be immersed in such an onward flow, a rush of life, a banquet of immedi-acy, that one lacks the degree of distance required for savoring.

But why does distance enter in at all here, if to savor is to be com-pletely present in the sense of tasting fully? Because such tasting, such presence, requires a certain hunger, a certain distance—a distance that arrives as the awareness of time passing.

My mother-in-law tells me, "What I miss most of all are those squeals that Ariel used to make when I came to the front door and she saw my face through the glass." Not only did I not make a tape of those squeals, but until she mentioned it, I had completely forgotten them. For a moment, I feel that sharp pang: I let something precious disap-pear and I failed to note its disappearance. But then I realize, "I couldn't record those squeals, I couldn't note them or even remember them," because in the moment of hearing them, they were too—I started to write "beautiful," but in fact, any adjective I might put in that slot is something added to them. The closest I can come is this: they were the sound of an emotion too huge for a small human being to contain, so that they came out like the high, vibrating sounds of a dol-phin. These sounds filled the air with something as fleeting and unut-terably present as a breeze, so that it is only now, feeling that pang, that slight constriction in my heart as it dawns on me *They're gone, and I failed to capture them* that I savor them fully for the first time.

PART IV

THE TEARS OF EROS
Love's Dark Shadows

1. The Bath

2. I Looked in Her Eyes

3. Play

4. Memories

5. Changelings

6. Who's at the Door?

7. *Noli Me Tangere:* The Family Photographs

of Sally Mann

Now we arrive at the realm that comes with a gate, and on the gate: a warning. For this chapter, along with "Goldilocks' Joy," which follows it, takes up directly the dark matter that we have known from the beginning, as soon as we put the two words together—eros and parenthood—cannot be ignored.

Some of this dark matter was touched on in the Introduction. I come back to it now, to expand the subject in somewhat greater detail—but also to delimit. And actually, as we discover just on the other side of the gate it is the limitations themselves, the revelation of a horizon beyond which we do not need to dwell, it is the limitations themselves, the revelations that turn out to be among the most significant finds of this exploration.

A virtual army of medical personnel, therapists, social scientists, educators, journalists, and adults in recovery has mobilized in recent years to address the issue of childhood sexual abuse. I leave to these experts and witnesses, whose passion and vocation it is, the urgent and important task of deepening our understanding of this abuse: the conditions that lead to it, that help to prevent it, and to heal from it. My own task in these pages has been, and remains, a different one: to carve out a bit more ground for the eros of parenthood to flow more freely in those families—the great majority of families—whose children are not in danger of being abused by their parents.

Of course, it is not possible to carve out this ground without coming up against the reality of sexual abuse as a horizon that defines the territory. To come up against this reality as horizon, however—to recognize when it is drawing closer, to discern where the boundaries are blurry and where they suddenly grow distinct—is not the same as to approach it as centerfield. In *choosing this approach, it is not for a moment my intention to minimize the suffering that sexual abuse inflicts. Rather, I see my project as a complementary one: to give voice to a dimension of family love that has been less heard from in recent years and that sometimes, in the current climate, can seem to belong to a realm "as far away as health."[1]*

This realm comes with its own darkness. For even the tenderest of parental love is shot through with ambivalence—an ambivalence that seems to be embedded in the very word "tender," with its root meaning "to stretch." The love of a child stretches us, demanding an impossible patience, an impossible generosity, an enormous sacrifice of time, money, sleep, privacy, order, peace of mind. . . . Resentment hovers around and within parental affection like a dark twin, like the thirteenth fairy, the one who, although we did not invite her to the christening, will crash the party anyway with her ominous message, "Think you can keep me out? Just wait. . . ."

But right here, face-to-face with this uninvited guest, something interesting occurs. While attunement *has been the prime navigational tool thus far, now* ambivalence *joins it. The parent who can attune discovers ambivalence not as an enemy of the eros of parenthood, but as a key ingredient. And simultaneously, the ambivalence that shadows ordinary parental love becomes an illuminating probe into the territory of the extreme. Abuse occurs when attunement fails. One way of understanding this failure is to see it as the inability to bear ambivalence—ambivalence in the form of complex and contradictory feelings. For abuse often occurs as a collapse of differentiation:* the other is myself; there is only one explanation for what I am doing; there is only one way to handle the impulse that I feel.

This is the very opposite of attunement, which is the via negativa, *the way that proceeds without certainty, without simple solutions, and that is ready—for the sake of intimate connection—to surrender its preconceptions again and again. We follow that way now into the shadows of family love.*

1

THE BATH

IMAGINE THAT IN setting out to explore the darkness of the eros of parenthood, we have traveled deep into the wilderness. Night has fallen; there are strange sounds in the woods, strange shapes in the shadows. At last, drawn by a single light, we come upon a clearing. In the center of it stands a wooden hut. Approaching quietly, we step up to its one small window. What will we see, in such a faraway place, surrounded by darkness?

A father is washing his small boy. The father is the poet Gary Snyder.[2] Here's the scene, in the father's words:

THE BATH

Washing Kai in the sauna,
The kerosene lantern set on a box
outside the ground-level window,
Lights up the edge of the iron stove and the
washtub down on the slab
Steaming air and crackle of waterdrops
brushed by on the pile of rocks on top
He stands in warm water
Soap all over the smooth of his thigh and stomach
"Gary, don't soap my hair!"
—his eye-sting fear—
the soapy hand feeling

> *through and around the gloves and curves of his body*
> *up in the crotch,*
> *And washing-tickling out the scrotum, little anus,*
> *his penis curving up and getting hard*
> *as I pull back skin and try to wash it*
> *Laughing and jumping, flinging arms around,*
> *I squat all naked too,*
> *Is this our body?*

Is this our body? the father asks. As he continues, he lets the question transmute slightly (*this our body, this is our body*) to become the poem's refrain. Even without these echoes of the Communion verse—*this is my body!*—we feel this bath to be a kind of sacrament, a dunking in the wonder of incarnation. As the poem continues and the poet's wife enters the hut, its celebration of intimate connection expands to include the wonder of reproduction: the transmission of seed from man, through woman, to child; the duplication of body parts, big and small; the life-giving difference between man and woman.

Yet this poem, which would seem to evoke the most primal, timeless dimension of human connection, gives off a strange kind of historicity. And though it is not a very old poem, it seems to belong to a different era, for the question it asks couldn't be asked today in the same way. Today, the amazed *Is this our body?* would ring out through an atmosphere thick with anxiety; it would be overcome by other questions. *Is something the matter with me? Am I damaging my child? Will someone spying on us in the bath think badly of me? Report me? Take my child away?*

Not long ago, I spoke with the father of a small boy. His name is Robert Danberg. He, too, is a poet, and he, too, was describing the experience of bathing his son, but as he spoke, there was an anxious overtone that was a world away from the world of "The Bath." And I noticed that he, too, had a refrain: *this is hard to say.* He would tell me, "You know, when I'm bathing Rubin, and I see his perfect little body, lolling—" and then he would stop and tell me, "This is hard to say—" Not once, but several times, his voice broke off like this.

Later, I found myself wondering *Why?* Why should it be so hard to say?

It's as though along with the Inner Child, we have discovered the Inner Molester. We proceed as if there were a latent pedophile, an incest-perpetrator, lurking inside each of us. And if we relax too fully in the company of our children, if we allow ourselves to experience and to express, without censure, the sheer pleasure and marvel of incarnation, surely this inner figure will fly out, like an evil genie, and commit some unspeakable deed.

Each time Robert's voice broke off, I felt that the natural and authentic refrain he wanted to express was something like *"Ah!"* or *"This is our body!"*—something that could express the awe, the *"I-can't-take-this-for granted"*-ness of a father gazing at his naked little boy. And it was as though each time he allowed himself to come close to expressing this *"Ah!"*, he had to censor himself, as if to ward off the invisible judge who is always there, hovering in the bedroom, in the bathroom, the judge who assumes that what any father taking such delight in his beautiful son *really* wants to say is *"When I'm bathing Rubin, and I see his perfect little body, lolling, I want to fondle him."*

But how close, really, is the fondling father to the father who gives unabashed voice to the *"Ah!"*? How close really, is the abusing father to the father *"laughing and jumping"* in the poem? Not as close as we have come to fear. Not as close. The atmosphere inside the hut is quite different from the atmosphere that comes through in so many actual accounts of sexual abuse: the hiddeness, the furtiveness, the *"this-is-not-really-happening"* quality. This bath is a noisy, exuberant interaction between parent and child, one that does not shrink from the light of the kerosene lantern, and one that permits the child a strong voice: "'Gary, don't soap my hair!'" he commands at the beginning, and later, "He gets mad and yells."

In the second stanza, when the child's mother comes through the door, it is clear that a deft and graceful ease exists between her and her child, and that there is a strong erotic connection between her and the child's father:

Masa comes in, letting fresh cool air
sweep down from the door
a deep sweet breath
And she tips him over gripping neatly, one knee down
her hair falling hiding one whole side of
shoulder, breast, and belly,
Washes deftly Kai's head-hair
as he gets mad and yells—
The body of my lady, the winding valley spine,
the space between the thighs I reach through,
cup her curving vulva arch and hold it from behind
a soapy tickle a hand of grail
The gates of Awe. . . .

What if—begging forgiveness to the poet now, for treating the poem as something not at all like a poem—we change some of the background facts of this scene? Suppose, for example, that the father is not a father, but a stepfather, or the mother's boyfriend. Suppose the mother does not enter the sauna because she is away working, as she is every day, leaving her little boy alone with her partner. And suppose that when she slips into bed at night, she turns her back to her partner, night after night—because she is tired, because she is ill, because she is angry, because she herself has been sexually wounded, because, because. . . And suppose that this man is a heavy drinker and has been drinking before he comes into the sauna. And suppose that this little boy is not the sort of child who can bellow, "Gary, don't soap my hair!," a boy who feels free to yell when he gets mad, but instead, a rather timid child, a child who has learned that it is dangerous to speak your mind to a grown-up, a child so anxious to have the attention of an adult that he will put up with almost anything, as long as it comes in the form of attention—even unpleasant attention.

With each of these additions, we have reason, as we gaze through the window of the hut, to become increasingly wary of the scene that meets our eyes. This wariness is borne out by any number of studies into the genesis of sexual abuse. In the words of the psychiatrist Brandt

F. Steele, who serves on the staff of the C. Henry Kempe National Center for the Prevention and Treatment of Child Abuse and Neglect: "Sexual abuse of children of all ages in the family is not an isolated phenomenon occurring in an otherwise healthy life situation. It is the obvious, overt, symptomatic expression of seriously disturbed family relationships and is always preceded by more or less emotional neglect or mistreatment. . . ."[3] Thus, as certain predisposing factors and certain signs of serious disturbance accumulate, we become positively irresponsible if we do not keep a steady gaze on the scene and a readiness to intervene.[4]

But in the absence of such omens—and given that the poet himself has invited our gaze—can we relax a little and enjoy the scene? Can we look at it less with a vigilante's eye and more, say, with a painter's eye? Renoir's or Cassatt's, for example, which, inviting us to immerse ourselves in the timelessness of the present moment, would show us a dappled light on flesh and water. Or Matisse, giving us in the linked bodies another dance called Joie de Vivre. Or, seeing the kerosene lantern set on a box, we might think of La Tour and of how he would take the light from this single source, intensified by the sense of darkness without, to reveal the sense of closeness within the small circle of family—The Holy Family. In the absence of these facts, why should these images seem so much farther away than the specter of abuse? In the absence of these facts, why should a father have to break off, in the midst of what so clearly wants to be a litany of praise, a spontaneous "Ah!" and say again and again, "This is hard to say—"?

Turning away from the window, ready to head back home from the scene of "The Bath," the question is this: is it possible to grow more refined in our model of sexual abuse?

Which is not to take it lightly.

Which is not to take it lightly.

Why?

We know why: because it happens with alarming frequency.[5] Because its effects can be both profound and long-lasting.[6] Because most sexual abuse occurs in the home, and on the part of someone a child knows—a family member or a friend of the family—and because the elements of shattered trust, confusion, and fear of speaking out greatly intensify the emotional wounding.[7]

And yet—

And yet? How can there be an "And yet—"?

We know that cancer is not something to be taken lightly. But we also know that its causes are many and complex. We know that a "one-size-fits-all" approach to its eradication will never work, for it involves an interplay of many factors: genetics, environment, nutrition, stress, weakened immunity. . . . The same is true of childhood sexual abuse. It takes a very complex set of conditions, an interaction of many factors—the perpetrator's psychology and history, the social environment, the psychology and the family situation of the child who is abused—to bring about an act of child abuse. Yet the current popular model of how to address the abuse is simplistic. In the words of Gail Ryan, director of the Perpetration Prevention Project at the Kempe National Center for the Prevention and Treatment of Child Abuse and Neglect: "Sexual-abuse prevention strategies have usually focused on preventing victimization. Children have been taught to 'resist and report' when someone attempts to molest them, and adults have been taught to reduce the access and opportunity of child molesters by screening and monitoring people who are in positions of authority with children. These strategies have placed the responsibility for protecting children from sexual abuse on children themselves and on their caregivers."[8]

This general strategy involves a kind of blanket vigilance, a pervasive anxiety, one that hangs like a dense cloud and that settles on all of us—children and caregivers equally. It settles on women as well as on men—though women are less likely than men to be perpetrators.[9] It settles on men who would never in their lives violate a young child, as well as on those who would and do. It settles on children who are not at risk of being sexually abused within their families, as well as those who are.

Perhaps there is no other way through the problem at this particular moment of our collective history. Ryan herself deems such strategies "appropriate and necessary," but points out that they constitute "secondary levels of prevention, based on the fact that children are 'at risk' for sexual victimization." In contrast, "The primary prevention of sexual abuse lies in preventing individuals from attempting to molest children in the first place—perpetration prevention."[10] Such strategies work—not to keep children out of the clutches of perpetrators, but to keep people from ever becoming perpetrators. Alas, such primary prevention has been the strategy least favored by public policy.

When scientists isolate a gene for a particular form of cancer, it stirs the hope for a form of "primary prevention" that one day will be able to treat the disease before it even begins. In the meantime, doctors are attempting to become more refined in their use of certain "secondary" strategies. In the case of chemotherapy, for example, there is the goal of targeting a specific site with the healing poison rather than drenching the entire body, including its healthy parts. Analogously, couldn't we, with regard to sexual abuse, aspire to arrive at a more refined approach? At best, "perpetration prevention" could be a form of "mending the gene." At second best, we could learn to focus our anxious vigilance in a way that while pinpointing the actual "malignancy," leaves more of our healthy selves free and exuberant. Does it really need to be so hard for a father, bathing his small boy, to exclaim, *This is our body!*"?

But what would this "second best" look like? It is easy to speak of "a more refined approach," but difficult to imagine the actual forms it might engender.

Not long after I met the father named Robert Danberg, he took me home to meet his wife, Mary Biggs. She has a degree in early childhood education from The Bank Street School and works full time in a day-care center in New York City. While their son Rubin was taking his afternoon nap in his bedroom, the three of us spoke. Mary told me: "When I first went to work at the day-care center, we were taught certain phrases to use at difficult moments. For instance, if a child seemed overwhelmed by another child's physical interaction with him, we might ask the first child, 'Do you like this?' And if the child said, 'No,' we might say, 'Remember, you can always say, "It's my body!"' At first I found these phrases very helpful: they offered a way to get through a sticky situation. But the longer I've been there, the less inclined I am to rely on catchphrases. It's odd, because I've actually begun to feel as though I'm shortchanging the child if I just give him a catchphrase. Each child, in each situation, is so different. More and more, I've learned to rely on the intimate knowledge I have of this particular child in this moment."

Intimate knowledge. I love the way that Mary put those two words together, reminding us that in letting go of a blanket policy, a rule-bound regimen, we don't necessarily fall into a wasteland, an anarchy. Isn't this what "emotional intelligence" is all about?[11] The idea that we can learn to read, with more accuracy, the varying signals that others give out and respond to them not by rote, but in true responsiveness, through words and gestures that hone themselves to the present moment? If we immediately hand out a catchphrase to the child, we miss out on developing this ability—both in ourselves and in our children.

The whole time I'd been speaking with Mary and Robert, Rubin had been sleeping. It seemed that he was taking an especially long nap. He hadn't made a peep in nearly two hours, but as the afternoon wore on, his presence began to permeate the conversation. From her stories of life as a teacher, Mary moved to stories of life as a mother, and from the latter, she gave me her own version of "The Bath." She told me that she and Rubin had always loved taking baths together when he was a baby, but that when he turned two, there was a marked change. Before, it had been easy to wash his hair, but now he became hysterical, squirming and crying. He also became intensely focused on her body, and he couldn't keep his hands off her breasts. She decided it was time for them to stop bathing together.

In part, Mary's decision rested on her professional training in the field of child development. She knew that Rubin was at the difficult, delicate stage of moving from infancy toward greater independence. He was beginning to see her as separate from himself, and—reinforced by his increasing awareness of gender—beginning to see the ways in which her body differed from his. All this stirred up intense and strongly ambivalent feelings: anxiety, sexual curiosity, a desire to merge again, a fear of merging. More important, however—and applicable to any mother, even one who hasn't been to The Bank Street School—Mary's decision arose from "intimate knowledge." Observing her child from up close—in the bath—she noticed a significant change in his behavior. Where once he was playful, and at ease, now he had lost his equilibrium. He had become agitated, overwhelmed, overstimulated by the intensity, the complexity, of the experience.

The decision to stop bathing with him wasn't without its sharp pang of regret. Bathing with her baby boy had been one of her great pleasures in motherhood, and as she doesn't plan to have another child, there is a particular poignancy for her at each step of letting go. Yet there was something bright in her tone of voice when she described the aftermath of her decision. "Rubin takes his baths with Robert now, and the entire experience is so much smoother. He's able to stay whole with his father in a way he couldn't do anymore with me. Just the other day, I walked into the bathroom as Rubin was waiting for Robert to join him in the tub. 'Mommy,' he said, 'do you want to get in the tub with me?' 'No,' I said. 'I'm just looking.' And he flashed me a huge smile, rolled over in the water and said, 'Look at me, Mommy: I'm a whale!' "

In the midst of what had become her son's ambivalence about bathing with her, Mary had to let go of her earlier "take" on the experience. This was a difficult, complex, and delicate process—one in which she had to make room for her own ambivalence, to feel simultaneously her desire to preserve the closeness that she and her baby son once had, her resentment of his invasive touching of her body, her protective concern for his development. Ultimately, she turned away from whatever gratification she had from this particular form of intimacy, knowing that she would probably never again in her life experience it. It is not hard to imagine a mother who couldn't let go at this juncture, who couldn't accept that what had been such an intense yet simple pleasure had become complex, shadowed, fraught with tension. Yet because Mary's focus was on Rubin and his needs, she took the next step. Though she took it on the basis of considerable knowledge, she took it with no simple catchphrase to guide her. She took it without fully being able to know what the outcome would be, and with no guarantee of success. She was richly rewarded.

In surrendering the pleasure she once had in bathing with her child, Mary discovered a different pleasure, a pleasure in seeing what she described as her son's "wholeness." *Look at me, Mommy! I'm a whale!* he shouted, expressing a huge pride in his powerful body and a huge affection for his mother. For even if he couldn't express it directly, somehow he knew that by withdrawing her big mammal-body from the tub, she freed him to experience his own magnificence.

Here we have come back to attunement, the royal road through the eros of parenthood. And in this context, we see again how far attunement is from the one-size-fits-all approach, with its comforting certainties. For attunement proceeds through an ongoing series of failures. Something that worked doesn't work anymore; something that was simple has become charged with complex and contradictory feelings, and finding the next step calls for something more than one simple solution. To attune to one child might mean reminding him to say, "It's my body!" To attune to another child, or to the same child in a different moment, might mean to call out, while laughing together, "This is our body!" Or yet again, it might be for a mother to cry out to a little boy who can't keep his hands off her breasts, "Hey! That's my body!" So that getting out of the tub, she leaves him room to be a whale.

2

I LOOKED IN HER EYES

"THE ONLY THING that seems eternal and natural in motherhood is ambivalence," wrote the American author Jane Lazarre.[12] And indeed, everything that underlies the passionate intensity between parent and child may go either way, toward tender interconnectedness or toward its opposite: resentment, withdrawal, violence.

Pregnancy can be traversed as the miracle of a life-within-a-life, an experience of fullness, wholeness, creativity—or as an invasion, an incapacitating loss of autonomy, a frightening passivity. Nursing a baby can be a blissful, life-giving experience of intimacy, or the painful, draining contact with a relentless succubus. The utter helplessness of an infant can melt a parent's heart, or cling to it like a parasite, a barnacle. The unconditional love the small child offers can feel redemptive, or both suffocating and cheap—for after all, they have no other place to be but with us, on us, beside us, and no choice but to love us. The way children perpetuate us, imitate us, duplicate our faces, bodies, expressions, and mannerisms can be flattering, or a reinforcement of self-loathing.

The list of opposites could go on and on. It's as though there were two worlds, mirror images of one another, one rising like an island above a lake, the other inverted, below. It's as though every parent has a double—or rather, as though every moment of parenting has its double.

Is this a problem? Certainly, it is hard to admit. It is hard to talk about. Looking through stacks of parenting magazines, through the sea

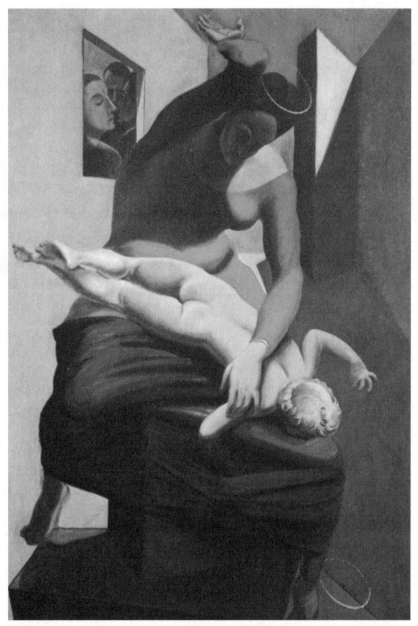

of cheerful tips on how to navigate the difficult moments, I am struck at how rarely there is the blunt admission that sometimes we hate our children. Sometimes we wish they would disappear. Sometimes they seem like tormentors, tailor-made by a malevolent god to our own most precise specifications. As the novelist Fay Weldon wrote, "The greatest advantage of not having children must be that you can go on believing that you are a nice person; once you have children, you realize how wars start."[13]

It is hard to admit just how many moments in a parent's life are double moments, moments that could so easily go either way. The milk spills all over the table, seeps into a pile of papers, drips onto the floor. What parent doesn't feel a flash of irritation, a curse on the tip of the tongue? This is a tiny fork in the road, but such forks sometimes arrive a hundred times in the course of a parent's day, and some are not so tiny. Is this in itself the fact that we are often "of two minds"—or more—a problem?

The British psychoanalyst Rozsika Parker has written an entire book, *Mother Love, Mother Hate*, on the subject of maternal ambivalence. In her view, ambivalence is a central and inescapable feature of motherhood, and it is not in itself the problem. Rather, "the issue is how a mother manages the guilt and anxiety ambivalence provokes."[14] When a mother is neither too psychically fragile nor too overwhelmed by her circumstances, ambivalence can be a powerful impetus that moves her to become more conscious of her child and of her relationship to him. Parker writes:

Where motherhood is concerned, I think the conflict between love and hate actually spurs mothers on to struggle to understand and know their baby. In other words, the suffering of ambivalence can promote thought—and the capacity to think about the baby and child is arguably the single most important aspect of mothering. Perhaps this becomes clearer if we invent a hypothetical mother who does not experience ambivalence but regards her child only with hostile feelings, or conversely, with untroubled love. In neither case will she find it necessary to dwell on her relationship with her child or to focus her feelings on her child's response to herself because she will not know what is missing. It is the troublesome co-existence of love and hate that propels a mother into thinking about what goes on between herself and her child.[15]

Though Parker's focus is on maternal ambivalence, much of what she says is applicable to fathers as well. Certainly the following story, told to me by a man named Rowan of his experience as a young father, could serve as a powerful example of her book's main thesis. This man, I should add, had been both physically and emotionally abused throughout his childhood.

"When my daughter was around two years old and being potty-trained, she learned the power of saying, 'I have to pee! I have to pee!' It was a sure way of getting her parents to stop what they were doing and attend to her. One day we were sitting at the dinner table, and she started up, 'I have to pee! I have to pee!' I was exhausted at the end of a day's work, and something snapped inside me. It was clear to me that she was just trying to get attention. I got up from my chair and yanked her out of her highchair in a fury. The moment I did, she began to cry hard and to pee all over herself, all over me. I looked into her eyes and I saw such fear, such humiliation. I recognized that look: I'd had those feelings often as a child. I handed her to her mother and I went into the living room to calm down. I said to myself, *That will never happen again.* And it never did."

This was one of those critical moments that could so easily have gone the other way. What made it possible for Rowan to go in the direction that he did, and for this moment to be a turning point—a point at which he not only changed his own pattern as a parent, but brought to an end the patterns of parenting that went back for generations in his family?

Empathy is the easy answer. But what is empathy? And how might it relate to the question of ambivalence—ambivalence understood as the simultaneous presence of contradictory feelings?

At first glance, the moment of looking into his daughter's eyes and seeing his own childhood self reflected there might seem, in its own way, like a narrowing of consciousness. The moment of grace is the moment when two become one and he feels as she feels. Yet what took place was not just a simple fusing, a collapse of his consciousness into hers. When a parent is fused with a child, the child does not exist as a separate being. (Indeed, it is not uncommon for abusing parents to express a feeling of "I have hit myself" and to cry along with the child whom they have abused. As Brandt F. Steele, M.D., explains, "The child's 'bad behavior' is somehow interpreted as an attack on the caregiver's already fragile self-image, the child considered as bad as the caregiver himself was as a child and consequently deserving of the same punishment or rejection that was meted out to him when he was young.")[16] In such a scenario, the only reality is the parent's reality, within which the child exists only in relation to the parent—to please or to torment, in fulfillment or betrayal of the parent's needs. In contrast, the moment when Rowan looked into his daughter's eyes reveals itself to be a moment of great complexity. Rather than a collapse into oneness, it involves a high degree of differentiation.

For in this moment, Rowan was aware of his state of intense anger and frustration and of what he was about to do. He was also aware of his daughter as a little person who, having her own set of feelings in response to his anger and frustration, was separate from him, and yet entirely at his mercy.

In this same moment, he reexperienced his primal feelings of fear and humiliation and was able to feel compassion—as an adult—for the child who was himself.

In the midst of this extraordinarily intense and complex constellation of feelings, Rowan made the conscious decision to hand his daughter to her mother and to leave the room until he calmed down. He was not capable of doing any more for her in that moment; he could not provide physical or verbal comfort—but what a great leap he had already taken!

This crucial moment of empathy—crucial in that it extinguished not only a single violent reaction, but a pattern of reaction that had been transmitted through generations—is in itself a kind of ambivalence. For it is a moment of being of more than one mind, a moment in which many different, and many contradictory, feelings swirl all at once.

For parents, it is not only with respect to protective and destructive feelings that ambivalence arises. The currents of erotic feeling that run between parents and children also provoke a powerful ambivalence. To experience anything resembling sexual feeling for one's child evokes the most powerful of all human taboos: the incest taboo. It violates the most culturally cherished ideal of parenthood "as the end product, not the site of sexuality."[17] In its pushing of boundaries, sexual feeling contains an element of aggression that runs counter to the parental impulse to protect. Not least of all, the growing awareness of the reality of sexual abuse intensifies parental anxiety. In this latter regard, Parker writes: "Revelations of maternal child sexual abuse have forced society to confront certain realities about motherhood. But such revelations have also encouraged a division in the way mothers are thought about: there are bad, unnatural mothers who abuse their children, and good, normal mothers who do not. Thus the always-present and always-disturbing elements in mother-child sexuality tend to be ignored and mothers are left feeling guilty and unnatural on account of the sexuality that is inevitably present to one degree or another between them and their children."[18]

Her point—which could apply equally to fathers—is that when this split prevails, when "normal" parents are not able to face the sexuality that is "inevitably present" to some degree in the parent-child relationship, they are cut off from the possibility of finding solutions to the complex and contradictory feelings that this sexuality engenders.

But what might a "solution" to such ambivalence look like? Parker provides the example of Nathalie, a mother who had this to say about her five-year-old son: "I do feel uncomfortable with the feelings Micky stirs in me. Recently he has really got into touching me—touching my breasts. It is nice, yet there has to be a line. I find it very difficult to know where to draw the line. I don't want to seem to shove him off, or appear really rejecting, but I need to be able to say, 'This is mine.' " Parker comments:

> Nathalie's description of the confusion her small son evoked in her . . . is a good example of how the management of ambivalence can assist the mother-child relationship. Although she says she does not want to "shove him off," she does feel invaded and irritated, as much by her sense of confusion as by anything else. Yet, as she says, "it is nice." She does love her child and does not want to seem to be rejecting. Love, desire, irritation, protectiveness and cultural taboo are all stirred in her and demand resolu-

tion. She appeals to the only certainty that she knows. She says, "This is mine," and thus lays down a containing boundary without constituting a rejection. The son's exploration of his mother's body could have led in another direction. The mother in her confusion could have exploited or rejected the child, while the son's desire and frustration could have motivated a sadistic wish to smash all boundaries. In other words, the element of sadism and aggression within the sexuality constellated between mother and child could have overwhelmed loving concern and creative ambivalence."[19]

The outcome of "creative ambivalence," Parker makes clear, is to *"think about what children themselves are trying to achieve, why and how it may differ from the parent's own experiences and aspirations."*[20] And here we are back with Mary and Rubin in the bath. In response to Rubin's invasive and hysterical behavior in the tub, Mary did not become overwhelmed. Rather, she allowed the welter of ambivalent feelings that had arisen to become a question: *What's the next step?* Attuning to the complex and contradictory mix of feelings that had arisen for both of them, she was able to think about Rubin, to think about their relationship, and to arrive at a decision that reflected her best guess as to what he himself was trying to achieve.

In the story of Mary and Rubin, in the story of Rowan who—having yanked his daughter up from her highchair in a fury, looked into her eyes and set her back down—we have examples of empathy as "the creative outcome" of a parent's experience of ambivalence.

Another friend, whose history was not quite as tormented as Rowan's, provides a further example, a moment of breakthrough that occurred when her daughter was around two. In yet another version of "The Bath," Jane Kingston told me: "It was the end of a long day, and all I wanted to do was go to bed. I was exhausted, and I wasn't feeling well. But unfortunately, I had to give Katya a bath because she'd been playing outside in the rain and was absolutely caked with mud, from the hair on her head to between the toes of her feet. She was ready to collapse, too, though, and she absolutely did not want to take a bath. She was resisting me already as I was undressing her, and—though I didn't hurt her—I had to lift her up quite forcefully to put her in the tub. Once in the water, she began howling. She wouldn't let me wash her. The howls turned into screams, and she wouldn't stop. I was so tired, she was being so impossible, and I felt as though I was going to lose it. Not that I would have physically hurt her, but I was going to collapse emotionally into the same state of helpless rage that she felt. And then somehow, I caught myself. I looked into her eyes. And when I did, I felt a pain, an actual sharp pain in my heart. I said to her, 'You're having such a hard time, aren't you?' Something let go in both of us. Something was calmed."

My friend told me that this experience was a turning point for her as a parent, one that has continued to resonate through all her years of parenting. She has since become a therapist, and when I asked her how her story might relate to the notion of ambivalence, she responded, "From the beginning, Katya has been a very intense child, much more challenging for me to handle than her older sister. At some point I learned that I have to acknowledge the ambivalent feelings that I often have about her, I have to acknowledge how stressful it can be for me to be her parent. If I didn't, I would just collapse into anxiety about her. All my energy would go into trying to control her. My ambivalence— allowing myself to acknowledge how difficult she can be—acknowledges her as having a separate psychic life from mine. That moment in the bathtub, I saw her. I saw how difficult life could be for her. And though I felt that as a pain in my own heart, it was actually a moment of differentiation. I saw that she wasn't trying to destroy me. She was just suffering. It was a moment of realizing 'Oh, that's who my child is.' "

These moments of release from the darkness and confusion of the parent-child relationship are not moments of simple fusion. They are moments in which a simultaneity of complex and contradictory feelings is experienced. And so it is that ambivalence is not an enemy of parent-child love—but a key ingredient. One that brings us back to the very beginning, to the root of true intimacy: the mystery of being not one not two, not two not one.

3

PLAY

✑

"TAKE A DEEP breath." "Count to ten." "Leave the room." "Pick up the phone." As rudimentary as they may seem, these tips for angry parents involve something quite complex: the ability to play within a rapidly constricting field of rising anger. For play, in its broadest sense, calls on us to entertain a range of possible meanings; to hold serious consequences at bay; to keep what is latent, latent; to refrain from, or at least to postpone, the moment of absolute closure. (As when one says, "Let's play with that idea for a while," meaning, "Let's entertain a multiplicity of possible interpretations before arriving at a conclusion.")

It is perhaps easy to imagine that adults who are violent with their children are people "without any values," people without the least ability to distinguish "right" from "wrong." But what often emerges is that physically abusing parents are so prone to self-condemnation that stressful situations readily trigger a collapse into hopeless, self-fulfilling disaster. A child cries, and a mother assumes, "I'm a terrible mother. I can't make my child stop crying." Having already condemned herself as "a terrible mother," there is that much less insulation between herself and the things that "a terrible mother" does. The leap to absolute negative judgment occurs so rapidly that there is little opportunity to expand the period of latency, to relax in it, to play with it—in the sense of testing its edges, experimenting with different modes of expression.

Does it seem outrageous to speak of "play" in such a context, when the stakes are so very high? Perhaps one of the reasons they get so high so fast is that there is so little play in the field. If, when a child cries beyond a certain number of minutes, it can mean only one thing: "This is a bad child who is trying to torment me," or "I am a failure as a parent," then things get very serious very quickly. According to Brandt F. Steele, M.D., "Low self-esteem and poor identity are common in abusers of all kinds and account for their inability to cope well with inevitable life stresses and their vulnerability to any behavior or event that is perceived as an attack on their fragile narcissism. Thus, something as 'normal' as a car battery going dead or a refrigerator or washing machine breaking down can create a sense of helplessness and can disrupt all daily routines. If it is a child's behavior that is perceived as a failure to respect or satisfy the caregiver's needs of the moment, it can be the crisis that precipitates physical abuse."[21]

Fortunately, the ability to play within the field of one's own mounting tension is something that can be learned; it is a skill that can be developed and refined. And one of the most important things a parent can learn is to recognize when no play is left, when the line between impulse and act has grown so short and taut that it will snap. That's when it's time to leave the room, pick up the phone. . . .

Once when Ariel was a baby, I was so frayed by sleep loss that when she woke up howling in the middle of the night, I said to my husband, "You go in to her," and I went out to sleep for a while in the car. I lay there for an hour or two, clenched like a fist on the backseat of the car. The driveway was dark, it was a cold autumn night, and I certainly didn't feel as though I was being playful. I felt, rather, like a terrible failure. Yet now, looking back, I can see that my escape was, in its own somewhat desperate way, a creative solution. Certainly it was preferable to collapsing into whatever impulse had welled up within me at the time, the desire to scream back at her or hurl an object against the wall or pick her up with so much fury that it startled her . . . or worse.

One way to describe what happens in abusive families is to say that there is a tragic absence of play. The adult who succumbs to the impulse to abuse has drastically narrowed his sights, reduced his own options—not to speak of those of the child he abuses. This absence of play is perhaps easiest to see in the context of physical or emotional abuse, but it can be seen in the dynamic of sexual abuse as well. The numbing of awareness, through drugs or alcohol, that so frequently accompanies sexual abuse is not one that permits the multiplicity and freedom, the spontaneity, of true play.[22] Rather, the "disinhibition" that follows such numbing is one that permits an adult to have his way with a child.

According to Gail Ryan, director of the Perpetration Prevention Project at the Kempe National Center for the Prevention and Treatment of Child Abuse and Neglect, "abusive' interactions are consistently defined by three factors: 1)lack of consent, 2)lack of equality, and 3)coercion (or pressure)."[23] Such an imposition of power on a child by one stronger, bigger, and older, one on whom a child may depend for his very survival, is anything but playful. Indeed, you might say that there is a dreadful seriousness that comes through in survivors' accounts of sexual abuse, in their memories of the compulsive repetitiveness of the behavior they endured, as well as in the atmosphere of secrecy, denial, and threats.

And here, in the name of multiplicity, I have a double story.

A Tale of Two Enemas.

Both are true stories, told to me by friends about their families.

One evening, in the 1950's, when the practice was still common, a mother and father were in the bathroom giving their seven-year-old son, who had not been feeling well, an enema. He was howling with apprehension and humiliation, and the parents were doing their best to remain calm and concentrated. The door burst open, and the older boy, eleven at the time, tore in with the kitchen scissors in hand. He strode over to his brother, cut the tube of the enema bag—and the whole family collapsed in laughter. No child ever again received an enema in that family.

The other is a story that went on and on. A mother gave her son enemas all the way through his childhood and well into adolescence. She never administered the enema to her daughters, only to her son. To this day, he does not like to be touched by his mother. Greeting him after months of separation, if she tries to give him a hug, he recoils.

Physical intimacy is difficult for him—for a number of reasons, but his mother's repeated invasion of his body is one of them.

In the first family, "the day Ronnie got the scissors" is part of the repertoire of funny family stories; it is told and retold with pleasure. In the second family, according to my friend, if he were to try to bring the subject up with his mother, she would not even remember that it ever happened.

What lies at the root of the difference between these two stories? If we could isolate and bottle the difference, how much suffering might be avoided! Doubtless, we would discover a long list of factors—social, economic, and psychological. But what I distill in the present context is this: one of the things that made the second family vulnerable was precisely that ambivalence, complexity of meaning, being of more than one mind, was not tolerated. A parent giving a child an enema could only mean one thing: "You are sick and I am helping you." The invasive aspect of the process, with its violent and its sexual connotations, could not in any way be acknowledged. Nor was it possible for the parent to have a change of mind. To be stopped, *in medias res*, by a son and his pair of scissors would have been unthinkable. It would have threatened the parent in the very marrow of the parental role, for to be a parent in such a family is to be firm, unwavering, an unassailable figure of authority. At the very foundation of such a family lies a rigid conception of parent-child roles. And because rigid: fragile. In this kind of family, a child who stands up to a parent is, in essence, giving the message that "You are a failure as a parent." It is not so far from this to "You are a failure as a human being." The stakes are very high in such a setting; is it any wonder that the possibility of laughter is so far away?

Indeed, not just laughter—but consciousness itself.

The rigidity of consciousness that characterizes the second family is of a sort that passes quickly into unconsciousness. To heal from this history, it has been necessary for my friend to bring it fully into consciousness, no small feat in itself, and to allow himself to remember the multiplicity of feelings: not only the humiliation and loss of control as the warm water entered him, but also the pleasure, a disturbing sense of arousal. . . .

To recover this complexity helps him to heal from the collapse of meaning that characterized the original experience, and thereby strengthen his confidence in his own powers of perception. For not only had he repeatedly suffered the invasiveness of his mother's ministrations, but these had occurred in an atmosphere that did violence to his consciousness in permitting the only possible interpretation of the experience: "I am a mother taking care of my sick child."

Personal accounts of childhood abuse frequently convey this sense of atmospheric pressure; it's as though within a cloud of dense fog, a voice both subliminal and booming repeated over and over again: *"This is not really happening,"* or, at most, *"The feelings that you are having are unwarranted."* This is the atmosphere that the Swiss psychoanalyst Alice Miller has described so compellingly in such books as *Thou Shalt Not Be Aware* and *For Your Own Good*.[24] For her, it is precisely this narrowing of consciousness that makes it possible for abuse to be transmitted from one generation to another. Rather than bearing the anxiety of complexity, of multiplicity, rather than adding to the pain of having been abused, the painful realization that "Perhaps my parents were wrong. Perhaps there might have been another way . . ." it is easier for some people to identify with the parents when their own turn comes to be a parent, and to do unto their children as was done unto them.

The intuition of a link between abuse and the absence of play is borne out by the profile of the typical pedophile as "highly Victorian" and "rigid" in his beliefs about sexuality. According to one standard text on abnormal psychology, "Convicted pedophiles . . . are often highly religious. They see themselves as devout, they read the Bible regularly, and they pray often for cure of their pedophilia. They are often beset with conflicts about religious piety versus sexuality, are guilt-ridden, and feel doomed."[25]

A certain rigidity and inflexibility also crops up in descriptions of families in which sexual abuse has occurred. In his book *Child Sexual Abuse, New Theory and Research*, David Finkelhor writes that:

the quality of a daughter's relationship to a father, whether natural or stepfather, makes a difference in her vulnerability to abuse. When a father has particularly conservative family values, for example, believing strongly in children's obedience and in the subordination of women, a daughter is more at risk. Moreover, when he gives her little physical affection, the same is true. Such daughters have a harder time refusing the intrusions of an older man, even when they suspect him to be wrong, because they have been taught to obey. Moreover, a child who is starved for physical affection from a father may be less able to discriminate between a genuine affectionate interest on the part of an adult and a thinly disguised sexual one.[26]

Turning to the role of mothers in contributing to a child's vulnerability to abuse, Finkelhor writes:

Victimized girls were much more likely to have mothers who were punitive about sexual matters. These mothers warned, scolded, and punished their daughters for asking sex questions, for masturbating, and for looking at sexual pictures much more often than usual. A girl with a sexually punitive mother was 75% more vulnerable to sexual victimization than the "typical" girl in the sample. It was the second most powerful predictor of victimization, after having a stepfather, and was still highly significant when all other variables were controlled.[27]

Though Finkelhor writes that "We can only speculate why," his conclusion is that "Sexually repressive practices backfire" and that "It is not sexually lax, but sexually severe, families that foster a high risk for sexual exploitation."[28]

The endangering familial atmosphere that Finkelhor is describing here is one composed of black-and-white polarities: parent/child, good/bad, touch/no touch; and monolithic identities: "Dad is boss." "Touch is sex." "Sex is bad." "You are bad." In such an atmosphere, there is little room in which to move around. Impulses are likely to be acted out in the most literal way. There is so little opportunity for modulation, experimentation, transformation. In such an atmosphere, a mother gives her son an enema again and again, well into his teenage years. *Be still*, she says, in so many words. *I am your mother. You are the child. We have no other way to touch in this family. Unless it's to hit. And I'm not hitting you now. I'm taking care of you. Because you are sick and I am making you well.*

How far this is from the house in which a boy, upon hearing his brother howl with anxiety and humiliation, rushed into the bathroom with a pair of scissors and sliced the tube of the enema bag. He came with the scissors like a *deus ex machina*—a god from without who arrived *from within* the bosom of his own family. For as brave and startling as his gesture was, it was one for which the ground had been laid. It fell within the boundaries of what his parents could permit, even as it released them from the tyranny of their own convictions. In the act of administering an enema to their howling child, they could remain in touch with their mixed feelings—their belief that the enema was curative, their discomfort at their child's distress, their doubt, confusion— and thus they could welcome their older son's insurrection and dissolve in laughter. This is not a family that is likely to require intervention from outside, because—when things break down or seize up—it is able to generate its own revisions.

More simply put, this is a family that permits a certain kind of play—a play in which the children themselves, in response to their own distress, are able to rewrite the rules. Such playfulness serves as a strong inoculation against abuse.

Not long ago, I met a psychotherapist named Sonia Beck, who works in a residential treatment center for troubled youth. Because many of the children come from troubled families, she is very familiar with the dynamics of physical and sexual abuse. Aware of all the terrible stories she's heard, when I talk to her, I marvel at how unarmored she has managed to remain, how willing to explore the darkness of the human heart without recourse to the steel doors of Yes and No, of Black and White. "Just think about the expression 'to entertain an impulse,'" she said to me the other day. "There's a wisdom in that expression. For if parents can *stay connected, in touch with, attuned to,* the part of themselves that transgresses, if they can *relate to it* rather than *being it,* then there's a chance of transforming it, being released from it. You might even say that the ability to entertain one's own dangerous impulses is a form of eros for oneself." A form of eros for oneself that in certain very dark and rapidly constricting moments between oneself and one's child, can open up some room in which to play.

4

MEMORIES

⌒

ONE NIGHT WHEN I was twelve, I went to bed with the radio on as a kind of background blur to which I was not really listening. A program came on about the Holocaust. The voices on the radio, voices of survivors telling their stories, mingled with my dreams, and that night I had the first in a series of nightmares. Though the plot and setting of these nightmares varied each night, in each one my father disappeared, leaving my mother and me in a desolate state—so desolate that it woke me, night after night, like an emergency.

Finally, one morning I went into my parents' bedroom and woke them to tell them about my dreams. That's when they told me that when I was three years old, my father had gone away for a year. He had gone to live in New Haven, Connecticut, while my mother and I lived together in a small apartment in New York City. From the moment they told me, it was as though a chunk of my life that had vanished fell back into place. In the days that followed, one memory after another returned to me, very specific memories that were confirmed by my mother: a dark-blue curtain in the living room that seemed drenched with sadness to me; a boy who threw a rock at my forehead, leaving a small blue dent; the time I fell forward from the windowsill, pushing the lead of the pencil I'd been sucking on into the roof of my mouth. In the background of each of these memories there was the feeling of desolation and danger that had come to me in my dreams.

Because of this experience, I know it's true that a cluster of memories can lie dormant for many years before being awakened by some spark from the outside world: a scent, a taste, a melody, a photograph, a fragment of conversation. . . .

But I also know that certain conditions can encourage one to reexperience the past in a certain way, and that the process of "remembering" is fluid and permeable enough that sometimes, with the right encouragement, it really becomes very hard to distinguish "real" memories from "false" ones. Some years ago—for whatever concatenation of complex and mysterious reasons—conditions arose across the country that encouraged the uncovering of childhood memories of sexual abuse. I know this even without needing to wade very deep into the controversy, and without needing to disprove anyone else's memories, for I experienced the power of this "encouragement" in my own life.

In the midst of this time—when everywhere, it seemed, on television, in the newspapers, among people one knew, there were testimonies to "recovered" memories—I went on a hike with my oldest friend on a mountain called "Sugarloaf." The very name seemed to invoke our childhood selves, and somehow, as we wound our way up a steep trail through the chapparal, we found ourselves confessing that we had each felt the need, of late, to go back over our childhood, scanning for incest. Despite all the media hullabaloo, it seemed an amazing thing to say to each other. After all, we were two girls who had been inseparable through childhood, who once could navigate each other's houses in the dark and supply, from memory, a complete and accurate catalogue of each other's toys, down to the scratched garnet ring found in the vacant lot, or the pencils that each of us nibbled differently; who knew every tic and odd expression of each other's parents, her father's small feet, my father's self-asphixiating laugh; whose lives, we'd always thought, had been open books to one another—could it possibly be that one or both of these lives contained a huge secret, a dark and terrible and utterly life-altering secret, a secret kept not only from each other, but from our very selves?

Until saying this aloud, neither of us had been fully aware of the powerful force that seemed to be bearing down on us, like a kind of atmospheric pressure, or a chorus of voices repeating, "You must look to be sure. Look. Look again." It was as though, in that time, a father, an uncle, an elder brother, was guilty—or at least worthy of intense suspicion—until proven innocent. And though in the scanning, neither Debbie nor I came up with anything, or even close to anything, I found that the impulse to scan remained, an impulse that felt oddly like a duty and a compulsion at the same time. It was not just the family memory-bank that I scanned, but other memories, too.

One day, when I was fourteen, an elevator man in Italy, a little man whose face was covered with freckles, rubbed his ears first on my face and then on my brother's. My brother, who was seven at the time, was dressed in a trench coat and matching beige cap, and when the man finished, Daniel told him solemnly, "Thank you." For years afterward, we told this as a funny family story—but now it occurred to me that perhaps it had been a great deal more than funny; perhaps it had even been traumatic? It's true that at one point, the man had taken the elevator to the very top of the building, and when the doors opened for a few seconds, I saw a barren, empty space under the roof and my stomach felt queasy. But he was such a little man, and obsequious in his movements, tentative as he nuzzled his freckled face, his freckled ears, against our faces, that he didn't really inspire much fear. After nuzzling us, he dropped us off at the proper floor, and when we went into the room, I told my parents what had happened as a funny story.

My mother laughed and said, "We'll have to leave him a big tip," and though I laughed when she said that, it seemed somehow off to me, as though she had taken the joke too far, as though she hadn't caught that being taken up to that barren space at the top of the building had made my stomach queasy, hadn't grasped the clenched, bravely stoic quality of my brother's "Thank you." But a trauma? No. It wasn't traumatic. It wasn't even seriously disturbing.

As a whole, it was an odd mix. Mostly it was "icky," a category that at the time included many things: certain foods like egg salad, having a teacher with bad breath bend over your desk at school, the thought of French kissing. There was the moment of my stomach going queasy, which now I would say was the start of fear—but the experience was also interesting, funny, touching. My brother was touching to me, so formal and polite in his little trench coat and cap, but the man, too, was slightly touching to me. He was so small and funny looking, and I was aware that he was only a little elevator man in the beautiful old hotel in which my family were paying guests.

How would I react today if this happened to my daughter? I've asked myself this many times, and here's what I arrive at: I would tell the hotel management. I would ask my daughter if she had been afraid. I would rehearse with her what she might have done if the man had led her out of the elevator to that deserted top floor. But I would wish for her that she could also hold some of the complexity of the experience, that it could also be a little bit funny to her, a good story to tell her friends about a man with freckly ears, and somehow touching, too.

And this, I realize, is one of those things that is hard to say, one of those places where I feel defensive, on the alert. How could you possibly wish for your daughter to find a pedophile, a man who molests children in elevators, even the least bit touching?

But that's precisely it: the words "pedophile" and "molest" don't resonate with my experience. I feel a strange shudder, a frisson, when I say them—but it's not a frisson of relief, not the *aha!* that comes from the right diagnosis, retroactively applied to a puzzling and disturbing experience (as when you realize "Oh! He was in a depression then" or "She must have already been ill at that time," and suddenly something big seems to click into place). In this case, it's a frisson that feels like something not quite fitting, like a friend coming up with an interpretation of your dream that sounds very plausible but somehow isn't right, "No, that's not it," you say—for reasons you can't quite figure out, and you want to shake it off.

"It does so little justice to the richness of a child's consciousness," a man said to me recently, "when the only narrative that can be told about one's childhood is whether or not one was abused." His remark helped me to understand the frisson, helped me to realize that when I wish for my daughter that she be able to see even a pedophile as not wholly described through the label of "pedophile," I'm not speaking so much out of deference to the pedophile, but out of deference to her. I wish for her to be safe from the violating touch of anyone she does not wish to be touched by, but I also wish for her mind and her heart to stay open to the richness and complexity, to the ambivalence, of her own lived experience.

And this brings me to another double story, about two daughters and their fathers.

During the same era that my friend and I had our hike on Sugarloaf Mountain, my friend Ruth and her husband received a letter from Jan, their youngest daughter. Jan was in her early twenties then, and had been living on her own for several years. Of Ruth and Stephen's four children, Jan was the one who had always seemed most attached to her parents, most prone to idealizing them, most eager to be like them. That's why the letter was so shattering to them. It announced that Jan was cutting off all communication with her father, because she had recently, in therapy, recovered a memory of having been molested by him when she was a child.

The entire family was stunned. Jan tried very hard to get her mother and her siblings to concur with her and validate her story, but none of them could. She felt increasingly estranged and alone. Though now, ten years later, she has referred to this period as a time when she "needed to blame all my unhappiness on something," she did not resolve the rupture with her father before his death. She was on a plane flying home when he died in the hospital, surrounded by his other children.

Ruth told me that after Jan sent the letter, it was a long time before they could get her to tell them the specific nature of the abuse that she had suffered. Finally, after weeks of silence, she told them: "I was nine years old, and I had fallen asleep on the sofa, and Daddy came and picked me up to carry me to my bed. On the way into my bedroom, Daddy put his hand on one of my breasts."

Ruth said that she had to suppress an immense desire to laugh when her daughter finally described this scene. Even if it was true— and Ruth felt strongly that it was not, that it wasn't like anything Stephen would do, and all of the other three children agreed—Ruth felt that it was not such a terribly bad thing for a father to touch, once, the marvel of a young daughter's new breast. I'd rather not plunge into an argument over whether or not it is a terribly bad thing—because what seems to me the most interesting part of the story is what Ruth went on to tell me. The main reason she felt such a powerful desire to laugh, she told me, was this:

"When I was the same age as Jan was in her story, about nine or ten, that is, my breasts had just begun to grow, and one night before I went to bed, I felt that I very much wanted my father to see them—not just to see them, in fact, but to touch them. Even if he was coming home late from work, long after we had gone to sleep, we knew that he always came in to kiss us good night. So on this particular night, when I got into bed, I pulled my nightgown up to just above my breasts. I pulled the sheet up to just above my belly button. Only my breasts were exposed, and I turned out the light, leaving just the night-light on. When my father came tiptoeing in, I pretended to be asleep. He saw my breasts, of course—he couldn't miss them—but he didn't touch them. He pulled the sheet up over them, and he kissed my forehead and tiptoed back out of my room. And I was so disappointed."

Ruth told me this story as though it were a simple story, the story of a daughter's straightforward desire and its disappointment. It seems likely that if we were able to delve a bit, we might discover that the story was not quite so simple and that under its simple, if startling, surface, there were layers within layers. Perhaps what permitted the daughter's self-display was the deep-down certainty that her father *would not* lay a hand on her. Or perhaps what prompted it was her father's refusal to acknowledge earlier, subtler signs of his daughter's growing womanhood; it was as if she were saying, "You're going to pretend I'm still a little girl. Okay, I'll show you!"

In the next chapter, we'll return to the theme of fathers and daughters, to the erotic charge between them, and the difficulty of finding its proper expression when a girl reaches adolescence. For now, I take Ruth's story as she presented it, for the way it subverts certain oversimplifications of our own era.

Ruth laughed when she told me her story. It was genuine laughter, even though it was resonating against an enormous sorrow, against the years of estrangement from her daughter and the unhealed rupture between her husband and her daughter. Still, she felt a level of irony at which she couldn't help but marvel. "Isn't it something?" she said. "My painful memory from childhood is that my father *didn't* touch my breasts."

5

CHANGELINGS

FOR YEARS, MY daughter would remind me of a certain protocol. If ever I suspected that someone had substituted a double in her place, I was to look for our sure and secret sign: between the third and fourth fingers of her left hand, there is a certain freckle that belongs to her alone.

As anxious rehearsals for separation go, my daughter's has always struck me as particularly rich with the contradictions of intimacy. For she seemed to be saying: *No matter how close we are, no matter how special I am to you, this closeness, this specialness, is not absolute, not fail-proof. Something could always slip in between us.*

Something paper-thin, something almost invisible, could form an irrevocable wedge. A distinctly different child could never steal my heart, she knew, but an exact copy would be a different story. By such an other, she could be defeated. Perhaps hers is the nightmare of a secure child, the child who knows that the only one who could really steal her mother's love away from her would be another version of herself, identical—save for something as minute as a single freckle hidden in the crevice between two fingers.

The myth of the changeling, a child secretly exchanged for another, has a long—and by its very nature, richly multiple—history. A mother bends over her child's cradle, and—lo! Her child is gone. In its place, wrapped in her child's blanket, lies a fairy child or a gnome. Or perhaps there is not a human child at all who greets her eye, but a

furry creature, a ferret or a mole. Or—most horrible of all—lying on
the pillow is something inanimate: a potato, or a block of wood.

Though it might persist in the dream-life of some contemporary
children, this myth of the substitute child seems mostly to have vanished from the common stock. Still, it's hard to imagine a parent for
whom the myth has no resonance. For our children are changelings.
Constantly in transformation, they are always substituting one version
of themselves after another. Faster and more convincingly than any
criminal or con artist, they change appearances: turning their blue-
black, newborn eyes into a different color, sprouting hair from their
bald heads, pushing teeth through their gums, spouting words from
their mouths, growing ever bigger, stronger, more capable. When going
in to get Ariel from her crib, I often had the feeling that I didn't quite
know who I would find there.

This quality of surprise—*Who are you today?*—was particularly
acute in the first two years of her life. And now, again, at the threshold
of adolescence, the pace of change has accelerated, and I often have
the feeling that I don't quite know who I'm living with.

In *The Magician's Assistant*, a novel by Ann Patchett, an older
woman tells a younger woman:

> When you're young and you want to have a baby because
> babies are so cute and everybody else has one, nobody ever
> takes you aside and explains to you what happens when they
> grow up . . . you should know that sooner or later they turn
> into teenagers, but somehow you just don't ever think about it;
> then one day, bang, you've got these total strangers living with
> you, these children in adult bodies, and you don't know who
> they are. It's like they somehow ate up those children you had
> and you loved, and you keep loving these people because you
> know they've got your child locked up in there somewhere.[29]

It's a strange, violent image—as if children grew by ingesting their
former selves, as though the older child was a kind of Hansel-and-Gretel

witch, who both ate and imprisoned young children. Or is it that the older child is somehow pregnant with his younger self? In any case, we have arrived at betrayal again. Growing children betray their earlier selves. "Every mother has to endure it, I suppose," Iris Murdoch's Harriet repeats to herself, observing her suddenly "untouchable" son. But parents, too, betray their growing children. A son takes off, leaving his mother as steadfast guardian of his past—but when he returns, he finds she's put a piano in his room, and arranged his things neatly in boxes in the garage. A daughter returns from her trip abroad to find that her mother, who at first grieved so hard in the empty nest, has taken up the tango. "She's out every night in some flouncy dress," she says, shaking her head like a Mother Superior. Children, too, can walk into the door of their parents' house and be startled by the unfamiliar faces that greet them.

Actually, though the grown child may no longer remember, the chances are good that even when he was small, he sometimes saw more than one face when he looked at his parent. In *Mother Love, Mother Hate*, Rozsika Parker includes a story told by Mary, the mother of a five-year-old daughter: "We were going upstairs because it was her bedtime, when she looked at me and said, 'Oh, there's no face in the back of your head.' And I said, 'Oh, there is sometimes?' She replied, 'Sometimes, the other one, the bad one, has her face on the other side.' I wondered at the time if the bad one was about my repressed negativity, which I was hardly aware of—but she was."[30]

Was "the other face" engendered by the mother's negativity, or by the child's? Or by both? In another story provided by Parker, a mother named Flick was making supper for her two young boys, who were sitting talking at the kitchen table: "I heard Jack, who was then five years old, say to Tom, who was seven, 'Do you think that? I do too!' It caught my attention and I asked them what they were talking about. Jack told me that they both think that after I put them to bed and kiss them good night, I go out of the room, remove my mask and clothes, and reveal myself to be a witch. I was a bit taken aback but at the same time, it felt that because they could say it, we could all know I wasn't really a witch. Sometimes I do feel a witch!"[31]

Sometimes I do feel a witch! the mother exclaims. For Parker, these stories are examples of the "relief" that is felt when the ambivalence that holds sway between parent and child can be spoken. In this sense, the image of the changeling or of the parent-as-other can be seen as cathartic, providing a channel for the release of negative feelings. It's not the good mother we hate; it's the bad one, the one with eyes on the back of the good mother's head. It's not our own lovely child we recoil from in horror; it's the mole that was put in his bed.

Usually we do think of it as something negative, as a lapse, a failure, an implied curse or rejection, when we suddenly see an intimate as a stranger. A man looks across the table at the woman he lives with, sees the way she smacks her lips against the rim of the teacup, and—in an instant falling through layer after layer of familiarity—he hits a hard, cold ground. *I have fallen out of love*, he thinks. No longer embedded in the shared texture of their daily life, his lover's gestures now stand out singly, starkly, like the collection of small clues one gathers from a stranger—he wrinkles his nose when he smiles, his laugh is more like a wheeze—that makes one decide, *No, this is not someone I care to know.*

Once, when I was a teenager, I walked into the kitchen of our house and saw a man standing against the refrigerator. As in a dream, I knew that he was someone very important to me, someone with whom I had a powerful connection—but I couldn't quite get who it was. Then it came to me: my father. He had shaved his beard, leaving his face white and pinched. I screamed and ran out of the room.

Even today, when I remember that moment, I feel my stomach drop in a mild version of the sudden groundlessness I felt all those years ago. It wasn't that I felt physically endangered; I did not fear that the beardless man who stood in the kitchen would harm me. What had seized me was the nightmare feeling of the deeply familiar turning suddenly alien. Implicitly, it contained the realization, akin to my daughter's fear, of how thin a wedge—the absence of a freckle, of a tuft of facial hair—could come between me and the primal, irrevocable sense of belonging to, of knowing and being known by, someone I loved.

Perhaps the intensity of my reaction does testify to a certain "repressed negativity." Indeed, when I think of the prolonged estrangement that occurred between my father and myself many years later, during which I frequently expressed the feeling that "He's not the father I used to know," I am tempted to think that there was something in this incident that was a kind of premonition of our falling-out.

Still, there is another way of looking at the sudden looming of strangers on familiar ground, one that has much less to do with the legacy of feelings we have about them, whether negative or positive. I am thinking of those moments when, in the very midst of our knowing, we are suddenly able to drop out of this knowing and meet them in a new way. Isn't there a part of us that longs to be known in this way, with a deep familiarity that nonetheless approaches us as one still-to-be-discovered? A long time ago, someone said to me, "I know you like the palm of my own hand," and though it was said with affection, I felt a shudder of horror. I wanted to be known . . . and not known.

"How endearing!" someone said once, watching my mother devour a sprig of parsley. The woman who said this was not a stranger to my mother, but she did not know my mother with a daughter's familiarity. "Familiarity breeds contempt," we say, and the word "breeds" seems apt. Within our brood, habits breed that despite the feeling of knowing each other inside out, actually obscure that knowing. When I was a teenager, my mother's physical presence inspired in me a profound irritability, especially her eating. When her friend exclaimed, "How endearing!" the words, like a kind of laser beam, pierced a hole through the layers of habit and irritability, and for a moment, I saw my mother freshly. Or rather, I saw her with a freshness that illuminated my familiarity. For there was something about the way she could gobble a sprig of parsley as though it were a delicious treat that embodied something quintessential about her: a certain mix of puritanical sparseness and a deeply sensuous nature.

By the time a brand-new baby comes into the world, it is not "brand new" to its mother. During the months that the child was forming in her womb, she has been forming images of the baby. That process continues from the moment of birth: "My baby is a calm baby." "My baby is restless." "My baby is like her father." "My baby is just like me." When all is well, these images serve the positive function of deepening connection, reinforcing the sense of loving familiarity and mutual belonging; but sometimes the way a parent believes she knows a child gets in the way of actually knowing it.

In their book *The Earliest Relationship*, Drs. T. Berry Brazelton and Bertrand Cramer include the case history of a mother whose fretful baby, from the very beginning, had activated her sense of having been herself a difficult baby whom her own mother had been unable to love. The fretful baby, Lisa, was taken to the doctor's office when she was three and a half months old because of her "relentless" crying. Both parents reported that she cried between eight and ten hours a day, and that the crying went on into the night. Nothing they had done could calm her, and they were desperate for help. What struck the doctor was that when the mother talked about Lisa's crying, she described the baby as "angry." He reports this exchange:

> "You do keep calling her crying anger or 'a temper' in Lisa. Does it remind you of yourself as a child? You told me that you were angry when you were little." Mrs. J.'s voice softened and became almost childlike. "I was a terrible little girl. I was angry all the time. My mother would just walk away and leave me, she got so exasperated. I felt she hated me at times. And I hated myself, until I could learn to control myself. Now Lisa is going to be just like me. Oh, God!"

A breakthrough came in his work with the family when the mother was able to see the extent to which her assumption that Lisa was another version of her own "bad self" was impeding her ability to care for Lisa. The authors continue: "To be able to remember how 'terrible' she was as a girl helps Mrs. J. decontaminate the present relationship from the angry ghost of her childhood. Then she can start seeing Lisa as if—indeed—she is seeing her for the first time."[32]

To suddenly see a child, a parent, through a stranger's eyes, as if for the first time, can be a powerful release from the prejudice, the pre-judging, of familiarity. Paradoxically, as in the story of Baby Lisa, it is sometimes only when we let go of what we *think* we know about others that we really have a chance to meet them. In such cases, who is the changeling? The baby we first put in the cradle or the one we found later, when the cloud of our "knowing" suddenly lifted and we looked, really looked, into those eyes for the first time?

6

WHO'S AT THE DOOR?

⌒

"A BABY IS born with a loaf of bread under its arm," the saying goes. There could as well be the saying: "A baby is born with an evil stranger in its shadow." Over the centuries, this shadow figure has appeared in many guises, both literal and imagined—the kidnapper, the ravisher, the eater-of-children, the seller-of-children, the slave driver, the harem-keeper, the wolf at the door. There are the she-devils, too: the witch, the dark fairy, the evil stepmother, the jealous queen. . . .

"Sometimes I *am* a witch!" a mother exclaims, having overheard her two young sons discussing her nightly conversion. In their minds, the good mother kissed them good night, then dashed off to remove her mother mask and costume, releasing her witchy self. The primal ambivalence that can turn a mother into an *other* in her very own house, a child into a changeling as it sleeps in its cradle, can also give rise to multiple dark figures who come from without.

Once, as a young child, I was walking through a department store with my father. We passed through the women's clothing department, and I saw a life-sized mannequin that was dressed in a severe navy-blue suit, with two rows of big brass buttons. "I wish she was my mother!" I exclaimed. I felt shocked at the words that had flown out of my mouth, and my father looked startled and didn't know what to say. It was many years before I could understand my exclamation as the wish that my own mother—whose playful, childlike quality I loved—could sometimes be more powerful and sure of herself. At the time, I felt that I had said something terrible that was a kind of betrayal. Now that I'm a mother, I know that parents commit very similar betrayals. What parent hasn't had a moment of wishing her child would disappear, become *other?* For both parents and children, it's easy for these momentary betrayals to transmute into the evil figure who makes our passing wish come true. "You wished for another mother? Well, here I am!" says the witch in the child's dreams. "You wished your child would disappear! Very well then!" says the thief in the parent's fears.

What gives the evil stranger such power is that he can embody both the moments of hatred and the intensity of attachment that exist between parent and child. "No, you can't stay up any longer!" an exasperated mother snaps, and going up the stairs to bed, the child sees two evil eyes in the back of the mother's head. Later, after the mother has read her child a story and stroked her hair and turned off the light, the child feels a terrible pang: *my lovely mother! What if a man with evil eyes climbs in the window and steals her away from me tonight?*

For parents, too, the evil stranger can appear both as punishment for the failure to properly value a child and as an expression of the extreme valuation of that same child. What links these two poles is not as simple as pure opposition: one of the reasons we sometimes resent our children so much is *that* they matter so much to us. They dash recklessly across the street or disappear for a long moment in a crowded place, and in one single moment, we can feel both an immensity of imagined grief and a fury that they could make us so vulnerable.

It begins . . . at the very beginning. Flesh of her own flesh, a baby comes at great cost to its mother. Having taken over her body in pregnancy, it then brings her body to the limit of what it can do, of what it can bear in childbirth. Once it is born, it takes over the rhythm of her days, ravages the sleep of her nights. Given the immensity of maternal "investment," the anxiety surrounding the fragility of an infant, and the resentment occasioned by an infant's devouring needs, is it any wonder that from the very beginning, the threatening Other follows so close behind?

Pregnancy is fraught with its own fears, but as soon as the child emerges from the shelter of the womb, it becomes vulnerable to a new kind of harm that comes from without. We've largely lost the ritual precautions that acknowledge this shadow presence, channeling them, perhaps, into newfangled fears: about SIDS, about car seats, about untrustworthy nannies. But once these precautions held firm, and they are still rampant in other cultures: among the Greeks, who keep their babies covered so as not to attract the evil eye, or among the Indonesians, who hang a wooden angel over their babies' beds. . . .

In truth, there is a much more intimate link between the parent and the evil Other than we often wish to acknowledge. Just look at the kidnapper. We posit him as the parent's pure opposite, but there is a strange bond between the parent and the kidnapper. There is a way, a terrible way, in which he values our child as we do: he wants her so badly that he risks losing his life. He also puts himself *in loco parentis*: our child becomes his charge. This is part of the ghastly irony that sometimes accompanies the newspaper accounts of such crimes. The same hands by which a child later perished at first procured her favorite cereal, a toothbrush, a small stuffed animal to make her feel at home.

Of course, the kidnapper has no true concern for the child. If he did, he could not inflict the greatest terror that a child could ever know. Still, there is a way that a parent can't help but identify with the kidnapper's covetous desire. And if a kidnapper should choose *our* child, there is a way in which his choice would seem horribly right to us, validating the overpowering nature of our love for her and its utter specificity. For we do not love "a child"—we love *this* child, with her stringy, mouse-brown hair, her blue-green eyes, the way she bites her lip when she is deep in thought, or, when she is feeling exuberant, suddenly reels off all the odd numbers between one and twenty.

Deep down, even though we often feel that we fail to love our children properly, we also know that there is something *de trop* in our love for them. In some cultures, mothers ward off the jealous gods by deflecting compliments to their children, or by outright insulting them. "Isn't he ugly?" a Japanese mother will say. For us, the evil stranger—the kidnapper, the pervert—is the other shoe, always about to drop. Keeping him in our consciousness, we announce to whatever vindictive power might control our fate, "I know my love for my child is outrageous. But look. I don't take my child for granted. I know that at any moment he could be snatched away. . . ."

There are still other aspects of parental feeling with which we invest the kidnapper. I have never forgotten the experience of leaving the hospital with two-day-old Ariel. Though I'm quite sure that my husband drove carefully, even gingerly, the sensation was that we were speeding in a getaway car. For even as I felt how utterly she belonged to me, at the same time, it seemed incredible that another human being could possibly be *mine*. At night, during the first two weeks of her existence, I would peer into the wicker laundry basket that she slept in, and it was not just to check that she was still breathing, but because I couldn't quite believe that she could still be residing at our house.

Gradually, through the immense and at times almost suffocating intimacy that care of a baby requires, this disbelief wanes. Then we have the opposite experience; the first time I took a walk down the street by myself after Ariel's birth, the air felt strange against my chest; it was as though some part of my body was missing. We clean their ears and their noses, wipe shit and spittle from their skin, and there is no separation between their bodies and our own. Still, at some level, we remember that our children do not really belong to us—and the kidnapper exists, in part, as the personification of this memory.

We also know that there is no justice when it comes to babymaking. I knew a woman named Yvette who struggled for years with infertility. In the supermarket once, she pointed to a small boy left alone in a cart in the vegetable aisle. The child looked quite placid, and his mother had no doubt just dashed to the next aisle for a loaf of bread or a carton of milk, but Yvette was indignant. "Look at that!" she said. "Anyone could come along and snatch that child! When I see such a thing, I want to take the child myself, because I know I would take so much better care of him." The fact that even someone like Yvette could harbor such a thought was chilling to me, and it raised the specter of a strange new crime: the preventive kidnap. In relation to Yvette and her anguished story of miscarriages, fertility treatments, and broken hopes, I always felt guilty. I didn't have to yearn so desperately before I got my daughter. And though I could say that I have worked hard to bear and to raise her, there is no way in which I could really say that I deserve her. She was bestowed on me. And that which has been bestowed can be unbestowed, swallowed back by the same mysterious power of destiny that bestowed her.

"Bestow" contains the word "place." Our children have been "placed" with us—the very word we use for foster care. When I peered into the wicker laundry basket during those first nights of my daughter's life, it was not only to see that she was breathing, but to make sure that she had not been placed elsewhere by whatever divine agency—as quixotic as any bureaucrat—had placed her with me. One way to understand our terror of the kidnapper is to understand him as the concretization of this fear of displacement. For, unlike other misfortunes that might befall our children, the kidnapper takes our child to some other place. This is in large measure the horror of kidnapping: the not knowing where.

Still, if we can understand the ways in which the kidnapper is our own creation, we can begin to put him in his place. The reality is that despite the immense publicity that has surrounded certain incidents, abductions by strangers remain exceedingly rare. Of these, the great majority involve short-term episodes, after which the child is returned. It remains true that for most children, the most dangerous place—because of the likelihood of accident or abuse—is the home.[33]

Yet even as we repeat this mantra to ourselves, the kidnapper will continue to haunt us, for reasons that care nothing for statistics. Living in earthquake country, my daughter is at much greater risk from the dresser in her bedroom than from a man who might climb in her window. But it is the latter who visits my nightmares, and not the former. In an analogous way, no matter how many times I repeat to myself, "I'm in more danger driving to the airport than I am in the plane," I will always feel more frightened when I am up in the air than when I am down on the ground. Knowing that a large chunk of my fear of flying is purely irrational does not eradicate the fear, but it does keep me from giving that fear too much weight. I may grit my teeth, but I don't permit my fear to narrow the horizons of my world by restricting my travel.

Similarly, when we understand the intimate link between the evil stranger and the eros of parenthood, we can to some degree defuse the terror that he inspires. For when we look him in the eye, we will see that though he does, alas, exist as a matter of fact, he also exists as an inner figure, embodying both the intensity and the complexity of parent-child attachment. As such, he is a repository not only for negative feelings, but for others—including, for parents, the sense of the undeserved arrival of our children into our lives, of the slender thread of ownership, and of the extravagant and risky nature of our love.

7

NOLI ME TANGERE

THE FAMILY PHOTOGRAPHS OF SALLY MANN

⌀

PHOTOGRAPY IS ONE of the primary sites around which anxiety over the eros of parenthood erupts. Once photographed, a human subject becomes an object. No matter how beautiful, strong, or proud the subject may appear, he or she—once captured in an image—must submit helplessly, like an animal in a zoo, to the gaze of others. In the case of a photographed child, this helpless submission is especially problematic. To what degree did the child consent to be an object for the gaze of others? Was it even possible for the child to withhold consent?

I am drawn to the work of photographer Sally Mann for many reasons, perhaps above all for the way that the most ordinary, and even slightly dilapidated objects in my own environment—a rusty watering can; a curving, leafless tree trunk—emerge with a kind of luminous strangeness after I've immersed myself in her world. In the present context, what draws me to her is the way that her photographs of children seem to walk along the very edge between observation and violation, the way that they delve into the very place where subject becomes object, then becomes subject again. And this place is charged with ambivalence: with a mix of tenderness and violence, of self-containment and exposure, the blankness of inexperience and the presage of powerful erotic feeling. . . .

On the cover of her book *Immediate Family*, Sally Mann's three young children stand in three different postures of *noli me tangere*: "Don't touch me."[34] Mouths set, absolutely not smiling, they stare

dead-on into the eye of the camera, into the eye of whoever would dare stare at them.

Yet they are bare-chested, and their chests look touching, vulnerable, undeveloped. Their arms, tightly held in defensive positions, are thin. Though they have mustered their most defiant faces, these faces look mustered. Even these fierce children cannot help but look like children.

Bare-chested, with their thin arms, their faces of mustered defiance, they have been captured, forever preserved, stilled in one of their mother's stills. They are transfixed, this fierce little triptych, on the cover of her book, and I who have bought it can stare at them for as long and as hard as I want to.

And yet, the very mother who has delivered them up unto me has also kept something back; again and again, when I open the book and look through the collection of photographs, I see that she has captured them at precisely this moment, on precisely this edge—this moment when they resist being captured, this edge where they draw back into themselves.

In fact, looking through the black-and-white photographs of these children, I get the same feeling I've had when looking at certain long-ago photographs of Native Americans that managed to preserve the fleeting moment, the vanishing edge, when a conquered people still rest so deeply in their own dignity that they can stare back into the eye of the conqueror with a look that says, *There is something about me that will never be yours*.

And, to go to the extreme, taking this edge to the very edge, isn't this the look that Sartre said was the last province of the oppressed? Even as the torture victim or the prisoner about to be executed are stripped of the last shred of autonomy, there is something they still possess: they can stare back into the eye of the torturer, the executioner, with a look that says *I see you, I see what you are doing to me, and in this very seeing, I declare myself separate; I withhold the conscious spark of my own existence even as you snuff my existence out*.

Whoa! Let's not exaggerate. . . . These are a mother's photographs of her three young children, Emmett, Jessie, and Virginia, in various moments of old-fashioned childhood: wading in water, sleeping in fields, playing a board game, trying on glamour, bearing the scuffs, scratches, dirt, and bites of young life lived *au naturel*. Why even bring up the subjects of torture and execution?

It's because there is something distinctly *noir* in these photographs, something with teeth that lurks in even the dreamiest. In one of the very few in which one of the children is smiling, she is standing only inches away from a recently killed deer. The curve of her body echoes the curve of the carcass as it hangs over the rear of a pickup—yet her look, with its vague and utterly private smile, could not be farther away from the animal's plight. Dressed in a white, lacy, make-believe dress, she sheds no tears. She is as sealed off in her fantasy world as the deer is in its death.

In other photographs, the bodies of the children look almost as if they, like the deer, had been rendered inanimate. Their postures look strewn, draped, crumpled, flung. In one, the smallest girl, with her beautiful pre-Raphaelite face, lies sleeping outside among what appear to be stuffed burlap bags. In her sleep, she looks utterly innocent, as if she had suddenly surrendered her heaviness to the ground. The bags echo this posture of surrender—as if someone had whispered, "Trust your weight to the earth"—yet they also look somewhat ominous, like those fairy-tale bags into which Three Little Kids might be stuffed by a wolf, like those bags in which kittens and stones are flung into rivers, a bag into which this very child herself might fit.

In many of the photographs, the children's skin—the very skin that another photographer might preserve in its smoothness, softness, and young shine—is gritty, dusty, sprinkled with leaves, covered with pocks. In part, these dirty-skin pictures come through as an ode to the freedom of childhood. But other tones resonate, too: the same bodies that look simply at home in the natural world can also look as though they were simply left to return to the natural world—as in "decompose." Although there is not a picture of a child's stilled, naked body covered with ants, such a picture would not look at all out of place in the collection. And many of the photographs—a pair of thin legs coated in flour paste, a belly and penis splattered with popsicle drips, a wounded face through surgical gauze—come close to the sort of blown-up symptomatic parts one sees in medical texts.

In some of the photographs, there's a duck-rabbit quality. You see a scene of serene, picturesque childhood and then you blink your eyes and something seamy appears, something that threatens to cross over into danger in the form of violence, poverty, grief, neglect. Uncovered, an angelic child lies fast asleep in bed, her hair, which one easily imagines to be soft and golden, in a blur around her head. You look again and see a vast urine stain spread out below her—and indeed, this dreamy photo is not entitled "Dreams," but "Wet Bed." Not too horrifying, perhaps—but still, it's a jolt, and in others, the jolts get sharper.

In "Emmet Afloat," you see a boy, voluptuously at ease on the earth, stretched out on an expanse of rippled sand that looks like water. Look again and you see a child's corpse, abandoned. In "Hayhook," you see the very white body of a naked girl suspended against a dark backdrop of house, tree, and family members, none of whom is looking at her. "Such innocent play," a friend said to me. He saw a girl swinging, utterly at ease in her naked body, secure in the bosom of her family. But what I saw reminded me of the very first time I learned that there was such a thing as child abuse. I was eight years old when I came across a newspaper article about a girl who was left to hang naked by her wrists from the showerhead while her family members went about their business.

A number of the photographs seem just about to erupt into something vividly erotic: two hugely white blossoms, "Night-blooming Cereus," are draped over a girl's nipples; the soft roundness of a little girl's body is nestled between the plump, hairy thighs of a man; little girls stare into the camera with the mixed-message, come-on looks of soft-porn models, those looks that say both "Try me" and "Don't dare."

It's no wonder that Sally Mann's photographs of children are considered controversial. Certainly they are a world away from those Ann Geddes babies, plastered on cards and calendars, who might so easily receive a Good Housekeeping Seal of Approval. Yet it is these babies—plopped in flowerpots, beaming out from garden beds, their dimpled faces glimpsed through bunches of hydrangeas, their plump limbs wriggling on a sea of petals—who are being unabashedly offered up for adult consumption. Presented as utterly innocent, in an utterly innocent setting, they allow us to gaze at the voluptuousness of smooth, curving baby flesh without the burden of awareness, without the least acknowledgment that there might be anything problematic in our gazing.

It's a fine line that Sally Mann walks. She comes so close to trespassing . . . and yet she doesn't. Even as she records her own experience of her children, it's an experience that—to return to Rozsika Parker's definition of "the creative outcome" of maternal ambivalence—wants to know what it is "that the children themselves are trying to achieve, and how it may differ from their mother's own experiences and aspirations."[35]

For no matter how naked and vulnerable the bruised, smudged, stilled, strewn bodies of her children may appear, they retain something inviolate. It's there in the gaze that looks back at her, and through her eyes at the eyes, of anyone else who might stare at them.

And it's there even when her children's eyes are shut—for though she steals upon them in sleep, she manages to present them in a sleep that belongs to them, and to them alone. Even when she renders her children thinglike, the photographs radiate a consciousness of what she's done: when not in the defiant gaze of the children themselves, then in the photographs' utter refusal to euphemize, to prettify, the thingness.

It has been said that what remains unconscious returns as fate. Which is really the more dangerous vision of children—the one that presents them to us scrubbed and cute among flowers, as décor and accessory? Or the one that acknowledges the edges we walk on?

PART V

GOLDILOCKS'S JOY
Finding the "Just Right"

1. The Forbidden

2. Edges

3. Innocence

4. Peaks

5. Hot and Cold

6. Fathers and Daughters

7. My Daughter's Dance

Having entered the dark woods in "The Tears of Eros," who could blame us for wanting to transit quickly, to leap back into a well-marked clearing, with bright lights and strong fences? For after all, simply to put the two words together, eros and parenthood, is to come up against what is arguably the greatest taboo of our time. And along the edge of a great taboo is a place where we don't want to linger. It is a place where it is difficult to waver, to wonder, to pause and take the measure of things, to find one's way. Most difficult of all, perhaps, is to be a wavering parent along the edge of a great taboo. It seems so unparental, to waver in a risky place where the stakes are high and children the potential victims. The temptation is strong to exit quickly, or to reach for the ready-made certainties, the black-and-white distinctions and clear-as-day ultimatums.

Yet the ability to waver—to pause, take in new information, and adjust oneself—is, in its own way, a form of parental protection. This is attunement again, the compass in Goldilocks's hand. Carrying this compass, a parent who comes to the edge of taboo does not recoil in horror or reach for the nearest posted "Do's and Don't's," but, bearing the ambivalence, is willing instead to put a toe in the water, a spoon in the bowl. . . .

That is why Goldilocks—daffy as she is, and quite unparental—is nonetheless the right guide at this juncture. For rapid transit is not her way. Having lost her bearings, she doesn't make a beeline for the world she left behind. She allows herself to be lured by the possibility of making herself at home, for a while, in the dark woods. She cannot do so by "being a good girl," by playing it safe and remembering her manners. She breaks and enters. She *tastes and sees. Perhaps most significant in her attempt to find out where she belongs and what belongs to her, she neither takes refuge in extremes nor avoids them altogether. Rather, she uses them to navigate, to come to know herself and what is good for her. At each point, what turns out to be good for her is the child's portion—the little bear's mush, his chair, his bed. But at each point, Goldilocks must discover this for herself. She doesn't arrive with a simple map. Too hot? Too cold? Well, then, that's how the next step presents itself.*

This chapter follows Goldilocks now, in her zigzag quest for the middle ground, in her search for the joy of the "just right."

1

THE FORBIDDEN

A MOTHER BENDS over her sleeping child. The child, who has clung to her all day, now appears astonishingly separate from her, a citizen of that enchanted kingdom where children go when they sleep, leaving their mothers far behind. And at the same time, here is that child, spread out before her, whose self-containment in sleep she could so easily violate. Some parents do, she knows. Even if she herself feels no strong impulse that must be suppressed, that impulse is there to some degree. It's there in the stories that fill the air, it is part of the human atmosphere.

And quite apart from the stories, violation is there as an element of eros. Erotic love—at whatever end of its continuum—always involves an element of transgression, the overflowing of ordinary boundaries. At the very least, transgression is present as possibility, as what we refrain from, as what we play with and balance on the edge of: the way a kiss can so easily become a bite, or a "squeeze" become painful constriction. The very permission that is granted to physical love in certain contexts, as in the marriage bed, occurs over against the backdrop of prohibition.

This is true between parent and child, no less than between adult lovers, though the parameters marking off the permitted and the forbidden are quite different. "It's actually my job to wash his penis!" my cousin exclaimed to me about her new baby boy. Latent in her exclamation of pleasure, and a certain amazement, was an awareness of all the penises in the world that it is *not* her job to wash, as well as the knowledge that there are some ways of touching her son's penis that do *not* fall within her job description.

But let's leave for a moment the charged atmosphere of the nursery and turn to a less threatening scenario.

A friend comes to visit, and—ignoring the heavy mugs in the cupboard, I serve tea in delicate porcelain cups. They are Russian cups from St. Petersburg, with a pattern of navy-blue and white, with gold rims and fluted edges. Part of what makes the experience of drinking tea from them special is the awareness that they could so easily break. Such awareness—the sense of how easily an impulse, a clumsy gesture, a lapse of attention, could disrupt the moment—is part of the savor of the moment. A similar awareness underlies the beauty of ballet, the Japanese tea ceremony, virtually any highly formalized art or ritual.

That is why laughter hovers so close to such activities. All it takes is one false move—the violinist who (as a friend reported to me once), standing for applause, revealed his fly to be unzipped. Through that narrow opening—an unzipped fly—an entire world, an inverted world of desire and impulse, so far from the world of practice and discipline, tumbled out onto the stage. Someone let out a single chuckle, and within seconds, an entire audience of several hundred serious, highly educated concert-goers was convulsed with laughter.

Yet the immanence of such laughter within the rapt listening of the concert hall is not an enemy of the listening; it is an aspect of the listening, a part of what makes it so uniquely rapt. Similarly, the experience of watching Tibetan monks in the painstaking creation of a sandpainting is inextricably mixed with the knowledge of what will come: the blurring of borders in the great sweeping of sand that follows. The anticipation of imminent destruction greatly intensifies the spectacle of creation. This is so even when the possibility of destruction is not inevitable, as it is in Tibetan sandpainting, but only quite possible, as with glassblowing, raku-firing, or other processes involving great precision in the handling of highly fragile, volatile, or precious materials. The same dynamic is at work in dangerous activities such as tightrope walking or flying on a trapeze. Inherent in the experience of observing such activities is the thrilling awareness of how close disaster looms.

Coming down the stairs with my baby daughter in my arms, I sometimes had the thought, *I could so easily drop her!* This thought was not accompanied by a feeling of desire to drop her, but still, the experience troubled me. I had the notion that "a good mother" wouldn't be capable of thinking such a thought. Now I believe that such thoughts are simply part of the experience of holding in one's arms the exquisite fragility of an infant. I believe that the experience of being "a good enough parent" often includes, if one is being honest, the palpable, if ghostly, awareness of all the things one imagines one could so easily have said or done—but didn't.

And now, back to the nursery, where a mother bends over her sleeping child. She stands there for a long moment, holding the edge of the blanket that her child has thrown off in sleep, gazing at his limbs that, flung this way and that, seem in their very stillness to vibrate with the small-boy energy that will burst out of the bed in the morning.

What if, however fleetingly, she does feel the pull of a forbidden impulse?

Perhaps she has a sudden desire to climb into the bed and clasp her arms around him, as tightly as a lover might—

Or, stirred by his beauty and the soundness of his sleep, she imagines pressing her lips to his, startling him awake—

Or, moved by something about him that appears so guileless as he lies there, his mouth slightly open, his chest rising and falling under her gaze, she has an urge to wake him up and confide in him, telling him certain important truths about herself, entrusting him with the story of her own deepest longings, her secrets, her fears—

Here are the extremes:

She can act on this impulse in the most literal way.

She can recoil from the impulse, burying it in unconsciousness, or perhaps adding it to her reservoir of self-indictments—"What mother would have such a thought?"

Or—?

Or what?

Where is the middle ground between blatant act and sheer repression?

In Milan Kundera's novel *Life Is Elsewhere*, a mother gazes at the face of her young son Jaromil, and finds herself in the grip of an "improper thought":

> It was turning dark, Dad was not coming home, and it occurred to Maman that Jaromil's face was full of a gentle beauty which no artist or husband could match; this improper thought was so insistent that she could not free herself of it; she started to tell him about the time of her pregnancy, how she used to gaze imploringly at the statuette of Apollo. "And you see, you really are as beautiful as that Apollo, and you look just like him. They say a child picks up something of the mother's thoughts when she's pregnant, and I'm beginning to think it's more than a superstition. You even inherited his lyre."
>
> Then she told him that literature had always been her greatest love. She had even gone to the university mainly to study literature and it was only marriage (she did not say pregnancy) that prevented her from devoting herself to this deepest inclination. If she now saw Jaromil as a poet (yes, she was the first to pin this great title on him), it's a wonderful surprise, and yet it is also something she had long expected.
>
> They found consolation in one another, these two unsuccessful lovers, mother and son, and talked long into the night.[1]

The improper thought was "so insistent that she could not free herself of it," and from this improper thought, she glides, as if pulled by a powerful underground current, into an outpouring that is not so much about Jaromil as about herself. Some might say that this mother is a world away from the mother who gets into the bed and commits an actual act of physical incest with her child, but I would locate her at one end, albeit the far end, of the spectrum. For in this scene, the mother is not for the child, but the child for the mother. She is using her child to fulfill her own needs—needs that in her case do not express themselves as literally sexual, but that press heavily nonetheless, and that violate his status as child. For she is asking him to compensate for the inadequacies of the grown men in her life—his face is "full of a gentle beauty which no artist or husband could match." Drawn to this gentle beauty, she uses him as confidante, entrusting him with the story of her life's greatest longings and disappointments. In doing so, she makes him the bearer of her subjectivity, the keeper of her past, the redeemer of her unlived life.

What if she hadn't moved so quickly from the power of the "improper thought" to the spilling-out upon her son? What if, right there where the channel narrowed and the current grew so strong, she had kept her sights wide? This is a perfect example of a moment when a mother might permit herself *to entertain the impulse*. When, instead of *being* the impulse, merging with "the improper thought," she might have found a way to express her desire to overflow, to swallow whole—while holding back.

When I ask myself what this might look like, what presents itself is some version—whether verbal or nonverbal—of "Oh, I could eat you!" For this is an exclamation that captures both the "too-muchness" that a parent feels, and the restraint. It's an exclamation whose magic resides in the conditional tense, for *I could eat you* implies *I won't*. And this in itself—the *could*, the *would*—opens up a middle ground. It gives voice to a strong desire, and in that sense, gives permission even as it reins in the desire.

"Oh, the things I would tell you if you were a grown man!" a mother says, sitting next to her son in the gathering dark. And then she squeezes him tightly, perhaps a bit too tightly, before getting up and turning on the light.

2

EDGES

⌒

A MOTHER WAS driving in the car with her son, who was in the back-seat. The mother slipped her hand in the space between the front seats to pat the boy on the knee, and he began to play a game with her. He touched her hand and said, "I'm putting caca in your hand!" "Yuk!" she said, quickly withdrawing her hand. This produced such gales of laugh-ter that to please him, she put her hand back again. "I'm putting caca in your hand" he exulted. "Yuk!" she said. Gales of laughter. Repeat. And then it came: a variation in the game. The mother put her hand back, and the little boy put his penis in it. She withdrew her hand quickly.

This is a big moment in the life of a small boy and his mother. The mother pulls her hand away instinctively, and then what? Does she erupt in anger, expressing horror or disgust? Does she plunge into silence? Even silence, at such a juncture, sends a powerful message: *What you have done is such a transgression that I am speechless; what you have done is of such consequence that I am going to act as if nothing hap-pened.*

Yet a casual response, as though putting his penis in his mother's hand was not a significant escalation of the game, is also not right. It makes too little of the boy's penis. And it fails to take account of the questions implicit in the child's move: *Does my penis surprise you? Hor-rify you? Make you laugh? Bring you pleasure? Is it okay for a boy to put his penis in his mother's hand? Where are the limits to how we touch each other, now that I am no longer a baby and not yet a big boy?*

How does a child know what is too much, too far, unless he starts to go there sometimes, unless he dares the edge? How does he come to terms with the latent forbidden unless he actualizes it from time to time?

The poet Theodore Roethke wrote: "I learn by going where I have to go."[2] Children learn this way, too. Such learning, which is experimental and without preconception, includes veering "where I musn't go." That is why, when children are small, they need their parents to be there for them when they reach an edge, to let them know that it is time to turn back, yet that no irrevocable harm has been done. Children learn by the going and by the look on their parents' faces, the tone of their parents' voices, the words their parents choose to say when they get there. The hot stove, the cat's bite when her tail is yanked, a parent's strong "No!": these intense experiences impress themselves in the memory, helping children to make a map of their world.

But how can they learn by the going if they can't go anywhere? How can they have any real inkling of why the forbidden—that apple on the tree—is forbidden unless, now and again, they have an actual taste of it? As a friend said, "You don't learn moderation by being moderate!" We were having a conversation about institutionalized child care. His wife, Mary Biggs, the teacher who spoke in "The Bath" (in the previous chapter) about learning to proceed through "intimate knowledge," told me: "To safeguard against the anxiety that is so prevalent in our culture, many day-care centers create a wall of rules so that the possibility of something going amiss doesn't even arise. In many centers, for example, it's a rule that children can't ever be without the supervision of at least two adults: a child can't be alone by himself, he can't be alone with an individual adult, he can't enjoy a private moment with his peers. It would be one thing if this were happening in places where children spend three or four hours at a time. But this is happening in places where children, from infancy, are spending the entire day, from morning till evening. It's happening in the places where they are spending their lives."

As she spoke, I found myself thinking of all the private places of my childhood. The dark, ferny place underneath the big redwood tree in our front yard that made a kind of secret house; the wild hillside behind the house, with its tangle of honeysuckle and nasturtium blossoms where we went to hide, to capture bugs, and to make our magical potions; the dark, cool, way-back room in the basement, where we went to pull each other's pants down and spank each others' bottoms; the bomb shelter in my neighbor's house, a hidden room with a dirt floor where there were candles, rolls of toilet paper, bottles of water, and tins of food, and where we went on purpose in order to be frightened, to imagine life after The Bomb, and to ask each other those terrible which-would-you-rather questions that children love. Would you rather be buried alive? Eaten by ants? Swallowed by quicksand?

I couldn't imagine my childhood without these edgy places. In some crucial way, I feel that without them, I wouldn't truly have had a childhood in the same way that a childhood without its bad dreams, its dark fairy tales, its falls and bruises and scrapes, its dirt and its messes, would not be a childhood. It would be something more like those clear bubbles that certain children, lacking white cells, have to live in, children whose mothers touch them through layers of plastic, whose food and drink must be sterile, whose skin never touches the least grain of dirt. It was frightening to think of: a childhood lived entirely in a safety zone, under bright lights and the watchful eyes of more than one adult.

Mary told me, "The center where I work is very unusual in its layout. The space we have is basically two very large rooms connected by a bridge. And underneath that bridge there are little cubbyholes where the children can be alone with each other—"

"I imagine that a lot of hanky-panky goes on down there!" I said.

"Yes," she replied, not the least bit ruffled. "We know there's a certain amount of hanky-panky, but we believe it's important to give the children some privacy, away from the gaze of adults. An important part of childhood is hanky-panky. We believe it shouldn't be policed."

From her description, it was clear that the children were not in a complete no-man's-land when they were down in the cubbyholes. The teachers were aware of who was down there, they were alert if the sounds grew too intense, or the silence too deep for too long. What seemed to matter was that within an essentially safe and protected space, the children could have the feeling of being private and alone.

She told me, "We do something else that's quite unlike the standard day-care center. When the children are resting on their cots, there's a certain time for visiting, when they can invite a little friend to join them."

"Hmmm. And what goes on with those visitors?"

"Some of them just lie pretty still next to each other, chatting quietly. But some of them get really intense. A lot of it looks just like adult foreplay, with all the groping and panting and nipping and giggling. The other day I saw these two little boys who were really going at it. They were smushing and gushing against each other, and their bodies were getting all sweaty. I was keeping an eye on them, and when I walked past the cot a little while later, they were both lying there, intensely quiet, sucking their thumbs. I nearly burst out laughing. It looked so much like the proverbial cigarette."

"When would you ever intervene?"

"Well, if it looks like it's just getting too overwhelming for one or both of them, or if it's disturbing the other children."

"What about masturbation?" I asked.

"Well, of course children do masturbate," she said. "That is, some do. Some don't. Some do much more than others. We had one little girl who really got into it. We'd find her lying on a cot with a pillow between her legs . . . it was intense."

"What did you do?"

"We would remind her, 'That's something that you do in private. You're not in a private place now.' "

"When would you start to worry that it was too much?"

"Well, we knew that the mother was aware of her behavior, and that seemed important. The mother was in touch with the situation. She was watching it, as we were. And we were watching to see if—like most intense phases that children get into, often when they've just discovered something about themselves or the world—it would turn out to be self-limiting. Which it did. After a few weeks, she just stopped doing it so intensely. If it had continued for a long time, and certainly if it had been accompanied by any other disquieting symptoms, then we would have felt that it was time to really take the next step in exploring what was going on with her."

"If it had continued for how long?" I asked. "I mean, at what point—"

She bit her lip. "Hmm," she said. "Maybe two months. I couldn't tell you exactly. It's hard to say. . . ."

Of course she couldn't say exactly. That's how "intimate knowledge" proceeds. Feeling its way—with some general guidelines, a few absolutes—it moves in the air like a pair of antennae, wavering, tentative, vibrating with sensitivity until, having picked up clues from its surroundings, it is ready to make the next move.[3]

Suppose, wavering, we go back to the little boy playing "Yuk!" in the backseat of the car and pick up more clues. Suppose we learn that his parents have recently separated, and that his father has moved out of the house. Now the child's transgressive gesture takes on another layer of meaning; now we can read it as a small boy's question to his mother, "When the big penis moves out of the house, what is the place of the little penis in your life?"

What's a mother to do? Somehow, without shaming him, without overreacting, she needs to let him know he has gone too far. Why does she need to let him know? Because he's an anxious little boy whose father has gone. He needs a mother who's a mother, not a desperate woman in need of a very small husband. *Yes, but what's a mother to do?*

There is no script here. Or rather, there's only the rough outline of one. Using the rules of the game that he himself has concocted, she might take her son's transgressive gesture as an invitation to tell him "Yuk!" If she manages to hit the right tone of playful warning, not too forceful and not too light, she just might find he's actually relieved. On the other hand, perhaps it won't go quite so smoothly and she'll falter: freezing in silence, snapping in anger or disgust. If so, will she hurt him? Yes. Irrevocably? Hopefully not. Most likely, her son will give her another chance, in a different guise, to play the game of "Yuk!" with him, to push this particular edge. And most likely—as long as she keeps her feelers supple and responsive—she'll feel her way along this edge. By going where she has to go, she'll find the way to let him know that he, learning by going, has gone too far.

3

INNOCENCE

⌒

"NOELLE, A BIT of research for your book!" my sister-in-law calls to me from the living room, where she is changing my one-and-a-half-year-old nephew's diaper. Lying on the floor with his legs up in the air, he has found a wooden castanet and, with a big smile on his face, he is rolling it up and down on his penis while chanting, "Pindy, pindy, pindy. . . ."

My sister-in-law looks at me with a look I've begun to recognize. It's a combination of amusement, incredulity, and a certain anxiety—a look that seems to say all at once, "Isn't this a stitch!" "Can you believe it?" and "Is this really okay?" By now, I've seen this look on the faces of quite a few parents as they've offered me their stories:

"We were traveling in Italy when my daughter was three. In Florence, we went to see Michelangelo's 'David.' She was in her stroller and she took one look at David and began masturbating. She got so flushed and excited that we had to wheel her out. . . ."

"My son is four, and ever since his little sister was born, he charges about the house shouting, 'I am King of the Vagina!'"

"My daughter is seven, and the other day on our way to the art museum, she announced, 'I like to see the naked statues. But when they make the women's vaginas, they don't do a very good job of showing their la-bi-as.' She absolutely loves to say that word."

"The other morning I noticed it was suddenly very quiet, and I called out to my son, who is five, 'What are you doing, Teddy?' 'I'm playing with a cannon,' he called back. 'A toy cannon?' I asked. 'No,

Mommy,' he bellowed. 'It's my penis, and one day I'm going to shoot it off into your mouth!' "

Such bold, unabashed images compete with an image of the child as a delicate vessel of unawakened sexual feeling, a vessel that must be protected from predatory adults. How do we hold these images together: the chanting, bellowing, masturbating child and the child whose precious and fragile innocence must be protected from those who would initiate him, too soon, into the realm of sexual knowledge and pleasure?

From the moment we say the word "innocence," we enter a territory where it is virtually impossible to make the elements cohere. The very concept of innocence is profoundly amorphous: it is a blank onto which, over the centuries, various images of blankness have been projected. Does "innocence" mean to have been conceived without sin, to be ignorant, to be without evil intention, to be inexperienced, to have never committed certain deeds?

Then add the word "child" to the word "innocence" and the blankness intensifies. For as unformed versions of the adult self, children make a particularly convenient blank on which adults can project various images of blankness, of the clean slate.

Over the centuries, one image after another has appeared on this slate, in an ongoing procession. When being innocent means to be free of the false pretense and layers of personae that constitute civilized adult life, then children, in their guilelessness, will be perceived as innocent. When being innocent means to have mastered, through will and rationality, the riot of desires that lead to sin, then children will be perceived as an untamed jungle of sinful impulse. And so on. . . .

"The innocence of a child" is a notion that has a highly mutable history.[4] And this means that whenever we find ourselves particularly obsessed with protecting the innocence of our children, we might take it as a cue to look more closely, to ask just *what is it we're so concerned to protect here? And why?*

———

Some years ago, in an episode called "Prisoners of Silence," the television program *Frontline* did an exposé of "facilitated communication."[5] This was a method by which highly trained facilitators learned to interpret, and to transpose into writing, the thoughts of a person whose communication was impaired. It was deemed to be particularly effective with autistic children, and there were many very impressive claims. Children who had barely been able to keep up at school were, with the aid of their facilitators, writing brilliant papers on Shakespeare. Children who had been intensely reserved all their lives were writing passionate notes to their mothers, telling them things like "You've never known how much I love you. . . ." After some time, however, a disturbing pattern began to emerge. Around the country, many of these children were communicating through their facilitators that they had been sexually abused by a family member early in life. One father, a pharmacist in a small New England community, returned home from work one day to be met in the driveway by his distraught wife. She told him not to enter the house, that there was a warrant out for his arrest and that allegations had been made that he had sexually abused his son. In his anguish, this father—who was not permitted to return to his home for months—reached out to other parents of children who were working with facilitators. Gradually he discovered that around the country, a striking number of these parents had also suffered accusations of sexual abuse via their children's facilitators. Banding together, they insisted that there be an investigation. A rigorous double-blind study was conducted by a team of independent researchers: it definitively showed that there was no objective basis for facilitated communication.

By all accounts, these facilitators were sincere and dedicated professionals, committed to helping the children in their charge. The training program they had attended was a rigorous one at the University of Syracuse. They had nothing to gain, in an obvious way, from concocting such stories; there was no money to be made, no vengeance to be wreaked. What could have compelled them to pull such stories out of the air, creating untold suffering for the families involved, and ultimately destroying the credibility of their own profession?

That the stories were in the media at the time, that the air was indeed thick with them, is true—but it begs the question: why were these stories in the air. And what is it that could be so compelling about finding, at the root of a mysterious malady—in this case, autism—a story of sexual abuse?

For human beings, uncertainty and helplessness are among the most stressful of emotions. (The relief that can be felt when war breaks out, after months of tension and confusion, is legendary.) One thing that can be said about such stories is that they greatly simplify a complex history of pain and difficulty, thus providing release from uncertainty. They also provide release from helplessness, for they not only present a single cause to focus on, but a cause that comes in the form of an enemy. To have an enemy calls for a plan of attack: remove the perpetrator from the family. Punish him. And, of course, where there is an enemy, there can also be a hero, a savior. This is especially so when the one being saved is a child, an innocent child.

Thus a painfully complex situation—one that from day to day requires a very patient, painstaking, and laborious form of caretaking—suddenly becomes clear, dramatic, and morally compelling. A child, a child who looks so normal, even beautiful (parents, teachers, and therapists who work with autistic children often comment that these children are particularly beautiful, a quality that seems to make their strange affliction even more mysterious) became difficult, troubled, and hard to reach because his innocence was taken away from him—his innocence defined, *tout simple*, as sexual innocence, sexual inexperience.

In other times, in other places, this particular story of lost innocence could not have been told. When the infant Louis XIII was not yet a year old, his court physician, Heroard, wrote in his journal: "He laughed uproariously when his nanny waggled his cock with her fingers." A few months later, he wrote, "In high spirits, he made everyone kiss his cock. . . ."[6] There are many such entries in this particular journal, and there are countless other documents from other realms and other eras that might be produced to make the point that our own

notion of childhood innocence is historically and culturally relative.[7]
To realize this can induce a kind of vertigo. There go the absolutes
again, precisely when—in the impulse to protect our children—we
most feel the need of them.

Are there any fixed points to help us move through this vertigo?

At its root, the word innocence means "no harm." We know that children are capable of inflicting terrible harm on others—so they are certainly not innocent in this respect. Whether or not they are capable of
understanding what it is they have done becomes, with regard to innocence, the relevant question.

And what about their sexuality?

One of the casualties of the current climate, with its extreme anxiety about sexual abuse, is that it becomes difficult to acknowledge the
degree to which children are sexual beings. Children vary, as do adults,
in the intensity and focus of their libidinal interests. Under normal circumstances, both sexual curiosity and desire grow more urgent with
the onset of puberty. Still, most children quite early discover their genitals as sites of a unique kind of pleasure. In her book *Your Growing
Child*, the British child psychologist Penelope Leach writes of the prototypical baby: "At somewhere between a few months and one and a
half years, he will discover that rubbing his genitals against something
hard (perhaps against the crib bars while he rocks backward and forward), or rubbing himself with his hand, is exciting. Some babies
become abstracted, turn red in the face, pat and appear to be working
themselves up to a climax. Left to themselves, they eventually relax
and go to sleep."[8] Moving from babies to a general summary on the
subject of masturbation, she writes, "Small babies touch their genitals
because they are there. Baby boys do so more than baby girls because
there is more to get hold of. Older babies, young children, older children, adolescents and adults deliberately stimulate their genitals
because it is exciting and enjoyable."[9]

While sexual feeling may begin as a baby's sheer physical pleasure
of rubbing up against the bars of a crib, by the time a child is three or

four, he is capable of an intense mix of emotion and physical sensations that is close to what we adults call "being in love." As children get older, they absorb the intense emotional charge around sexuality, so that the physical sensations become infused with complex feelings such as shame, excitement, love.

Love. How often do we acknowledge that children can fall quite passionately in love? The Italian sociologist Francesco Alberoni has written a book, *Il Primo Amore* (*The First Love*), on this subject. Having observed children in school settings, from ages three and up, he insists that children experience a state of being in love that is similar to its adult counterpart. In the presence of the beloved, children have many of the same sensations. He quotes his ten-year-old nephew, Angelo, who confided in him that he had a new love: "I don't understand anything anymore; when I see her . . . I sweat, I shiver, my heart pounds, and I blush. With Annachiara, even my ears turn red."[10] What is more, even very young children distinguish between friendship and the special feeling they have when they are in love. Alberoni writes:

Children use the expression 'I fell in love, it was like a bolt of lightning' to indicate an unexpected attraction, a strong desire for the other person. It is in this way that 'innamoramento' is different from friendship. A friendship is formed little by little; it is constructed on a secure base and founded on trust. Instead, innamoramento is from the beginning in this infantile form an attraction, an immediate preference. And it doesn't know if it will be reciprocated. Until an instant before, we didn't know that person, or if we had seen him/her, nothing about that person attracted us. Then we're smitten by something that makes her/him appealing, attractive, desirable. Something unexplainable and unforeseen. And the desire can even last a long time.[11]

Young children are also capable of developing strong crushes on an adult that are similar to the infatuations of one adult for another. One of my own earliest memories is of being, at age three, so excited that a particular friend of my father's was coming over that I was quite literally unable to contain myself and threw up all over my mother's lovely blue curtain!

Another friend recalls her daughter's nursery-school crush on her male teacher, "a handsome young man with long, flowing blond hair." She recalls, "Katya would become so paralyzed by her crush that when the teacher spoke directly to her, she would get completely mute, blushing, biting the collar of her blouse." Years later, Katya told her mother that she would refrain from going to the bathroom all day, because "I couldn't bear the thought that he would hear me pee." Her mother, a psychotherapist, believes that Katya's extreme self-consciousness in this regard indicates that at some level, she had already made a connection—though not one she could yet begin to understand the implications of—between her "private parts" and the special intensity of feeling that she had for this handsome man.

When we acknowledge that children are capable of intense romantic and sexual feeling—feeling that is similar in many respects to what adults feel—does this weaken the case for their need of protection? No. For the other fixed point that enters into the equation is the radical difference between children and adults. Young children are physically smaller and weaker than adults. They are dependent on adults for their emotional and physical well-being. A child who has sexual feelings that arise spontaneously in his own body, feelings that he himself acts on through his own initiative—whether in masturbation, through a passionate exclamation or gesture toward a parent or other loved adult, or sex play with another child—is a world away from the child whose sexuality is appropriated by an adult for the adult. It's not just that a young child's small body is easily hurt, torn, or bruised when an adult uses it for his own pleasure; it's the intensity and complexity of adult sexual feeling that can overwhelm, frighten, and disturb a child. To witness an adult's loss of control in sexual pleasure, to absorb the shame that almost inevitably accompanies acts of incest and pedophilia, place an enormous burden on a child's emotional life, one from which he may never recover and that may permanently color his sexual experience.

Yet even these criteria are culturally relative. There are parts of the world, and there have been times in history, in which certain interactions between adults and children have been accepted practices: grandmothers fondling their little grandsons' genitals to calm them; older men fondling boys; adults performing the first sexual initiation of a young person at puberty. . . . To acknowledge this cultural relativity need not result in a sense of utter groundlessness within our own culture, for there is a radical gap between a practice that is acknowledged and sustained by the culture as a whole and one that is not.

In the first scenario, the child who participates in such a practice has—in one form or another—been preparing for it his entire life. He has witnessed it, heard it whispered about, observed its aftermath in others, so that even if the practice itself is a secret practice, it is a secret that he has anticipated, one that he knows has been passed on from grandfather to father to son through generations of his people. Though he may have a certain dread of the practice, and though the practice itself—scarring, circumcision—may be both frightening and painful, its rootedness within the culture assures that he does not also have to bear a burden of shock, horror, shame, or profound disillusionment with his elders. And this makes a world of difference.

Where does this leave us?

To believe that children deserve to be protected from the trauma of sexual abuse, it should not be necessary to render them, for the adult imagination, "innocent" of sexual feeling and desire. Such a rendering is in its own way a form of exploiting children, of using them once again as a convenient blank onto which to project certain images. Even if, in this case, the images might seem to be flattering, they exist primarily for the sake of adults, assuaging adult anxiety by presenting a clear, unambiguous picture, a world of absolutes in which the pure and innocent child is corrupted by the sexual predator.

If we try to look at children without this layer of imagery, we are forced to acknowledge something much more complex about children and their sexuality. As I've talked to parents, I've noticed that among the things that have become *hard to say* are those that reveal the passion, intensity, and even sometimes the aggressive sexual curiosity that they observe in their own children's behavior. "We were sitting on the sofa. It was a hot day and I wasn't wearing a shirt, and Devon started really exploring my nipples. He was rubbing and tweaking and twiddling and I sat there and took it until I couldn't take it anymore," a father tells me about his seven-year-old son. "I was in bed reading," the mother of a seventeen-year-old girl tells me, "and Andrea came in, sat down next to me and told me that she felt that she was ready to lose her virginity with this new boyfriend of hers that she'd been going out with. We talked about it for quite some time, and it was very emotional for both of us. Finally, she stretched out on top of me. She was crying, and she had her face pressed against my breasts, and her crotch sort of pressing against mine through the blankets, and I felt like she wanted to dive back into my body. Finally, I had to push her off me!"

Yet the same boy who so vigorously explored his father's nipples is the boy who needs to know that he can say "No!" and be heard if an adult—even his father—should say to him, "Rub my nipples, run your hands over my body. . . ." The same girl who lay on top of her mother, wanting for a few moments to dive back into her mother's body before leaving her girlhood behind, needs to know that if an adult—even her mother—should say to her, "Lie on top of me. Press your body onto mine. . . ." she can say "No!" and be heard.

The task for parents is to bear the ambivalence they feel about their child's sexuality—whatever the mix of embarrassment, protectiveness, amusement, pride, hope, anxiety, or envy that might be—in a way that stays focused on the child's needs. For adults to protect their children, it is not necessary to render them sexless, but rather, to ensure that their sexuality unfolds without interference from adult needs. This includes the need, so pronounced in our own era, to see children as "innocent" of sexual feeling.

4

PEAKS

THE FIRST TIME I heard the sound of my daughter's laugh, I had done no more than blow a paper party favor before her eyes. The surprise of that paper tube, flying out like a tongue and curling back again, made her erupt into laughter again and again. This was a peak moment for her, and it was for me, too. I rushed to the phone and called my mother long-distance to tell her, "I just heard Ariel laugh!"

In this peak moment, I felt a melting of the vast difference between us. To feel that I could get through to this tiny speck of flesh who could not speak a single word—and not just get through, but get such a rise from her, to provoke such intense delight through my ges-ture—was, in its own way, a miracle akin to Annie Sullivan's spelling "water" on Helen Keller's hand.

It was akin to something else, too—this peak moment, this melt-ing of difference—but here we are again at *this is hard to say.*

In a passage from the novel *Victor Gets Back* by the late Andrew Richter, the main character Victor is feeling a little left out as he watches his wife Lila play peekaboo with their baby daughter Pearl:

Lila smiled a perfect baby smile and covered her face. And Pearl did it at the same time, in the same way, the same perfect smile, the same gesture of her hands that expresses both cover-ing and lifting to the mouth, as if each of them, in hiding, were also gathering handfuls of the other to eat. Then the long wait as Pearl peeks first and then Lila separates her hands like stage

curtains opening on her face, but her face is very still, expectant. Lila's eyes go wide, her mouth turns to an "O" and Pearl
does the same. But not until the magic word, Peekaboo!, do
both of them erupt in laughter and affection, Pearl's eruption
more like an engrossing orgasm, her hands and feet clenching,
back arching and relaxing and arching again, and her wild peal
of baby laughter, something so sexy and complete Victor was
only sorry that he couldn't get Lila to do the same.[12]

Orgasm. He's put a baby and an orgasm together in one breath. Do
we reel? Do we recoil? This is Goldilocks' territory, that house in the
woods where we lose our bearings, and find them and lose them and
find them again. . . . [13] You put baby and orgasm together in one breath
and it's like tasting soup that's too hot. Much too hot.

How about we cool it just a little bit? How about we look at the
word that comes before: not "engrossing" but *like*. He says it was *like an
orgasm*. The small word *like* has great significance for the eros of parenthood, for there is a world of difference between *is* and *like*, between
identity and similarity, and many difficulties arise from the failure to
see this.

When my daughter dissolved into laughter at the party blower, I
dissolved with her. A thirty-four-year-old and a one-month-old dissolved into the same laughter. That's true and it isn't. For I didn't completely dissolve, and though in some ways it was, in other ways it
wasn't, the same laughter.

Within the intense feeling of mutuality, there was—for me, the
parent—an awareness of the vast differences between us. I was acutely
aware of her as a tiny new being, a being in formation. She was so small
at the time that I could still hold her in the palm of one hand; she was
so new to the world that a paper party blower could transport her into
a paroxysm of delight. Part of my intense pleasure in the moment was
that something that meant so little to me could mean so much to her.
Simultaneously, another part of the pleasure for me was the intimation
of our future relationship. *She's going to be witty*, I thought to myself,
and suddenly I had an image of her grown up and the two of us laugh-

ing, as two people of truly equal mental sophistication might laugh together over a funny story.

What about the peekaboo mother? In the passage before the one quoted above, the author writes:

> In the evenings just when Lila came home from Fabric World, the two of them played Peekaboo. It was obvious that Lila had been playing peekaboo forever. She said that it trained infants in the persistence of reality. You cover your face, and to the infant, your face disappears; then you uncover it, with a big *Peekaboo!* and your face is back. Repeat enough and the baby gets the point. Your face is behind those hands; it was there the whole time.

A parent and her baby partake of the same experience. "Lila smiled a perfect baby smile and covered her face. And Pearl did it at the same time, in the same way, the same perfect smile, the same gesture of her hands that expresses both covering and lifting to the mouth, as if each of them, in hiding, were also gathering handfuls of the other to eat." Yet the mother also retains an awareness of herself as mother, of her child as child. She retains an awareness of what the experience is "to the infant." She retains an awareness of her child as a being-in-formation.

This is sameness in difference, difference in sameness. Physical love between parents and children may not have the same climactic drive as love between adult lovers, but it has its own peaks. For the child, this peak may indeed be a moment of pure dissolving into the experience, as Pearl's is in the passage above—*her hands and feet clenching, back arching and relaxing and arching again*—but for the parent who remains parental, it is not. Even as Pearl's mother, Lila, joins her daughter in the paroxysm of the child's pleasure, and the differences between them melt, Lila keeps something to herself. Between adult lovers, this would be a less than "engrossing" orgasm. Between parent and child, it is a perfect moment of melting into separate, and unequal, peaks.

5

HOT AND COLD

"I WORRY ABOUT those families in which there is no incestual love."

A woman I know, a psychiatrist, repeated that line to me. When she was in graduate school, it was something that a professor of hers had been fond of saying.

He wasn't advocating sexual acts between parents and children; that goes without saying. Implicit in his statement—which might equally well have been phrased, "I don't worry about those families in which there is some incestual love"—there is a sense of dosage, measure. But what would it look like, this "some," this dose of incestual love, and how would we know when we had found it?

It's not hard to picture what he meant by "families in which there is no incestual love." Haven't we all had a glimpse into families whose predominant atmosphere is one of coldness, indifference? Once, when a friend and I went to stay at a beach house on the Jersey shore, we met a mother who was also staying in the house with her six-year-old daughter. The little girl was in a year-round boarding school, and the week that they were spending at the beach was to be her brief summer vacation with her mother. The mother was there with a female friend. The two women lay on the beach all day, tanning, talking about the various doctors they hoped would notice them in their clinics at nursing school. The mother appeared to have no interest in the little girl, who was left to play by herself near the water.

One day my friend and I invited her to make a castle with us.

She joined us with a delight just barely hidden by her shyness, and after we'd been digging for a bit, I remember thinking it curious that a girl her age seemed to know so little about making a sand castle, as though no one had ever shown her how. The three of us worked on our castle for a long time and it became very elaborate, with turrets and a drawbridge, high walls, and a moat around it. The little girl wanted very badly for her mother to admire it. "Will you ask my mother to come look?" she whispered to me, as though asking for something quite dangerous or extravagant. It felt like a strange errand to me—like being asked to kiss someone else's boyfriend on the lips, or to brush a stranger's teeth—but I went up to where the mother lay on the sand and invited her to come and see her child's creation. Half an hour passed before she ambled down to us. Without showing the least curiosity about the castle, without peering through its windows or examining its different sides or asking any questions about how we'd lugged the water or where we'd found such perfectly round stones, she made a perfunctory exclamation, something like "Very nice." Then she asked the little girl if she would like to go and get an ice cream, a triple-decker if she wanted. As they went off, the woman told me, "I tell her she can have anything she wants, as long as she doesn't bother me." I watched the little girl, on her way to anything she wanted, trailing behind her mother and her mother's friend.

Though it was entirely undramatic, I've never been able to forget the encounter with this pair. It was vivid in its pallor, memorable in its quality of absence. A little girl digging, using two adults she barely knew as prongs to try to capture her mother's attention. She couldn't. Eros had failed to pierce her mother's heart. This was twenty years ago, and I have no idea of what became of them, but I remember feeling that something terrible was bound to happen in the future, some eruption or implosion of grief or rage. The lack of love was such a giant hole, and the little girl so careful to tiptoe around it.

In his book *The Plural Psyche*, Andrew Samuels writes that "The function of incestuous sexuality is to facilitate the closeness of love.

Desire in a relationship guarantees the importance of that relationship to both participants. It can go tragically wrong. It can get acted out, it can possess generation after generation of a family. But incestuous desire has the function of providing fuel for the means by which we get close to other people and, hence, grow."[14]

How is it possible to provide just enough fuel for a fire that neither burns too hot nor goes cold? The extremes aren't hard to locate, but what about that elusive middle?

Perhaps it's not so elusive.

Aren't there those times when the "just right" announces itself through its boisterousness, through the very freedom and frankness of its pleasure? A friend who has a three-year-old boy told me that the other day he had come barging, stark naked, into her bedroom in the morning. He threw his arms around her and said, "I love you, Mommy!" Then, turning around and facing himself in the long mirror, he told her, "And look at my penis!"

"Isn't it something?" my friend said to me. "He made the connection." The connection, she meant, between his penis and his love for a woman. She was beaming when she told me the story. It was a look that said *my cup runneth over.* I saw amusement in it, and a mother's pleasure in her son's enjoyment of his own magnificence. But there was something else as well. I saw a woman's pleasure at being so appreciated by a man, however small that man might be. "It's a romance," she told me. "What do you mean?" I asked, eager to hear her definition. But we seemed to have arrived at the irreducible. "It's a romance," she repeated.

Unabashed, unashamed delight—the atmosphere in Gary Snyder's "The Bath"—is one way of recognizing "the just right." And so perhaps one way of recognizing that one has strayed is when the unabashedness departs, when something that began as simple, wholehearted pleasure alters and becomes more complicated. My cousin told me, "There was this ritual that Rosy and I had from when she was very little. When we were in the bath together, she liked to sip water from my belly button. It always made us giggle. But then, ever since she turned four, I started to feel kind of strange about it. I mean, here was this rather large person in the tub sucking water from my belly."

"What did you do?" I asked.

"I got pregnant and my belly button disappeared!"

Her solution, drastic as it is, may not have wide practical application, but the gauge does. The gauge of slight discomfort, of feeling "kind of strange." It was a similar gauge that my friend Sorrel had used on that very hot day when he and his seven-year-old son were sitting bare-chested on the sofa and Devon began exploring his father's nipples. Sorrel allowed him to rub and twiddle and tweak until "I got uncomfortable and told him 'Okay! That's enough!' "

After Sorrel told me this story, it occurred to me that he had been exemplifying a kind of yoga principle: you hold a posture just until it starts to hurt. This principle, this gauge, works both ways. You can use it to find your own sense of limit, and you can use it to find your child's. For children, too, have their ways of signaling "That's too much." The tiniest baby can shut its eyes or turn its head away when a threshold has been reached. Older children have many ways of letting you know they've reached a limit, as when they ask a question about something rather difficult—a family sorrow, a tragedy in the news, where babies come from—and they're listening quite intently for a while to your answer, and then suddenly stop. They break the gaze, they bring up something completely unrelated, they suddenly remember that it's time to feed the turtle.

The word "embarrassment" contains the word "bar" and derives from the notion of hitting a bar, a block, an obstacle. Embarrassment itself, whether the child's or the parent's, can be a gauge of when the "just right" has been lost. Something that has been a simple flow between parents and children—bathing, dressing and undressing—hits an obstacle: the obstacle of self-consciousness. It's as though parent or child or both suddenly realize that "You're not just an extension of my body anymore. We are two separate selves." And this realization tends to be experienced as embarrassment, as a clue that it's time to treat each other with a little more formality.

"Natural modesty" is the term that I heard several parents use when describing this process. One woman told me, "My son turned seven recently, and the other day something happened that had never happened before. He walked into the bedroom when I had just gotten out of the shower and I was standing naked by my dresser. And I suddenly realized that he was looking at me in a different way than he ever had before. And he suddenly seemed to realize it, too. I threw my arms across my body to cover myself, and he looked away. It was like a sort of natural modesty had just kicked into gear."[15]

Feeling "kind of strange," a sensation of slight discomfort, self-consciousness, the experience that something that once felt simple and wholehearted has become more complicated, shadowed; these are some of the ways that "a sort of natural modesty" announces itself, and these are ways to gauge our distance from *the just right*. There is also the gauge that the young mother (in the last chapter) used when she noticed that their baths together were becoming "too intense" for her young son. He was overexcited, overstimulated, increasingly unable, as she put it, "to remain whole." A parent can watch for this too-much-ness. Imagine that a father takes his little daughter in his arms and is swinging her up in the air. At a certain point, he notices that she is looking at him with such rapture, such adoration, that there is such intensity to her cries of "More, more!" that she can really not contain herself. And so he sets her down and says, "We're getting dizzy. Let's sit down and read a story. . . ."

There is still another gauge that can be used, one that is perhaps a bit more difficult to calibrate. One woman who had been married twice and raised five children told me, "My second husband, Stephen, always bathed with our two daughters when they were very small. At a certain point, I noticed that he had stopped. When I asked him why, he told me, 'I felt that I was starting to feel too much pleasure.' "

His wife was deeply impressed by this. It was such a striking contrast to her first husband's behavior as a father. Speaking of this man, she told me, "I have a memory of Tony sitting on the landing of the staircase with our two youngest children rolling his socks up and down on his ankles. When they stopped, he said, 'No, keep doing it,' and he had this dreamy sort of expression on his face." She shuddered in horror as she described this scene, and what struck me was the seeming disparity between the gravity of the act—after all, it was just a pair of socks being rolled up and down on a father's ankles—and the intensity of her reaction.

This woman, a psychologist who directs a well-known institute for child study, feels very strongly that her first husband crossed the boundaries with her children. Yet when she speaks about what he did to them, she does not mention genital contact, the kissing or fondling of small breasts or buttocks. The acts in themselves—having his children roll his socks up and down, coming into their rooms and stroking their backs as they lay on their beds—would not be likely to appear on an official list of inappropriate touch, but this does not alter her conviction. What tipped the scales for her was the predominant feeling-tone in the father's interactions with his children: an intense neediness, a dreamy self-preoccupation, a lack of attunement to the children's reactions. She told me that one of her sons, now a young man, had recently described to her the dread he used to feel that his father might come into his room. Even though his father would not do "more" than sit beside him on the bed and stroke his back, this was much too much. It was unbearable to the son—unbearable in its root sense of too much to hold, too much to carry—because it was so freighted with the father's need.

From her son's experience, this woman made a segue to the day-care center that she directs as part of the institute. "I tell the students who are working with me at the center to pay attention to how they hold a child. You want to sit with your back relatively upright, providing sheltering but firm support for the child—not all slumped over them, collapsed into them. If I observe someone who, day in and day out, seems to need too much from their physical interactions with the children, seems too dependent on affection from the children, then that's a warning sign for me. It's not so much that I fear a literal act of sexual abuse as that the adult is letting the child down because she's not being fully adult. She's merging her own needs with the child's."

In the words of another woman, herself a psychologist and a mother of two: "It's greed that makes the difference. It's not really so much about what part of the body is being touched, or how." When I repeated this to my neighbor, a woman who spent two years in Malaysia with the Peace Corps, she vigorously agreed. Describing the village where she had lived, she told me, "Inside the high wooden buildings where the people live, there are these swings that hang from the rafters, where they put the babies. It's not uncommon when a baby boy is fussing for the woman who's tending him to diddle his little penis. It's mostly the older women—aunts and grandmas—who tend the babies during the day, and no one would ever think that there's anything the least bit wrong in what they do. It's simply their way of taking care of a baby, of distracting him with pleasure when he's unhappy."

The distinction between literal acts and the emotional context in which they occur is an important one. Indeed, the long-term effects of sexual abuse are far more closely correlated to the quality of psychological interaction between parent and child than by such blatantly concrete factors as the severity and duration of the abuse or the child's age when the abuse began.[16]

Among the factors that determine the quality of psychological interaction is *intention*. David Finkelhor writes: "Professionals who work with children believe for the most part that children are very good at distinguishing touch that is affectionate from touch that is sexual and intended for the adult's genital gratification."[17] A normal child, whose boundaries have not been seriously violated, can learn to feel when there is something *de trop* in the atmosphere because an adult is allowing his own pleasure to supersede, to take over the experience. The child can feel this as a curious raptness on the part of the adult, as a kind of absence, or as a complication in the form of shame, embarrassment, an odd giggle, a furtiveness, an injunction to whisper. . . .

All this raises an interesting question. What happens to the internal gauge, in both children and adults, when the static from outside becomes more and more powerful?

One mother told me, "We're very free about our bodies in my family. I let my boys run naked, I thwack their little tushies, and they laugh. It's a game. Of course there are some things I never do. Once beyond diapers and potty-training, I would never touch their genitals, for example. There's a very powerful internal sense of what's okay and what's not."

But increasingly, she told me, she felt an anxiety "from outside" seeping in. "The other day my youngest son came home with a project he'd made at school for Mother's Day. The children had been asked to respond to the question 'What is a mommy?' and on a big sheet of paper, he had written, 'I love to take hot tubs with my mommy and play games with her.' In our family, one of our favorite things is being all together in the hot tub. But seeing this in his big letters on bright paper, imagining it through the eyes of school officials, I noticed that I felt anxious. I felt that social screen that comes up between you and your own child. And I had that 'what-if' feeling. What if somehow I'd done something wrong? I hadn't done anything wrong. I knew that, I know that—and yet there's something in the air that's so powerful, so oppressive, it makes you doubt yourself, it alienates you from what you know to be true. Increasingly, I've begun to feel discomfort in all sorts of places where I never did before, and it doesn't even really feel like my own discomfort. I don't know whose discomfort it is."

Whose discomfort is it?

I've never been a shoplifter, and I have no intention of shoplifting. But sometimes when I go into a store, I can feel the clerk looking at me with such vigilance that I begin to feel as though maybe I am, indeed, a shoplifter. I can see her eyes following me in the round mirror up on the wall, and suddenly what I know to be true about myself carries no weight. Feeling a growing unease, I begin to lurch around, picking up now this item, now that, with increasing randomness—an ashtray, although I don't know anyone who smokes anymore, a pair of puce socks, although I hate the color puce. By now, the clerk is shadowing me; wherever I go, she's a couple of feet away, pretending to arrange things on the shelves, darting sidelong glances at me all the while. In a last-ditch effort to collect myself, I mumble something to her and stumble out of the store. Back in the light of day, it will be a while before I can shake off the suspicion that has settled on my skin and penetrated to my sense of who I am.

Perhaps there is a clue here, one that can be used to navigate through the eros of parenthood. Perhaps it is possible to distinguish the sense of discomfort, of feeling "kind of strange," that comes from within from a discomfort imposed from without. A question one might ask oneself is *Does the discomfort arise primarily when I feel or imagine that I am being watched?*

For the mother whose son brought home the "Mommy is . . ." collage, it was when she imagined school officials looking at his joyful "hot tub!" exclamation that she felt unease, an unease that she had never experienced in the hot tub itself. Such unease is far away from the mother who suddenly felt an impulse to cover her naked body when her son walked into her bedroom. It also seems rather far away from the mother whose daughter sucked water from her belly button in the bathtub. She was proceeding from her own internal sensation ("I started to feel kind of strange")—not from the imagined gaze of others.

Not that it's always easy to distinguish within from without. One mother, who lives alone with her twelve-year-old daughter, told me, "My daughter still likes to sleep in my bed at night, and I like it, too. She's usually asleep when I get into bed, and we each are curled up on our own side of the mattress, but it's very cozy. I like to hear her breathing as I fall asleep, and sometimes when I wake for a moment in the middle of the night, I realize that we're holding hands. For about the past year, though, I've been asking myself if it's okay. It feels okay to me, but I notice that I feel a little anxious or embarrassed if I tell my friends about it. And I can't really tell where that anxiety is coming from—if it's my own sense that it's time to grow out of something, or if it's just that I feel self-conscious about what others might say."

This woman told me that the way she handled her uncertainty was to regularly do "a sort of scan": "I make myself pull back and look at the whole picture. For instance, I observe myself, to see if I seem to need too much for her to sleep with me, if I feel too lonely or have more trouble falling asleep if she spends the night at her dad's or with a friend. And the answer is: I don't. I've also asked myself if my daughter seems especially clingy in other ways. And she absolutely doesn't. In her everyday life, she's extremely independent of me, always out with her friends, an ace on the softball field, excelling in school without even much help from me. In fact, I think there's a way that sleeping next to me at night actually helps her to be more independent of me during the day. I suppose you might call it a kind of regression that happens at night, if you wanted to label it. The way it feels is that there's something that gets reknit between us at night. Then, in the morning, she leaps out of bed and unravels it. . . ."

Simply to pose these questions—"Do I need this too much?" "Is this too much for my child?" "Is it impeding her in some way?"—is a way of pausing, of buying oneself a little time, creating a kind of buffer between oneself and the gaze, or the imagined gaze, between oneself and the catchphrase. Such questions lead to the way of attunement, of reorienting oneself to the path of intimate knowledge.

This path, as we know, does not provide the comfort of certainty, of absolutes. But isn't this precisely the question, whether in fact we all need absolutes, the same absolutes?

The mother who told me that "I don't even know whose discomfort it is" is a counselor who works in a detention home for delinquent youth, many of whom have been sexually abused as children. She is very familiar with children who have a poor sense of where their bodies end and another's begins, children who sexualize virtually every relationship, because that's all they have ever known. She recognizes the need for such children to be supplied with a very firm sense of boundaries. She talked about working with one child, a deaf boy, who had been so consistently treated as a sexual object in his early life that the category of nonsexually exploitive touch really did not exist for him. She told me, "We drew a diagram, with two boxes, one inside the other. The box inside was labeled 'Good Touch' and the box around it was 'Bad Touch.' It was absolutely basic, blatant, black and white. That's what this child needed. But my sons don't need that. I don't want people indoctrinating my children with fear. I worry that they're going to lose their own sense of intuition. I resent, and it worries me, that increasingly this black-and-white mentality—which really is needed for certain children—is being foisted on all children. And I resent that this very fear-based mentality is being foisted on me."

To release ourselves from this fear-based mentality means that we will travel a more meandering path. It means that sometimes we will go a little too far in this direction, sometimes a little too far in that.

A friend of mine, Irene, has one child, a son to whom she has always been very close. When Jesse was in his twenties and had his first serious girlfriend, she gave the girl a very pretty negligee for Christmas.

"Jesse went bonkers," she told me. "Absolutely bonkers."

"Why, do you think?" I asked, always curious to hear how people will say these things that are *hard to say.*

"Because it was like, in giving her that negligee, somehow I was going to be in the bed with him."

Irene won't make that mistake again. No doubt her life will offer her, as it does all of us, the opportunity to make new mistakes. But better a son going momentarily bonkers over his mother's slightly too intense or misdirected heat than the little girl playing alone on the beach.

And, of course, there is a way that with or without the faux pas of the negligee, Irene *is* in the bed with her grown son. Just as when my other friend's three-year-old son grows up, she'll be in the bed with him and his girlfriend, too—in the bed, that is, as the one to whom he once exclaimed, nearly in the same breath, "I love you, Mommy!" and then, "Look at my penis!" *He made the connection,* my friend said. The primal connection between his penis and his love for a woman that will sustain him through all the loves of his life. Lucky for the future women in his life that he made the connection, that he had a mother who beamed with pleasure when he did.

And woe unto those whose lovers came from families in which there was no incestual love.

6

FATHERS AND DAUGHTERS

IN "A FATHER'S Story," by the late Andre Dubus, the fictional narra-
tor says of his teenage daughter:

> It is Jennifer's womanhood that renders me awkward. And
> womanhood now is frank, not like when [her mother] was
> twenty and there were symbols: high heels and cosmetics and
> dresses, a cigarette, a cocktail. I am glad that women are free
> now of false modesty and all its attention paid to the flesh, but
> still, it is difficult to see so much of your daughter, to face the
> deep and unabashed sensuality of women, with no tricks of the
> eyes and mouth to hide the pleasure she feels at having a
> strong young body. I am certain, the way things are now, that
> she has very happily not been a virgin for years. That does not
> bother me. What bothers me is my certainty about it, just from
> watching her walk across a room or light a cigarette or pour
> milk on cereal.[18]

This father seems to be asking for veils, for something to come
between him and his clear perception of his daughter as a sexual being.
Why? He doesn't say. He only says that what bothers him is not *the fact*
that she is not a virgin anymore, what bothers him is *his certainty about
it*, a certainty that comes "just from watching her." It's as though simply
to see a daughter as a sexual being feels like a transgression to him, like
getting dangerously close to the violation of a big taboo.

And what about the daughter in the story? Is she really so unabashed in her sensuality before her father? Does she sense his awkwardness? Is it hard for her, perhaps like a veil coming between herself and the father who was once so much more open and unabashed in his affection for her? In his awkwardness, does he no longer reach out to put his arm around her or kiss her on the cheek or tell her how pretty she is? The reader doesn't get to glimpse into her mind.

When I ask real-life women about this passage, there is sometimes a comic element in their stories, as with the friend who told me about practicing dance steps with her father, a large pillow wedged between their bodies. More often there is sadness that comes through. In different versions, I hear very much the same story again and again: about fathers rendered awkward by their daughters' womanhood; about fathers, once warm and spontaneous, who suddenly grew distant and cold. At precisely the moment in their lives when these daughters were feeling most insecure about themselves—*Who am I now? Am I still lovable? Will men find me attractive?*—their fathers withdrew and often became critical, withholding the encouragement that their daughters so craved. When my friend Jenny was a little girl, her father never hesitated to tell her how pretty she was. They used to go through the names of movie stars and he'd tell her all the ones that reminded him of her mother: the soft, doe-eyed, red-headed types. Then he'd list the ones that reminded him of her: certain sassy, cerebral blondes. One day when she was a teenager, the name of one from the Jenny list came up and he declared, "Oh, I can't stand that actress!"

In a paper entitled "The Innocence of Sexuality," the psychoanalyst Jonathan Slavin speaks of the way that a parent—as long as he is careful not to allow his own agenda to interfere with the child's needs—can respond positively to a child's budding sexuality in a way that is acknowledging and affirming "what it is that the child is trying to become."[19] This seems to me a particularly lovely formulation, one that gives permission to the parent to bestow, in an appropriate way, what the child desires. Though the specific example he uses involves a mother and her small boy, this form of acknowledgment and affirma-

tion is one that adolescent girls seem to long for with special intensity—but, alas, theirs is a longing that is often sharply disappointed.

In other times, in other places, fathers and daughters weren't left so
adrift and so alone to navigate this difficult passage. When a girl
reached puberty, she might move into a different hut in the compound,
away from her male relatives. She might be given away in marriage and
sent to live with her husband's family. She might come under the sway
of an elaborate set of customs—formalities of speech, gesture, eye contact, clothing—designed to regulate her closeness to her father. The
contemporary father in Los Angeles, New York, or Toronto does not
have a great deal more than his own sense of awkwardness to steer by.
Much as children, as they grow older, rely on disgust to help them separate from their parents' bodies—flinching at the sound of their parents' eating; recoiling at the sight of a mother's least physical flaw, her
unshaved legs, her crooked tooth—so fathers, it seems, sometimes rely
on disgust to help them separate from their daughters' bodies. "Oh,
look at Jenny's long fingernails!" her mother exclaimed one evening at
the dinner table. "Well, they might be nice if they were shaped," her
father snapped in a tone he'd never used on his daughter before she
turned twelve. What's sad is that in the absence of a supportive social
network to guide the transition, daughters tend to perceive their
fathers' behavior as a form of personal rejection.

The stories I heard were from women who are now in their thirties
and older. What is it like for fathers and young daughters today, when
the atmosphere has become so saturated with fear of sexual abuse, with
suspicion of the predatory male?

It doesn't take much, I learned, to get men talking about the heavy
pall in the air. It's there in the parks, in the playgrounds, in grocery
stores, and train stations. If you're a man, you feel self-conscious if you
smile at a child, or look at her for more than a few seconds. You don't
dare lay a hand on a shoulder or tousle a head of hair, or even give a
friendly wink. If you happen to be a "Mr. Mom," whose wife is at work
while you manage the household, the other mothers look at you with
alarm and suspicion when they drop their children off to play with

yours. And if you're one of the rare men who's drawn to work with children as a vocation—perhaps because you're an exceptionally gentle, playful type; a man who has kept a certain curiosity alive, who loves to peer at bugs and make volcanoes inside jars, to teach small children how to swim or juggle or build campfires or do magic tricks—then you're really suspect. One young man I briefly met on a ferry in Seattle told me that he felt particularly drawn to work with inner-city boys, many of whom were living without contact with their fathers. He had worked for a while in various government-subsidized preschools. He had greatly enjoyed working with the children, and his supervisors had given him very good reports. "But," he told me, "the ink would hardly have time to dry on the last set of fingerprints before it was time to make a new set to prove I hadn't done some hideous deed, and I just got tired of it." He's making a lot of money in computers now.

How could such rampant anxiety in the public sphere not affect the private sphere? And what does it do to the private sphere when it becomes so sealed off from the public? If touching a child becomes, increasingly, something a man can do only in the privacy of his own home, does this make touching his own child even more charged?

The layering of different pressures that bear down upon a man can be extraordinarily complex. Not long ago, when I was traveling back East, I talked with a friend who is stepfather to his wife's daughter, a beautiful and very intelligent little girl named Lisa who has been diagnosed as having Asberger's Syndrome, a condition related to autism. It is never easy to be a stepparent, and the challenges for Michael have been particularly acute. Because of her condition, Lisa has great difficulty in understanding emotional and social cues, and it takes enormous patience and sensitivity to interact with her, almost as if one must learn a new language. She is very affectionate, however, and very physical in her expression of affection. Her mother, Rebecca, told me, "Lisa is like a little animal in some ways. For instance, she's very attuned to people's scent. From the time she was tiny, she has loved to burrow next to me and smell me. She loves the scent under my neck, and, if I let her, she would go up to other people and check out their scent, too. It's her way of getting to know someone. I knew that she had really bonded to Michael when I saw her sidling up next to him and catching a whiff."

For Michael, opening his heart to Lisa has meant opening himself to the deeply idiosyncratic ways in which she expresses her affection and attachment. It has required great subtlety and generosity on his part. Along with the inherent difficulties of the situation, he has also had to contend with an environment that, to put it mildly, has sometimes been less than supportive. A year ago, the family left the town they had been living in and moved to their current residence. Lisa entered second grade, and after only a few weeks into the school year, a very painful incident occurred.

Because of her condition, Lisa often feels overwhelmed by sensory input, by sights, sounds, and odors that are piercingly vivid for her. To release her tension, she sometimes masturbates—and because she does not have the same sensitivity to social cues that other children have, she can be quite uninhibited in her behavior. A substitute teacher noticed her masturbating in the classroom and was also startled to hear Lisa speak very frankly about where babies came from, using words such as "semen" and "vagina." (As it happened, Lisa had recently asked Michael to explain how her baby sister had come to be, and he had told her in very simple, but explicit, language.) The substitute teacher put her observations together with the fact that Michael was a stepfather, and she decided to alert Child Protective Services. Fortunately, the classroom teacher, who was experienced in working with "special-needs" children and with whom Rebecca had already established a strong rapport, insisted on calling Rebecca and Michael first. In talking it through, the teacher became convinced that Lisa was not in any danger, and the matter was finally dropped—but not until Rebecca and Michael had gone through several weeks of anguish. In Rebecca's words, "We were new in town, there was no one locally to vouch for us. It seemed so unfair to Michael, and it was a very vulnerable, helpless feeling for both of us." Indeed, one of the things that struck Michael most powerfully was the realization that "There was really nothing I could say to defend myself. I knew I had to watch myself very, very carefully, to act very, very calm. I knew that if I betrayed any intense emotion, it would work against me." To this day, he is extremely circumspect about sharing this story, knowing how quickly and deeply such accusations, no matter how unsubstantiated, can take root.

As for Lisa, she is nine now. The other night when Michael was putting her to bed, she asked him, "Will you tickle me down there?" Michael took a deep breath, knowing how careful he had to be in the way he said No. "That wouldn't be appropriate," he told Lisa. "But I can rub your back and kiss you good night."

What a complex landscape he's walking through. Under the felt gaze of school officials, bearing the stigma of the stepfather, he has to be ready to respond spontaneously and sensitively to Lisa's curiosity and longings without hurting or shaming her. His situation is particularly complicated, but in its own way, it represents an intensification of a challenge that faces fathers in general. In another bedtime story I came across, a nine-year-old girl asked her father, "When you kiss me good night, do you get the same funny feeling that I do?" "I feel the same way when I kiss you as I do when I kiss your brother," the father replied.[20] Don't we feel somehow that the father isn't telling the truth, that he's leaving something very significant out of the equation? It's a different eros that a father feels for a daughter than for a son. But what a difficult path to walk. Living under a stern and censorious gaze, how does he respond to a daughter's budding sexuality in a way that is both tender and appropriate, encouraging and yet restrained?

One father I met told me that when his daughter was eight, she suddenly asked him one day, "Why can't you and I have sex?" He took a deep breath and told her, "Because it's something special between me and Mom." In its very simplicity, this seemed to me an inspired response. Without recoiling in shock and embarassment at his daughter's question or denying the eros that existed between them, he let her know that his sexuality was safely contained within his marriage. This same father is a massage therapist, and from the time she was very little, his daughter has always loved to be massaged. He told me that as her body has become more womanly, and hence the experience more charged for him, the easiest thing would have been to simply stop giv-

ing her massages. She let him know that she would be bitterly disappointed, however, and so he chose the more difficult route: to observe
himself carefully along the edge that these massages brought him to.
He told me, "When I massage her now, I am aware of a sexual energy. I
can see how it comes in. I can see how it could be abused. But again
and again, I bring myself back to intention. I remember the difference
between sensuality and sexuality. And sometimes what I do is, I tell her
what a beautiful body she has. That's my way of making the experience
be *about her, for her*."

It's not hard to imagine that another father, in the same situation,
might communicate something altogether different when he
exclaimed, "What a beautiful body you have!" Indeed, I imagine that
there are few fathers who could navigate this edge without burdening
the daughter with an excess of their own need, desire, or anxiety. Still,
it serves as a powerful example of a parent trying very consciously to
find for himself, and for the sake of his child, the line between too hot
and too cold.

With such a large pressure field bearing down from the atmosphere, it's
perhaps good to return to a less charged example and to remember the
power of small acts.

When I was a teenager, my father exclaimed more than once when
my long hair was pinned up, "I love to see the back of your neck!" The
sheer fact that I've stored this small detail for so many years is an indi-
cation of how much it meant to me. It wasn't a furtive comment, made
carefully out of earshot of my mother, which might have made me
uncomfortable. I remember it, rather, as something that he said quite
openly, in the kitchen or at the dining-room table, perhaps even saying
to my mother, "Don't you love to see the back of Noelle's neck?" Yet
because it was not something he had said when I was a little girl, and
because it was about a somewhat hidden part of my body—the back of
my neck, which was exposed only when my hair was up—I experienced it as a confirmation that I was growing gracefully into a woman.
It did have a slightly erotic quality. Just a little. Not too much.

7

MY DAUGHTER'S DANCE

IT'S EVENING, AND in that rushed slot before suppertime, I head for my daughter's room with a heap of her clean laundry. The wicker basket balanced on my hip, I pause for a moment before knocking. Music leaks from her door. *Don't try to catch a flying thing. . . .*

"Come in!" she calls. I enter, feeling a bit like a shy, clumsy charwoman in the den of her worldly and exotic mistress. It's clear that I've entered in mid-scene: clothes, jewelry, and shoes are strewn about, a candle is lit, and a stick of fruity-sweet incense is burning.

"Look at me!" she commands, and I set the basket down on her bed. She turns the music louder. *Don't try to hold a bird that sings. . . .* She resumes her dance, and I see that it's a *pas-de-deux*: a "Dance for Girl and Mirror." Moving around the room, she keeps coming back to touch base with the mirror—as once she did with me in her toddler's explorations around the kitchen or the living-room floor. Then I was the ground zero, the still point from which she gathered strength to move in ever-widening circles through her world. I feel a pang for her: will the mirror reveal flaws to her that are invisible to me? So far, she seems to be holding her own. Gazing into the glass, she tosses her hair behind her head in a gesture that imitates—or does it incubate?—confidence. She begins to sway to the music, undulating her hips in a way I didn't know she was capable of. As a child, I knew the range of each of my dolls' movements, precisely what the joints could do or not do. But my daughter's repertoire of movements has already taken me by surprise. I feel slightly awkward again, as though I don't quite know who I'm with. Her lips are pushed forward in a dreamy, glamorous pout that seems to belong to someone else. The look in her eyes is complicated, like a child's gaiety being blown at me through a sultry exhalation of smoke.

"Dance with me!" she says, grabbing my hand. I feel a sudden anxiety. My undulating, preteen daughter has grabbed my hand and asked me to dance. This is one of those moment for which I have no map. I could give in to the anxiety, slip my wrist out of her grasp, murmur something about supper burning, and march out of the room with my empty laundry basket. Or, I could decide to stay.

Tightening her grasp on my hand, she twirls me around the room, spinning me out and reeling me in. She laughs: she's captured her busy mother and brought her under a spell. I always did love to dance. It's been a long time since I did, and the beat of this tune is strong enough that I could let myself go. *Don't try to catch a flying thing. . . .* How easily I could give in to my own *pas-de-deux*, and do the dance of a "Mother and Her Youth." She catches my eyes with a look that brings me back from the verge. I see that for her, the dance is now a *pas-de-trois*: a dance for "Girl, Mother, Mirror." In fact, she's using me as another mirror. *Look at me, look at me* her body says without words. *I'm turning into a woman before your eyes.* I let my heartbeat slow. Now it's my turn to reel myself back in and consent to being used by her. For I'm not just a mirror, but a stand-in, for some as yet, I suspect, only dreamily imagined Other, or succession of Others.

It's one of those bittersweet moments—growing ever more frequent—when I can feel her shedding me like an outer skin, and at the same time, know that what makes it possible for her to do so with such abandon are the deep layers of connection between us. I think of the moment when I first touched her, skin to skin. There, already, was the play of surface and depth. They handed her to me, and I held her cheek against my cheek. I felt, for the first time, the outer layer of the one who had been so deep inside me, and whom I already felt I deeply knew.

Remembering that moment, I realize I'm not just any stand-in. I'm the stand-in par excellence. And actually, "stand-in" isn't quite the right term; the heat I feel from her is real—which is why it made me slightly anxious when she grabbed my hand and told me to "Dance!" Rather than marching out of the room, I had to stay with my anxiety in order to understand that she really was dancing with me . . . and that she was not dancing with me. She was using the sparks from our connection to send heat in a different, if for now mostly imagined, direction, away from me.

Now I let myself go back into her dance, but I do so on her terms, holding myself in check even as my hips begin to sway—a bit—and I can see from the look on her face, which is dreamy, mirthful, rapt, and ever so slightly wicked, that whatever this moment is for which I had no map, I'm doing it right.

PART VI

CONCLUSION
Beneficent Boundary Loss

1. Zones

2. Rapprochement

3. Ashes

4. Tending the Small

5. Dilation

6. Boundary Loss

7. Time Overflowing

8. The Hardest Thing

Like the pairing of eros and parenthood, *the words "boundary loss" carry a dangerous charge. It is fear of the latter that haunts the former and cries out for fences and signposts, for clear, unambiguous charts of the body and sharp lines between "Good Touch" and "Bad Touch."*

Yet from the very beginning, children explode our sense of boundary, of "me" and "you"—and sometimes, if only for brief, fleeting moments, even between "me" and the rest of the world. They come to us through the dissolving of boundaries that is the act of love; they inhabit our bodies, emerge, and then flood through our lives. In this flooding, they ask that we give ourselves to them completely, with no holding back. "It's not God I want, it's someone in skin!" the child exclaimed.

He was right to put God and parent-child love in one breath, to apprehend that the sense of totality, of you are my all, *that belongs to one realm holds sway with equal intensity in the other. Yes, the eros of parenthood is shadowed by the lure of idolatry: the child becomes god to the parent, the parent god to the child. It is also shadowed by exclusivity: "My child means the world to me, but not* your *child." Nonetheless, it does carry within it the possibility of a genuinely universal vision, one that in its very essence extends beyond the narrow confines of the single self. Without denying the dangers, this last chapter celebrates the act of overflowing—thus seeking to restore to boundary loss its rightful place.*

1

ZONES

A WOMAN I met, a Latin-American who lives in California, was giving her young grandchildren a bath one evening not long ago. She and they were sudsing, sloshing, rinsing, laughing, when all of a sudden one of the little girls stood bolt-upright and bellowed, "Red light!"

Unbeknownst to Grandmother, who had given a scrub to a slippery behind, the children had just that week, in kindergarten, been indoctrinated in the difference between "Green light touch" and "Red light touch."

It took Grandmother a moment to catch her breath—for it had been almost as if an alien voice had taken over and spoken from the mouth of her grandchild, and the term at first made no sense to her. What was a traffic light doing in the bathtub? Then, suddenly remembering that it had been Child Safety Week and thus grasping the subtext, she bellowed back:

"No! It is not Red light touch! Everywhere I touch you is Green light because I am your grandmother and I love you!"[1]

Blasphemy! When she told me these words, in the midst of a dinner party, I reeled a bit. Suppose the secret police were in our midst, the traffic cops taking note? They'd been in the bathtub, after all, speaking from the mouths of babes, transforming a fluid experience, a melee of slippery bodies—whose arm? whose ankle? whose fingers pouring water from where?—into a grid of yours/mine, here/not here, yes/no.

How much easier life would be if we could navigate its swirling waters with the aid of such a simple and simplifying tool. It's one so readily taught to young children, so clear, unambiguous, and even gamelike, as when you play "Red light/Green light" and try—whenever the person who's "It" isn't looking—to steal closer to the frontline.

But to what degree can the nature of a touch be defined by *where* on the body it occurs? A baby, a lover, a doctor touch a woman's breast; is it even the same breast that they touch? Here we have entered the realm of Heraclitus, the ancient Greek philosopher who tells us: "Upon he who steps into the same river, different and again different waters flow—"

Different hands might impart to the same child, in the same bathtub, and on the same body parts, very different versions of touch—and versions whose difference is vastly more complex and subtle than the grid of "Red light/Green light" can express. For the difficult truth is that in one context, it might in fact be useful for a child to be armed with such a tool. But in another, this tool itself might be a violation, a manhandling, an inappropriate intrusion into a family's inmost space.

Not long after I heard the story from this grandmother, I heard a story about another. A woman I met, whose mother is Mexican, told me about the day that her mother arrived in California to meet her newborn grandson. Taking him from her daughter's arms, she kissed his naked little body "all over." Saying these two words to me, the woman's voice dropped to a whisper and she looked at me a bit anxiously. Then she went on, " 'Mother,' I told her, 'be careful! This is the United States!' " Her mother looked surprised and confused. What could her daughter possibly mean? She was a grandmother welcoming her baby grandson. It wouldn't occur to her to separate his little body into parts. Her kisses were a way of anointing him, pronouncing him perfect, whole.

What does it mean that in stories like this our own culture functions like the snake in the Bible, introducing shame and self-consciousness into what began as a garden of sweet delight?

2

RAPPROCHEMENT

*

A FEW YEARS ago, when my French friend Claire and her eight-year-old son, Roch, came to visit me in California, we went to spend the day at a hot-springs resort not far from my home. The building is rather labyrinthine, and since Roch doesn't speak a word of English, I had planned on having him come into the dressing room with us, so that he wouldn't feel anxious or disoriented. "That will be all right, won't it?" I asked the clerk at the front desk. She gave me a startled look of intense disapproval and told me, "I'm sorry. That won't be possible."

Claire and I looked at each other. What struck me was that the woman's concern was clearly not that Roch, who happens to be an exceptionally beautiful little boy with golden curls, might be at risk of being approached by a man in the dressing room, but that he would bring a disturbing element of sexuality into the women's dressing room. For her part, Claire was experiencing genuine culture shock. She was stunned at the thought that a little boy could carry such sexual power as to make a roomful of grown women uneasy. In France, where men, women, and children routinely change into and out of their bathing suits in open view on public beaches, where young girls and women frequently go bare-breasted when swimming or sunbathing, and men and boys drop their pants to piss on virtually any pillar or post, there is much less charge around the naked body. (And here I can't refrain from including this excerpt from an interview with the artist Louise Bourgeois: "When I was a little girl growing up in France, my mother worked sewing tapestries. Some of the tapestries were exported to

America. The only problem was that many of the images on the tapestries were of naked people. My mother's job was to cut out the . . . what
do you call it? . . . yes, the genitals of the men and women, and replace
these parts with pictures of flowers so they could be sold to Americans.
My mother saved all the pictures of the genitals over the years, and one
day she sewed them together as a quilt, and then she gave the quilt to
me. That's the difference between French and American aesthetics.")[2]

Given this difference, in France there is not only much less charge
around the naked body, there is much less charge around the image of
an unclad or naked child. The recent furor over the Calvin Klein ad
that featured children in underpants jumping and flopping on sofas
could never have happened in France, for it would not have been seen
as explicitly sexual in the first place. What made that ad so provocative
to the American eye was precisely that it played off against such deadly
seriousness, such intense fear of the forbidden. As such, it became an
emblem of hypocrisy, of the way we express horror at the sexual
exploitation of children—while sexually exploiting that very horror.
For myself, I found that the ad disturbed me in America in a way it
never would have done in France.

And here it is possible to see that the eros of parenthood is beset by
a twin danger. On the one hand, the forbidden impulse is so terrifying
that it goes straight into unconsciousness, thereby reducing the possibility for conscious sublimation, transformation. On the other hand, a
peculiar feature of human nature is that the more something is forbidden, the more it beckons, the more it calls out, "Don't you want to play
with me?" This is particularly true of the erotic life—which is why, for
example, there is nothing less erotic after a while than to be in a nud-
ist colony among scads of naked people who are raking leaves, barbe-
cuing hamburgers, and playing croquet. When nakedness is *de rigeur*,
nakedness loses its thrill. Just as in the marriage bed's endless expanse
of permission, the force of eros tends to wane.

What might this tell us about the current climate? That the more
energy we pour into obsession with the forbidden, the more we
heighten the gap between what is permitted and what is not, the more
relentlessly serious we become in our policing of the territory—the

more we sexualize the atmosphere. Like my friend Claire, visitors to the United States frequently remark on this phenomenon.

"*Mais pourquoi?*" Claire's son Roch asked me as we left him at the door of the men's dressing room. Trying to explain to him why he couldn't come with us was a painful and awkward experience. In the name of a strange propriety, I found myself implanting an idea in his head that had not existed before. Before my very eyes, I could see him acquiring a new vision of himself: as a little man who leered at naked women. An atmosphere that is obsessed with the forbidden is a sexualized atmosphere. And simultaneously, an atmosphere that is so highly charged that the merest thought of a forbidden act is horrifying threatens to push such thoughts into the deep unconsciousness from which sorry deeds erupt.

Is there a way through?

"It's actually my job to wash his penis!" my cousin exclaimed to me while washing her baby boy. Remembering this, I find something that is like a small key that might unlock a very big door, or like a thin strand of thread that might lead through a labyrinth. In her humorous use of the word "job," there is an implicit acknowledgment of the limits that our own peculiar heritage, with its puritanical and utilitarian values, prescribes. Idle hands are the devil's playground, but a mother who is rinsing grit from her baby's foreskin has a bit of immunity. In her very play with the word "job," my cousin was pushing the boundaries—a bit.

In her exclamation, she is not so guarded as the father who, describing his son in the bath, kept breaking off with "This is hard to say—" She is also not as free as the poet in "The Bath," who exclaimed, "This is our body!" Her exclamation is somewhere in between, and in its betweenness, in the way it moves between two poles, I find a clue, a glimpse of the way through. It is a way that is already deeply rooted within the field of parenting, already very much a part of what it is to be "a good enough parent."

I am thinking of *rapprochement*, that crucial phase in which a child, while moving out toward the horizon of his environment, continually "checks back" with the parent—whether simply through eye contact or actual physical contact—using the parent as point of departure and source of security. In its combination of moving toward the horizon while checking back with the parent as the ground of stability and reassurance, the process might be described as a form of *bounded moving beyond the boundaries* that have hitherto defined the child's world.

Rapprochement is not simply something that the child does; it is something that the parent permits. And at the heart of rapprochement is trust. The child trusts the parent to be there as he wanders toward the edge of the room, the playground, the sandy shore of the creek. And the parent, though she keeps her eyes open and is aware of certain dangers that hover at the edge—he could stray too far and get lost, he could climb too high on the jungle gym, or wade too deep into the water—trusts her child to stay within her orbit. It is through a certain balance of watchfulness and laissez-faire that she permits her child to confidently discover his world in a way that itself is balanced between extremes of fearfulness and recklessness. When a child is either extremely fearful or extremely casual about exploring the circumference of his environment, it is often taken to be a sign of insecure attachment between parent and child.

What if, as parents, we were to use this model *to enter into a state of rapprochement with ourselves?* For in the present atmosphere, we are like the insecurely attached child—clinging anxiously, with no trust in the "good enough parent" to be there, the parent who neither abandons nor invades. And we are also like the parent who sits on the bench at the playground releasing a steady stream of anxiety into the air: "No! Don't go into the sandbox! Don't go near the swings! Don't put your mouth on that railing! Don't go down the slide. . . ."

What would it take to acquire just enough trust in ourselves as "good enough parents" to surrender—not too much, but not too little—into a more playful and exploratory mode? Then our experience would be more like that of the child who can let go and experience the joy of having a body—feeling his legs pushing high into the air as he swings, the pull of gravity as he *whooshes* down the slide, the rough-and-tumble camaraderie of other bodies—knowing that his parent is there to catch him if he falls, to warn him if he strays to close to an edge. Perhaps the very voicing of the question, which is itself a form of pushing against the edge, can open up the place where we presently find ourselves, as if we were small children clinging anxiously to an anxiously overbearing parent, the sort of parent for whom even a play-ground is a field of buried mines.

3

ASHES

"THERE IS A way to wash ashes with ashes," said the thirteenth century Zen master Dogen.[3] This is literally true of ashes; the friction of ashes on wet cloth can remove the stain of soot, and ash is an ingredient of soap. It is true metaphorically in other dimensions of experience: in the way that tears of sadness can cleanse sadness, for example, or that the Zen student's intensification of doubt can fuel release from doubt.

What about the wounds of eros? Is there a way to bring eros to heal the wounds of eros? Is there a way of overflowing boundaries that can correct the violation of boundaries?

These are not the usual questions. For usually, in the wake of violations of boundary, the first questions are, "How can we shore up the boundaries?" "How can we expand the distance between people?" Usually the first line of defense is to build more walls, create more *cordons sanitaires*, find more ways to regulate touch. And so we arrive at the day-care worker who must never be alone with a child, who may not hold a child in her arms; at the crossing guard who must not lay a hand on a child's shoulder; at the high school where, as a friend who is a teacher near Tacoma, Washington, recently told me, "Basically we've been taught that there's a little piece of a student's forearm that it's okay to touch, briefly, but nowhere else."

Do such regulations of touch really curb the violations of touch? Perhaps they do. I do not believe that the data are in yet, and I'm not sure how exactly such data could be collected. What form would they take? Fewer reported cases of child molestation among crossing guards, school-bus drivers, scoutmasters, child-care workers, high-school teachers? Fewer convictions? Even such criteria as these can be highly influenced by atmospheric anxiety.

But let's imagine that, nonetheless, we had proved beyond a shadow of a doubt that the present trend toward vigilant regulation of touch was necessary. Then, at the very least, could we add the word "sadly" to the word "necessary"? Without sentimentalizing, and without making light of the true violations of touch, is it possible to acknowledge that there is a cost to our vigilance? There are other vanishing life-forms that we mourn: the animals going extinct; certain long-held customs that now seem to us redolent of another, much less harried age, as well as one less fearful—the family dinner hour; the relaxed evening stroll through city streets; school corridors that had no need for metal detectors and armed guards. Could we also include *touch* in our sad litany?

I think of that father who told me, "I coach my eleven-year-old daughter's soccer team. I'm an affectionate man. I used to reach out to tousle a child's hair or pat a shoulder for comfort or encouragement— but I don't anymore." I think of my own thirteen-year-old daughter, who happened to mention to me the other day, "Did you know that P.D.A.'s aren't allowed at my school?" "P.D.A.'s?" I asked. For a moment, I actually thought I might be reassured by her answer, as if she were being protected from something noxious—something like an S.T.D. (sexually transmitted disease), or P.I.D. (pelvic inflammatory disease). But then she explained: "Public Display of Affection."

To realize that around the country, perhaps several thousand times a day, the affectionate impulse is being restrained, held back, is to grasp the reality of a kind of global cooling.

A handful of days ago, I was in the dressing room of the health club where I swim. A little blond-haired girl, whose mother was preoccupied with her other child in another corner of the room, fastened her eyes on me while I was changing into my bathing suit. I smiled at her and told her what a pretty dress she had. She didn't respond, but she kept her eyes on me—so intensely that although I think she couldn't have been more than four, I actually felt a slight shyness in front of her. In its raptness, hers was the gaze of a voyeur, except that it was completely without shame, without self-consciousness. I think it was this combination that enchanted me, overpowering the slight awkwardness I felt, so that I could go on unpeeling. When she broke her silence, it was to exclaim, "What a nice brassiere you have!" "Thank you!" I told her. When finally her mother called to her that it was time to go, she called back, "No! I need to see this lady finish!" She said it with true urgency, and it confirmed for me that for some reason of her own, she really did need to see me undress—perhaps to satisfy her curiosity about a grown-up woman's body that was quite different from her tall, blond mother's; perhaps simply to experience the world as a place safe enough to permit a certain kind of discovery, a place where you could trust an adult you'd never met before to reveal to you—in a way that was entirely at your behest—what lay below her outer layers.

It was a moment of intimacy between two strangers, a tiny moment of eros between a child and an adult—not one the little girl is likely to remember, but not insignificant for her, I think, in the way that it added to her reservoir of trust in the world around her and her ability to obtain just the sort of adventures that she needed. For me, it will be a memorable moment because even as it was happening, I was aware of it as the kind of moment that is vanishing, overshadowed by a very different kind of interaction between adults and children.

Only a few days earlier, I had experienced this other kind of interaction. I had passed a little boy in a shopping mall who was licking a huge ice-cream cone. He held it out to me in a kind of triumphant gesture and I exclaimed, as he so clearly wished and expected me to do, "That looks delicious! What flavor is it?" But before he could answer, his mother came up from behind him and yanked his elbow. "Scott!" she hissed. "How many times have I told you never to talk to strangers?"

When I think of these encounters, what I feel is a kind of nostalgia, a delicate sadness—albeit one that does carry ominous undertones. We've heard about the flap of a single butterfly's wings that can set off a storm on the other side of the globe. Who can say that these small disappearances—of a certain kind of warmth, a certain degree of self-revelation, of reassurance, admiration, confirmation between an adult and a child—scarcely noticeable one at a time, aren't adding up in some as yet incalculable way, to something huge?

But if these phenomena seem almost too subtle to dwell on, there are other disappearances that seem already to flash a bright warning light. What of the small children who are spending the greater part of their most formative years in day-care centers where touch is so highly restricted that adults are not permitted to hold children on their laps or to hug them tightly in their arms? What effect does this have, day in and day out, on children who spend most of their waking hours apart from their families? As a friend of mine, commenting on his experience with his two-year-old son, said, "At this age, Rubin can get so overwhelmed by his feelings that he just disintegrates. You can't reach him by words alone when he's in that state. The only thing that really calms him is to be held. It seems to me that for many children at a certain age, there are moments that occur each day when the only way they can be contained is physical—through strong, warm, encompassing touch. And I ask myself, *What if my son didn't have that in his life?*"

It's a question that bears asking in relation to children in general, but most especially to boys, who tend to be exiled from the warmth of comforting, affectionate touch even earlier and more rigorously than girls. A mother I know, who is also a specialist in early childhood education, shared this observation with me: "When I look at how boys are raised in this country, I see so much of this 'big-boy, big-boy' stuff. Little boys are hurried along to become 'big boys'—that's the main thing they're praised for. 'He's a big boy, he drinks from a cup now.' 'He's a big boy, he sleeps in a bed now.' 'He's a big boy, he doesn't wear diapers anymore.' 'He's a big boy. He doesn't cry.' And at every step of the way, if you look at what it means to be 'a big boy,' it almost always involves a step away from touch. 'He drinks from a cup' means that he's not being held to be breast- or bottle-fed. 'He sleeps in a bed' means that he's not being held as he's set down or picked up from his crib. 'He's not wearing diapers' means that all that interaction of touch is gone.

'He doesn't cry' means that when he's upset, he doesn't need to be comforted with a hug or a kiss. . . ."

Why are we in such a hurry to exile small boys from the realm of affectionate touch, and what are the consequences of that exile? In a recent comparison of the playground behavior of French and American boys, it was found that though the American children touched each other far less frequently than the French did, when the American children did touch each other, it was more likely to be in an aggressive manner.[4] The meaning of this finding is not necessarily clear and simple. Does it mean that while both sets of boys experienced a basic need to touch, the American boys channeled that need into aggression, as the only socially acceptable mode? Or does it mean that the absence of affectionate touch actually made the American boys more aggressive? Or both?

What does seem clear is that when the results of this study are set alongside others, the warning lights begin to flash brightly, revealing the strong possibility that affectionate touch may actually protect against violations of touch. In his book *Childhood Sexual Abuse*, David Finkelhor notes a correlation between sexual abuse and families in which there is very little physical affection.[5] In a way that might at first appear to contradict the evidence, he also suggests that greater, not less, close contact between men and children might actually help to prevent sexual abuse. He writes:

> Based on the sex distribution of offenders, it would be easy to imagine someone's suggesting that to protect children from sexual abuse, we should keep them as far away from men as possible. Although in its extreme form, this is ridiculous, such attitudes reach expression in prejudices against male baby-sitters and single-parent fathers. In fact, the exact opposite may be what is needed. As they take more and more equal responsibility for the care of children, men may well come to identify more closely with children's well-being and learn how to enjoy deeply affectionate relationships that have no sexual component. This step may be one of the most important we

need to take toward transforming men from offenders against children to defenders of their well-being.[6]

Other researchers have found the absence of maternal affection to have a particularly strong bearing on the genesis of violent behavior. Summarizing such research in relation to boys from broken homes, the authors of *Ghosts from the Nursery: Tracing the Roots of Violence* write: "As we look even more deeply at the underlying factors shaping children's behavior, it appears that the mothers' degree of warmth and affection are variables that fundamentally mediate the link between broken homes and crime. Where mothers are highly affectionate with their sons, the marital status of the home seems to make little difference in the outcome for adult crime. The highest levels of crime are found among boys who had both a broken home and an unaffectionate mother.[7] Taken together, these examples would seem to indicate that when there is an absence of healthy, affectionate touch, children are actually at greater risk of becoming both the victims and the eventual perpetrators of abusive touch, whether violent or sexual.

Compared with people of other cultures, Americans are relatively touch-deprived in the first place. As a recent newspaper article reported, "Cross-cultural studies have revealed that the United States has one of the lowest rates of casual touch in the world—about two times an hour (although the same does not hold for Puerto Ricans, who claim one of the highest rates of casual touch—about 180 times an hour). French parents touch their children three times more often than America parents." The article continued, "And, in spite of a new and growing body of evidence that touch is good for both soul and body, escalating concerns about 'inappropriate' touch and sexual abuse have made Americans touchier about touch than ever. Some schools have instituted 'Teach, don't touch' policies."[8]

When we respond to violations of touch by banishing, or severely limiting, touch, we incur a cost. For while touch can be violating, destabilizing, dis-integrating, it can also be stabilizing, containing, reassuring. Recently, Sonia Beck, the psychotherapist who works in a residential treatment center for delinquent youth, told me, "There's more and more fear about touching the children that we work with. For instance, male probation officers won't go inside the home of the young person they're checking in on anymore. Everything can be so misperceived. So they'll just stand there, talking on the doorstep. It makes it so much harder for some genuinely healing form of human contact—in the form of encouragement, support, or counsel—to take place. That probation officer may be one of the very few adults who could really make a difference in that young person's life, and there he is, talking through a peephole. When we try to take away bad touch, we need to remember to put something good in its place."

In its original context, "There is a way to wash ashes with ashes" is a metaphor for spiritual healing. It invites us to remember how many modes of healing there are, some of which can appear quite paradoxical.

In the medical realm, there is the antiseptic approach: a sterile field is created, vastly reducing the risk of illness. Along with this approach, there are other preventive measures. There is early detection: nipping illness in the bud before it has a chance to take hold. And there are ways of warding off illness by strengthening the body and keeping it resilient. There is the surgical model of healing: to cut off, to transplant, to re-connect, clean out. There is the medicinal solution, and it is many-faceted. Some medicines operate through opposition: the antidote neutralizes the poison; the antibiotic attacks the toxic organism. Some medicines operate through compensation: iron tablets for anemia, insulin for diabetes. Then there is the vaccine, in which the proper dose of like meets like.

When it comes to abuses of touch, we have favored certain metaphors for healing at the expense of others. We have favored the antiseptic approach, declaring ever wider zones wherein touch is severely limited, or prohibited altogether; scouring the atmosphere with that ubiquitous, inquisitive glare; drumming into our children the tenets of "stranger danger" so as to keep them safe from noxious outside influence. And we have favored the surgical approach, removing the offending parts: "Send more sexual abusers to prison," we say. "Send them younger." "Send them longer." "Castrate them. . . ."

But what about other models for healing?

One evening I gathered together several people I know to help me think about these questions. Among them were three social workers and one psychologist who have each given years of their lives to work "in the trenches"—three of them dealing with seriously troubled youth in residential treatment centers, and one with the criminally insane in a state hospital. Because of the population they work with—so many of whose lives have been marked by a history of both physical and sexual abuse—they were not the least sentimental in their responses. This was a group of people who understand the reality of transgressive touch and who grasp the need for limits. They made it clear that when you're working with people for whom affection—if they've been lucky enough to receive any—has been intertwined with aggression and/or sexuality, you have to be extremely careful about how you touch them. You don't just reach out and tousle the hair of a young person who's been a sexual object for adults for much of his life. The same is true if you're dealing with someone who has abused others. For such people, the gauge as to what constitutes appropriate and inappropriate touch is radically off, and you can't assume that what looks like a simple affectionate gesture—on their part or yours—is really so simple.

Yet, as the group spoke, it became clear that they were distinguishing two very different kinds of limits. There were the limits that you might say arose organically from their knowledge and experience of working with severely troubled people, limits that had grown out of their attempts to understand them and to help them heal. Then there was the other set of limits: those that were imposed from outside, from on high—and when they spoke about these, it was with a deep sense of frustration. These were the limits that in their view existed not so much to help the clients themselves, or the people who work with them, but primarily to protect the institution from litigation. They told me, for example, about the elaborate regulations that surround the transporting of young people—because you need to be able to prove, beyond a shadow of a doubt, that an adult drove a youth from Point A to Point B with adequate supervision, with no unaccountable moments during which someone might have done something for which someone could sue. They told me about the endless documentation that surrounds every move and that takes away from time that could be spent in healing interaction.

My friend Susanna has worked for fifteen years in a state hospital for the criminally insane. She said, "The way I've learned to work with people is to be real with them. That includes allowing them to see my vulnerability. And it also includes the fact that real affection develops for people—yes, even for the criminally insane—when you work with them day in and day out, sometimes for years at a time. But it seems that more and more is getting in the way of my being real with the people I work with. There are so many restrictions. You can't exchange gifts; there can't be exchanges of any kind. And there can't be any touch. The other day I was walking through the grounds and a patient I had worked with for a long time suddenly came up to me. We hadn't seen each other in a long time, and we just spontaneously gave each other a big hug. Inside of me, I knew it was so right. But in the back of my mind was that anxiety: *Maybe someone is watching us.* You could lose your job over something like that."

There it is again: the gaze, the feeling that *maybe someone is watching us*. Hearing Susanna's story, Sonia Beck described how in the treatment center for troubled youth where she works, she has tried to find ways to get out from under this withering gaze. She said, "It seems that more rules keep coming between us and our capacity to make genuine connection with the kids. Increasingly, there's a short-term treatment model in therapy, and so we don't have the luxury of building up a long and deep relationship. And there's that pervasive fear that makes you feel you have to keep a tight rein on what you can allow yourself to express. So more and more, what I try to do in the short time that I have with these kids is to help them make a connection *with themselves*. For example, I've become interested in the power of artistic expression to help them make contact with something real inside of themselves. I had a young man who was obsessed with listening to violent rap music, and I got him to sit down and write his own rap. It was very powerful for him. He didn't know that there was enough inside of him to do that. I'll work with a group of girls on making something with their hands—something out of clay, for example—and you wouldn't believe how hard it is for them to imagine that they could make something of value and that if they did, they could keep it. Always their first impulse is to give it away; they just can't picture themselves as legitimately deserving anything. So I tell them that they can give something away, but first they have to make something they like for themselves. . . . There are so many ways in which we don't have the luxury of touching them, whether physically or emotionally, and so I try to help them to be touched by themselves."

As Sonia spoke, there flashed in my mind a line of graffiti that I had seen years ago in a collection of photographs of the 1968 student uprising in Paris. *Sous les paves, c'est la plage!* Which means: "Underneath the cobblestones, there's a beach!" It suddenly struck me that often when I told people what I was writing about, what I was investigating, there was a certain underground quality in the conversation that followed, the sense of a secret life that pulsed just below a hard and impacted surface. Sometimes it was actually not so far away from the stories reporters tell about visiting countries under oppressive regimes, regimes where they feel watched all the time and have to carefully mind what they say. When I posed the first few questions, I often got a slightly startled look, a wariness, perhaps some nervous laughter. If I pushed a little farther, we might arrive at *This is hard to say.* Farther still—and if the conversation didn't suddenly come to a halt, then often something seemed to bubble up, something that had a life of its own. It was this quality I felt as Sonia spoke about her work. It was as though she was describing a process of tapping into a vibrant and secret life, an irrepressible energy that would find a way to express itself under even quite straitened circumstances.

This underground quality was present, too, in an image that Susanna returned to several times throughout the evening. When she was transferred to a new position at the state hospital, a party was held for her in a room at the "unit" where she had worked for five years. "I opened the door and went inside that room and there were balloons and music and sweet things to eat. There were patients and staff whom I had come to know well. There was so much love in that room. Everyone was so happy. It's rare that we get to have that experience." The image, I find, is rather like the famous duck-rabbit diagram. Look at it one way and it's a celebration of something vibrant and irrepressible, the beach that lies below the cobblestones. Look at it another way and it's a lament. Why should such happiness have to be a rare experience in a closed-off room?

And is there a point where the layer of cobblestones becomes so heavy that it begins to change the very nature of the beach. Is there a point at which the atmospheric anxiety becomes so thick that it begins to alter the very field, the intersubjective "space," that exists in therapeutic encounters, interfering with some of the most delicate and complex aspects of the process of healing?

In "The Innocence of Sexuality," Jonathan Slavin, a psychoanalyst and director of the counseling department at Tufts University, takes up the difficult question of erotic feeling in the therapeutic relationship.[9] With great depth and subtlety, he explores the ways in which, through the therapist's skillful use of "innocent sexuality," a patient can find release from a childhood legacy of sexual feeling that was complicated and overburdened by a parent's need. The paper concludes with a story, brought to him by a therapist in consultation, of a young woman and a very "small" moment that held enormous power for her.

As a girl, this woman's relationship with her father had been intense and deeply enmeshed. One of the ways that she had learned to defuse the intensity in the relationship, her analyst suggested, had been to repress her own sexuality. During a session, the analyst noticed that one of the patient's earrings was lying on the couch. When he picked it up and handed it to her, their hands touched for a moment. He looked away. At the next session, the woman spoke about this moment, wondering aloud why he had looked away. She imagined that he had wanted to protect her from a certain embarrassment, which indeed she had felt, about having lost her earring. At this point, the analyst thought for a moment and decided to tell her that though what she imagined was true, there was something else as well. He had felt moved when their hands touched, and so his looking away had also reflected his sense of the moment's significance.

In the sessions that followed, this tiny incident—the dropped earring, the hands touching, the looking away, the therapist's disclosure—continued to reverberate in ways that were clearly healing for the patient. For the first time in her life, she said, she could imagine the possibility of having a relationship with a man that was not "complicated," that left her feeling freer and less vulnerable than in previous relationships. "I know that what has happened here is not temporary," she told the analyst. Slavin concludes: "Were it not for the analyst's readiness to share something of his own experience of the patient, his muted but nevertheless real sexual experience, and experience of her as a sexual person in the moment when their hands touched, this unfolding of a crucial aspect of the patient's denial and then repossession of her sexual experience might not have occurred."

Muted but real: for the therapist to have shared in this way took great courage. Under the pressure of the vigilant gaze, of the censoring voice that says, "You could lose your job," he risked a moment of authenticity.

Real but muted: what is crucial in the interaction is that he took this risk for his patient out of his understanding of her injury from the past and of her need in the present. He also did so with great sensitivity, in a gesture that was contained within the moment, self-limiting in the sense that it was not an open invitation to escalate or intensify an erotic interaction. In their exploration of the incident, he referred it back to her, to her past and to her work in the present, rather than drawing it toward himself and his own personal need.

In these ways he was able to make the move that was neither too hot nor too cold. He was able to be authentic to his own experience in a way that was "just right" for her—neither too withholding nor too intrusive. Through his willingness to take a risk, to depart—a little—from the totally "safe" stance he might have assumed, he was able to facilitate for her a moment of immense significance. How easy, under the pressure of the withering gaze, it might have been for him to miss this moment. For the withering gaze and the voice that says "I could lose my job" inhibit the willingness to take a risk, even a small risk.

Perhaps even more significant, anxiety can disturb a therapist's mind, making it difficult to attune, with the exquisite sensitivity that was present in this interaction, to the complex needs and history of the patient. What often transpires between a therapist and a patient might be called a form of deep, intersubjective reverie. The patient says something or makes a gesture and the therapist hears the words, sees the gesture, in the context of a whole procession of images that have arisen before, a procession that might include fragments from the patient's dreams and memories as well as moments of interaction from previous sessions, all of which mingle with a host of impressions in the present moment.

Such reverie does not flourish in the Big Brother atmosphere. The withering gaze, the threatening voice can bear down with so much pressure that the therapist is forced, again and again, to do more check-ing in with his own anxiety than with the patient who sits before him and with the flow of images that circulate in the air between them. In the words of one psychotherapist I spoke with, "For me, that sense of a censoring gaze doesn't interfere so much with what I do—with whether or not I put my hand on a patient's shoulder or exchange a hug as we say good-bye—but it interferes with *how I think*. It interferes with my free-dom as a therapist to feel the fullest range of evocations—in mind, in body, in heart—and to parse them out slowly, over time, sifting through them, not prematurely foreclosing the impact through anxiety."[10]

His emphasis on thinking reminds us that therapeutic touch need not be literally physical and that what is crucial in the healing interac-tion is for one human being to be present to another in a way that authentically communicates "I see something deep and essential about who you are. I see you in your separateness and your uniqueness, and I appreciate what I see." For a therapist to extend this form of presence without freighting it with his own need, his own agenda, is the crucial thing, and it requires a degree of skill and sensitivity that, with all the focus on blatant transgressions, we sometimes lose sight of.

Once more, then, we are back to the search for the middle ground. Given that certain guidelines must be in place to protect patients from flagrant violations of the therapeutic relationship, is it possible to maintain an atmosphere that is fluid enough, free enough from outside intrusion, to permit the creativity of true responsiveness? While assuring a basic background level of safety, is it possible to refrain from interfering with the ability of sensitive, highly trained and experienced people—whether teachers, counselors, or therapists—to make the moves that seem right to them?

In Susanna's case, the right move was a spontaneous hug delivered to a client whose life she had shared, day in and day out, for years. In other cases, the right move is something much more measured and subtle, what one therapist I spoke with called "a homeopathic dose of eros." Such a dose might not involve an act of physical touching at all, but rather, a certain quality of exquisitely attuned attention that allows one human being to feel profoundly exposed before another and in that exposure to feel—in a safe way—profoundly accepted, embraced.

In the very use of the word "homeopathic," there is a reminder of how many models of healing there are. Along with that earlier litany, then, for the vanishing life-forms, there is another that has a place here, one that represents a different kind of remembering. For to remember that there are many ways of healing can move us out of nostalgic sadness toward something more hopeful, and more forward-looking.

Gathering examples of different kinds of solutions is an expansive approach, one that moves in the direction of waxing, not waning, and that frees us from the grip of the surgical/antiseptic dyad. It's an approach that can lead us away from lamenting the lost touch to discovering new ways for touch—whether in its subtlest or most literal forms—to heal the violations of touch. In its very expansiveness, in its multiplicity and fertility, this is an erotic approach to healing the wounds of eros, a way to wash ashes with ashes.

4

TENDING THE SMALL

✎

LIKE ALICE IN Wonderland, who grew small and then big and then small again, to write about the eros of parenthood is to encounter a constantly shifting sense of scale, one in which the public and private, the macro and micro, dimensions of life not only alternate with, but permeate, one another.

One moment we're in a small apartment where a father, gazing at his son in the bathtub, begins a sentence with, "When I look at Rubin lolling naked in the tub—" and ends it with, "This is hard to say." The next moment we're in a big city day-care center where a toddler has collapsed howling on the floor. A day-care aide is bending over him, saying comforting things and patting him on the back. "He's beside himself," she murmurs to herself, or "He's falling apart," and the very words express her sense that he's gone over the brink of what he can contain within himself. She has years of experience in working with children, and a deep familiarity with this particular child, but she doesn't dare do the one thing that she feels would really calm him: pick him up and rock him in her arms.

It used to be that the model for good institutional care was a place that was "like home," but now the metaphor begins to work in the opposite way. "What if someone were watching us?" says the counselor, having shared a spontaneous hug with a client on the state hospital grounds. "You could lose your job for something like that," she explains. "It's actually my job to wash his penis!" exclaims the mother, diapering her baby son. The thought amuses her, but there's a definite edge to it, as if she might need to appease someone or put her case before a disapproving judge—a judge who might take her job away. The well-run institution becomes the one most permeated by the vigilant gaze, and the home that is safe for its children becomes equally permeated. Indeed, the vigilant gaze and the disapproving judge may emerge in the form of the child herself, trained at school to be a traffic cop in her own tub, bellowing "Red light!" to her startled grandmother.

Nowhere, it seems, is it currently more true that "the personal is political" than when we enter the territory of eros and children. And nowhere, it seems, is it more difficult to find a gauge for the "just right" than when we ask, "What form of monitoring is appropriate within the small and intimate frame of the family versus the wider institutional sphere?" Like so many questions that arise in this territory, this one is difficult not only because of its complexity, but because the stakes are so high. In the name of the family's inviolate privacy, terrible things have happened—mostly to women and children. Yet when the family is made too permeable to outside influence, there are other costs, which it has been the focus of this book to explore.

Whether the vigilant gaze beats down on the home or the institution, it presents the same alibi: extremity. The extreme acts of some individuals create a situation of extreme urgency, this alibi goes, necessitating an intrusion into the ordinary lives of all of us. As one mother told me, "My sons run around naked. I love to grab their little tushies—but I've become self-conscious. I hear this fearful voice inside me; it's a voice based on how others have violated their children. It's as though *they*, the people who have violated their children, provide the guidelines. We've given them so much power."

When a state of emergency can be declared, the reward is clarity—a strange kind of clarity that though greatly reinforcing some boundaries ("No gifts! No exchanges of any kind! No hugs!"), weakens certain others. Above all, the boundary between public and private is weakened; the better to allow that vigilant gaze to permeate the home and shore up the boundaries. . . . "More and more, an anxiety from outside seeps in," a mother says. "I don't even know whose anxiety it is. . . ." Resonating in her words is what might be called a not-so-beneficent boundary loss, an invasion of the small space of her family's most intimate life by the same big cloud of atmospheric anxiety that makes the counselor fear lest someone see her offering a client a hug on state hospital grounds.

If it's extremity, a climate of emergency, that leads to the not so beneficent boundary loss, what if we tried a different approach to the question of scale? What if rather than focusing so intensely on the extreme actions that provide the rationale for our big and invasive public solutions, we focused on the roots of these actions? Then we might discover a very different kind of shift in dimension, one that reveals the great power of the small.

Who are they, those who do extreme things to children and thereby create a climate of emergency for all of us? "They," of course, are many different people. The person who exposes himself to a child is different from the one who causes her bodily harm; the habitual pedophile is different from the close relative who succumbs to a single incestuous relationship, and so on. And each emerges from a different life-history. There is one constant strand, however, that runs throughout any excavation into the origins of child abuse. More often than not, those who abuse children are people who suffered some serious form of abuse or deprivation in their own early life.[11]

Not all children who suffered such injury grow up to inflict it on others. Indeed, for some, the experience of their own childhood suffering serves as a powerful incentive to break the pattern. But to a significant degree, those who do abuse children—whether as strangers or as family members—did not receive adequate care when they themselves were children. In some combination or another, they experienced one or all of the following: they were physically injured or sexually violated by their caregivers; they were deprived of affection and encouragement; their basic needs—for food, shelter, love, stability, guidance—were neglected. In the words of Brandt F. Steele, M.D., "Probably only about one-fourth of all people abused as children grow up to be diagnosed as abusers. . . . On the other hand, it is rare for a child-care professional to see anyone who has maltreated children who does not give a personal history of significant neglect, with or without accompanying abuse, in his or her own childhood."[12]

This, then, is the broad outline of the pattern: inside the abusive adult we find an abused or a neglected child. When looked at more closely, the pattern seems like one of those Russian wooden "nested" dolls, and the small opens up to the smaller and smaller. . . .

Particularly when it comes to violence, there have been dramatic discoveries in recent years—dramatic in their very subtlety. As if someone had handed us a powerful microscope, we are able to look far-ther and farther back into the histories of violent individuals and to peer with ever more discernment into the network of contributing fac-tors. Increasingly, what emerges in these histories is a complex pattern of damage beginning in earliest life, indeed often beginning in utero. Complicated pregnancies, difficult births, genetic anomalies, neurolog-ical malfunctioning, and other physical problems present at birth, head injuries in early life—to different degrees and in different combina-tions, these are recurring elements.

When a baby, already to some degree abnormally fragile, is born into a chaotic, violent, or very deprived environment, the stage is set for later difficulties. In a landmark study of the origins of violent behavior, the distinguished criminologist Dorothy Lewis traced adult criminal violence back to the interaction of two or more internal fac-tors (for example, cognitive and/or neuropsychiatric deficits) with early negative family circumstances. Summarizing such research, authors Robin Karr-Morse and Meredith S. Wiley write: " As we begin to discover the previously unimaginable impact of the smallest insult to the brain at crucial times in development, we are beginning to see that much of what we have formerly written off as unknowable in ori-gin, and therefore unchangeable, can and must be prevented."[13]

Of all forms of child abuse, the most insidious is psychological abuse: words and behaviors that while not physically or sexually violat-ing the child's boundaries, communicate to the child "You are unloved. You are unwanted. You are bad." Short of physical abuse leading to death, psychological abuse on the part of a parent is the most devastat-ing form of child abuse.[14] It generally accompanies other forms of abuse, rendering them even more traumatic and making children more vulnerable to yet other forms of abuse. Reviewing the research on child abuse and neglect, Marla Brassard, Ph.D., and David B. Hardy, a statistical consultant, write: "This research suggests that it is the psychological concomitants, more than the severity of the acts themselves, that constitute the real trauma and are responsible for the damaging consequences of physical abuse, sexual abuse, and neglect."[15]

A child who has grown up believing "I am worthless. No one cares about me" is more likely to become the victim of an act of physical or sexual abuse than the child who has grown up with the self-confidence that healthy parental love bestows.[16] He is also more likely to become the perpetrator of such acts. And children who have come to believe they are worthless are more likely than their counterparts to transmit that message to their children.[17]

Robin Karr-Morse and Meredith S. Wiley write:

> The interactive process most protective against violent behavior begins in the first year after birth: the formation of a secure attachment relationship with a primary caregiver. Here in one relationship lies the foundation of three key protective factors that mitigate against later aggression: the learning of empathy or emotional attachment to others; the opportunity to learn to control and balance feelings, especially those that can be destructive; and the opportunity to develop capacities for higher levels of cognitive processing.[18]

Of all the negative factors to which a tiny human being can be exposed, lack of affection is among the most powerful. This has been relatively common knowledge since the foundlings who "withered" in institutions were described some fifty years ago, but now in this category too, we can observe the process and its consequences at a much subtler level. Using "tiny units of behavior: reciprocal eye contact, vocalizations for babies and mothers, a variety of touches and voice tones," it is possible to discern a lack of positive attunement in the earliest interactions between mother and child that in combination with other negative factors, puts a child at high risk for later delinquent and criminal activity.[19]

The absence of affection acts upon the growing human self as would a toxic chemical, mercury, or plutonium. The comparison is not "merely" metaphorical; among recent discoveries is the fact that the absence of affectionate care in early life affects the human brain at a cellular level in ways that can permanently alter its structure—indeed, sometimes even altering the very genes that will be transmitted to the next generation of children.[20]

The new research is both awe-inspiring in its confirmation of the vital necessity of affection and frightening in its revelation of human vulnerability. For just as a child whose brain is not exposed to language before a certain time will never be able to acquire an adequate grasp of language, so it appears that there is a crucial "window" during which the human brain takes shape emotionally. Just as language activity is centered in a certain region of the brain, so is the processing of emotion. If this region is not stimulated or it receives damaging stimulation in early life—whether through the unresponsiveness of a depressed parent, or the unpredictable or violent responses of another—it appears that the consequences are profound and long-lasting. The ability to self-comfort, to control impulses and regulate powerful feeling, and above all, the ability to empathize with others—these vital emotional skills need to be learned in earliest life, and when they are not, the very regions of the brain from which they emanate may be permanently damaged.

Paradoxically, even as we become more discerning as to the smallest seeds of dangerous behavior, the broad societal response to this behavior has become less discerning. In responding to crime, we are taking ever broader strokes, making ever fewer distinctions. Increasingly, juveniles are being punished as adults. Increasingly, minor crimes are being punished as though they were major. With the three-strikes law in California, someone who steals on three different occasions is as liable for life imprisonment as is a three-time murderer.

Even as we understand with greater precision that those who injure others are, overwhelmingly, people who have sustained multiple injuries themselves as babies and young children, we have become more punitive in our response. "No," says a mother to the little neighbor who has rung her doorbell in a *New Yorker* cartoon. Why can't her son come have some fun? Because "Danny's on death row."[21] Even as we become more aware of "the little things" that interact to lay the ground for dangerously extreme behavior—damage to the fetus in utero, lack of affection in early life, learning disabilities manifest in preschool—we choose to put our focus at the other end of the scale, pouring far more resources into the criminal justice system than into preventive and supportive care for parents and young children. Imprisoning and executing diminish the number of criminals out on the streets and satisfy the desire for revenge, but they do not address the seeds of dangerous behavior, and it is from those seeds that danger grows.

And this brings me back to my friend Jane (last seen in "I Looked Into Her Eyes"), who was giving her howling two-year-old daughter a bath.

Jane does not have a violent proclivity, but in the scene she described, she was about to "lose it," to lose it in the way that most of us lose it when we lose it, which is to regress to what we have known, to what we have lived, to whatever represents for us the most familiar, most primitive, fallback response to stress, the response that seems imprinted in our very brains, whether we reach out and hit, yell damning words, collapse into helpless frustration ourselves, or get up and walk out of the room, leaving the child to howl alone.

What kept her from going over her brink?

She looked into her child's eyes and she felt a pain in her heart.

She felt her child's pain in her own heart, but she did not become her child, nor did she collapse into her own childhood self. She saw her child in the tub as separate from herself, a separate little person with her own needs. Feeling her child's pain as her own, she was simultaneously able to remain a parent.

This is empathy. Empathy understood not as fusion, but as the ability to feel another's pain in one's own heart while seeing the other as another, and thus avoid collapsing into identification. "Identification," it is said, "is being, not seeing." Unconscious activity follows from identification, and is part of the mechanism that transmits child abuse from one generation to the next. In the words of Gail Ryan, of the Kempe National Center for the Prevention and Treatment of Child Abuse and Neglect:

> Empathy [is] the ability to recognize the cues of others which indicate what they are needing or experiencing, even when those needs and experiences are different from one's own. The lack of empathy (failure to perceive harm to the victim) and lack of accountability (avoidance of accurate attributions of personal responsibility) are ultimately the most significant deficits of abusers. Empathic foresight (the ability to imagine the impact of one's behavior on another before making a decision to act) and personal accountability are the highest deterrents to abusive actions . . .[22]

When my other friend, the man who had himself been abused as a child, rose in fury to yank his howling daughter from her high chair, he was at great risk of collapsing into identification with her and of simply repeating what he himself had experienced as a child. But he didn't. He looked into her eyes and saw her pain. He felt it as his own, but he also saw her as separate from himself, a separate little person with her own huge pain, her own terror and humiliation. He set her down. He walked out of the room and said to himself, *That will never happen again.*

Isn't this the moment we need to penetrate with the light of understanding? Aren't these the questions we need to ask: What permits such a moment? What encourages such a moment? What enables one parent, himself abused as a child, to arrive at such a moment despite the odds? For this is the moment that does not happen when a child is abused. It is this missing moment—the moment of feeling the child's pain while seeing the child as separate, with needs, longing, desires of its own—that permits all manner of abuse. And from this abuse spring the extreme actions that through the fear they engender and the reactive solutions they inspire, increasingly structure our experience of both public and private life.

What if, by using the knowledge we already have, we were to devote more of our time, energy, and resources into understanding *this* gaze—the gaze of an adult into a child's eyes—that brings release from suffering? This might bring us a measure of relief from the other gaze, the vigilant and invasive gaze that bears down not only in the prison yard and the state hospital grounds, but in the day-care center and the home where a father is bathing his son. It might also lead the way to a very different form of intervention than that which occurs when we wait to respond in rage and terror to the big stories, the full-blown horrors, that sustain the climate of emergency. Prenatal care, support for parents of young children, preventive care for "at risk" families, a serious commitment to finding ways to address the complex and recalcitrant nature of psychological abuse, further research into the phenomenon of "resiliency"—these are forms of intervention that in their combination of subtlety and generosity, might well be considered a form of beneficent boundary loss.

Tending to the small, and the smaller and smaller, we might find that we had broken through some very huge barriers indeed.

5

DILATION

"THEIR EYES DARKEN with kindness" is one of my favorite lines from the poem "The Blessing," by James Wright.[23] The eyes in the poem belong to two horses, and though I know little about horses, the line has always held a powerful resonance for me. First there is the reversal of the cliché that inexorably associates anything good with what is bright. But beyond the beautiful surprise of the pairing of darkness and kindness, there is something about the image that has always seemed quite accurate to me in a literal way.

Years after I first encountered the poem, I came across research on "the biology of love" that confirmed my impression. In his book *The Human Animal*, the anthropologist Desmond Morris writes:

> One way in which we can find out how our new companion is reacting towards us is to prolong our periods of close proximity gazing. During the early stages of courtship, the eyes transmit vital signals. If we stare closely enough, we can detect the degree of pupil dilation as they look back at us. Since the pupils expand slightly more than usual when they see something they like, we can tell whether we are 'being liked' or not. If our companion's eyes show huge, black pupils, we know that they find us appealing and that the next stage in our courtship sequence will probably meet with success. If, on the other hand, the pupils shrink to pin-points when we gaze closely at our companion's face, we might as well give up.[24]

As the eyes of lovers darken when they gaze into each other's eyes, so do the eyes of parents darken when they gaze at their babies. Indeed, most women's eyes darken when they look at any baby. Among men, it is those who are the fathers of small children themselves whose pupils will dilate at the sight of a baby.[25]

There is a connection, then—at a most elemental, even cellular, level—between widening, spreading, expanding, and love. (And don't we readily think of eyes as narrowing with hatred or suspicion?)

"But pupil dilation is merely a phenomenon of attention," a well-known scientifically inclined writer said to me, as if thereby dismissing the connection. He frequently writes about children, and I felt that he was uneasy about the link that I was drawing between the parent-child gaze and that of lovers.

"Merely"? There are many forms of attention, of course—some beneficent, and some not—but isn't attention a primary ingredient of love? We bestow our attention on those we love, and we long for attention from them. The very word *attention* carries the notion of expansion within it, for it derives from the root word *tendere*, meaning "to stretch." *Tender* is a related word, as are the root words to "tend" and to "attend." Even when we talk about relatively mundane acts of kindness, we use expressions such as "She really extended herself for him," or "He went out of his way for her." There is something at the root of caring for another that involves stretching, an expansion of boundaries.

The ultimate act of stretching for another is the act of giving birth. There are few numbers as momentous as those that announce the centimeters of dilation during labor. For many women, the experience of birth is that of being taken to an extreme of openness—so much so that there is a fear of bursting apart. And though one doesn't break apart, there is often tearing, the need to be sewn up—confirming the sense of having opened beyond the capacity to open. A midwife told me once she'd attended the home birth of a woman from one of the South Sea islands. When the woman went into labor, her family rushed about the house, opening everything that could be opened: boxes, drawers, windows, doors.

What brings about the preposterous expansion of birth is, of course, contraction. The whole rhythm of birth is one of contraction and expansion. With each powerful contraction of the uterus, the cervix is coaxed into opening a little wider.

The sexual act itself is also a rhythm of expansion and contraction. In both men and women, it is the swelling of blood vessels in the sexual organs during arousal that leads to the powerful rhythmic contractions of orgasm. And in the midst of the contractions of orgasm, as in childbirth, there is the experience of expansion beyond limits. *Petit mort*, the French say: "little death." In this little death, the boundaries of one's own separate skin are shed, and so for a few moments, are the narrow straits of ordinary consciousness.

It's a terrible truth that the human capacity to break the boundaries can manifest itself as violation, as wounding, and even as destroying, the integrity of another's being. But there is a going beyond boundaries that lies at the heart of love, of true caring for others. There is a breaking out of one's own skin that is linked to the very meaning of ecstasy—*ec/stasis*: "standing outside." From the minute movement of the pupils darkening with kindness, widening with attention, to the extreme sensation of breaking open at the peak of sexual love or childbirth, the movement of expansion beyond boundaries is quintessential to human connection.

Such expansion always carries an element of danger with it. A mother looks too long, too intently, into her baby's eyes, flooding him with her presence. A lover opens his heart, and not only delight, but grief, walk in the door. There are so many ways in which love can go wrong and contact become injury. No wonder that the impulse to shore up the boundaries, to wall off, seal up, bind tight, is strong. It's what led Sleeping Beauty's parents to lock a certain door in their castle and to destroy all needles in the kingdom. Wishing to keep their beautiful daughter safe and inviolate, they vowed that nothing should pierce her delicate skin. But she and the needle found each other—so that her prince, in time, could find her. It's a quiver of arrows that Eros carries, not a pot of glue, for love requires a piercing-open.

Yet even as we are pierced and thrown open, even in the very peak

of peak experiences, there is an underlying reality of measure and proportion. Expansion and contraction exist in alternation. The experiences themselves are limited in time. The body does not break open;
the lovers do not merge forever into one flesh. Our eyes come with eyelids, and even a newborn, flooded with his mother's gaze, can shut his
eyes and turn his head. There is a sense of measure, of proportion, that
is rooted in our very bodies.

This sense of measure is deeply embodied, but it is also sustained
by one of the unique gifts of human consciousness: the ability to imagine. For in the act of imagining, and in the expression of what we imagine, we can play at the very edge of boundary loss. Here, at this edge,
we can find release for our most ecstatic impulses without violating
anyone or anything.

James Wright's poem "The Blessing" begins with an acute awareness of boundaries: a man must pull off the freeway to discover the
horses in the meadow, he must get out of his car and step over the
barbed wire to come closer. Coming closer, he at first feels achingly
separate from the horses and from the love they bear for one another.
They appear to exist in a tender universe of two from which he is
excluded.

But then something changes. It's as if the speaker allowed his open
eyes to widen, to let his own being extend and mingle with the atmosphere that surrounds the horses. The poem ends with these words:

> I suddenly realize that if I stepped out of my body
> I would break into blossom.

Here it is again, the imagined possibility, the conditional tense,
the *if*—

If I stepped out of my body, the poet says—but he doesn't, and he
doesn't need to. For in such an expression of ecstatic longing, which
stays on *this* side of the edge, there is already a breaking into blossom.
The act of imagination, and the exclamation itself are already a kind of
blossoming, an overflowing, a breaking-out. A breaking-out that does
not violate, that leaves whole. Having become, for a moment, both

horse and blossom, field and sunset, the man remains a man who will get back inside the small space of his metal car.

"Oh, I could eat you!" the mother says—but she doesn't. She lets the shudder pass through her body and lays the baby back down in his crib. Expansion, contraction. Not one, not two. Not two, not one.

myself. Except for the awareness of dissolving, which remained,
[m]yself dissolve utterly. There was great joy in that moment, and
[sen]se of seeing directly into the face of who it is we really are, with-
[scr]eens. I would have liked to remain inside that moment, but I
[couldn']t. It passed into another moment; I told myself, "I'd better eat
[be] hungry later," and I finished my soup, washed my bowl and sil-
[ver] and returned to the place that had my name on it in the med-
[itation] hall.

[At] that time, I wasn't yet a mother, but the moment was similar to
[the mo]ment of pulling the plug from the socket, that moment when
[who]le world became a child's mouth and a mother's breast. There
[is some]thing at the heart of the eros of parenthood that is truly radi-
[cal—ra]dical in its literal sense of *root*, and radical in the sense of its
[potenti]ally transforming power. What if we were to tap the power of
[bou]ndary loss that lies at the root of each of us? The vision fades,
[the scr]eens return, but it remains true that *everyone is either the child of*
[a paren]t or the parent of a child or both. Even the most unwanted child
[on]ce held by his mother's body, which made itself over for him.
[Fo]r at least a moment, as he emerged from her body, her own
[body b]roke open to give birth to him, and he filled the whole world.

[Tw]o sunburnt, dusty girls tramp along a summer road. Virginia's
[car]arrow and she sees them as *other*—and in their otherness, as
[coars]e, awkward, self-assertive. Then, for a moment, the screens fall
[away.] The door that "shut(s) people off from our sympathies" opens,
[the] boundaries dissolve. Her eyes widen, darkening with kindness,
[for] a moment, she sees these two human beings in that other way,
[the wa]y a mother or a father, eyes widening, sees the baby who burst
[throug]h the opening they made in their lives.

6

BOUNDARY LOSS

TOWARD THE END of my pregnancy, I found myself in the grip of a
strange compulsion. Though the day was hot and my belly huge, I
heaved myself the six long blocks to the public library and came home
with a pile of books on the Middle East. In those last two weeks before
the birth, even as I experienced the signs of imminent labor—the
waves of tightening in the abdomen, the mix of acute cellular vigilance
and overwhelming drowsiness, the impossibility of getting comfortable
on any surface, in any position whatsoever—I ate and slept and read
about Lebanon, Israel, Jordan, the Palestinians, about borders, ethnic
hatreds, civil wars. . . .

Only a short while before my reading binge, I'd been immersed in
an irresistible and very classic form of nesting. With manic intensity,
I'd painted a great many things in my house—walls, sills, chairs, a toy
box, a lamp—a rosy peach the color of women's thighs and babies'
rumps by Rubens. But what had come over me now could only be
described as anti-nesting. I read with a mysterious, and even desperate,
necessity, making charts of the various factions and tragic milestones,
the assassinations, the hostage-takings, the coups and bombings. If
anyone had asked me "Why?" I would have told them, "Because it's my
last chance in a long time to understand the world."

Then my daughter was born, and all the factions fell away. She was
all there was. As she slept beside me the morning after her birth, I
leaned out of my hospital bed to pull the plug out of a socket, and in
that moment, I felt a rush of sadness for the socket. For in that

moment the socket was a mouth and the plug was a nipple, and everything in the world was either a mouth or a nipple, hunger or food, need or fulfillment.

In the days that followed, my field of vision gradually expanded around the small circle of mouth and milk. For a few days, everyone I saw was either a head or an opening that had made way for a head. If I saw a tall, distinguished-looking man talking on the television in elegant and lightly accented English about the NATO alliance, I would think to myself "What a large head he has," and a wave of feeling would move through me for his mother, whom I could see as though she were there before my eyes: a young girl lying on a cot in a hallway in Amsterdam, in 1944 or so, bombs falling in the city around her, their sound obliterated as someone with their hand on her sweating forehead says to her, " *Drukken!*" ("Push!").

From head and opening, my circle of vision grew to encompass mother and child, then parent and child, and I was struck by what seemed to me the blinding truth, a truth I'd never seen before, that *everyone is either the child of a parent or the parent of a child, or both.* I experienced this not as an idea, but as an immediate perception so that I could not look at an individual human being without perceiving at the same time a parent or a child, as if everyone were at least a double image, everyone pregnant, in a sense, with someone else.

From this vantage point, violence and war were not even wrong, they were simply impossible, absurd. For the value of a single human life was not an abstract concept; it was the most tangible reality, a reality borne in my own flesh and as apparent to the naked eye as the color of a person's hair or skin, or the size and shape of his body.

This vision—with its utter clarity and simplicity—happened to crystallize for me from up close, in a condition of extreme nearness, at the moment I reached to pull a plug from a socket. But it is identical in essence to visions that others have had from a vast distance. When the astronaut Russell Schweickart was spinning in outer space, he saw our small blue planet floating in its vast sea of darkness, and saw simultaneously the fragility and the preciousness of the earth and all its inhabitants:

The contrast between that bright blu tree ornament and the black sky, tha the size and significance of it really small and so fragile, such a precious lit that you can block it out with your everything that means anything to yo and death and birth and love, tears and little blue-and-white spot out there wh your thumb.[26]

The intensity of such visions fades. The the mother comes home from the hospital v life with its mix of fatigue, irritability, exh resumes. It is necessary that the intensity of is hard to navigate the sphere of daily life if plug from a socket. Even the Jains—wearin and clearing a path through the grass whe inhale or trample insects—have to admit th callousness, is necessary in order to survive.

In 1926, Virginia Woolf recorded in her

Two resolute, sunburnt, dusty girls in je with packs on their backs, city clerks o along the road in the hot sunshine of once throws up a screen, which condem in every way angular, awkward, and self is a great mistake. These screens shut m making habit, though, is so universal tha our sanity. If we had not this device fo from our sympathies, we might dissolve would be impossible.[27]

We might dissolve utterly, she writes. Once tation retreat, I experienced such intense mouths of the faces opening and closing arour

to feed
I felt m
the sen
out scr
couldn
or I'll b
verwar
itation

At
the mo
the wh
is some
cal—ra
potenti
the bo
the scr
*a paren
was or
And f
being

Tw
eyes n
angula
away.
and th
and fo
the wa
throug

7

TIME OVERFLOWING

"I HAVE NEVER wanted to freeze my children," my friend Eleanor said to me severely the other day. Eleanor is in her sixties, she has raised five children and is a grandmother several times over, and if Botticelli had painted "Inverna" as he painted "Primavera," he could have used Eleanor as his model. There is something wintry in her large blue eyes and flowing white hair, but there is nothing cold about Eleanor. She can often be found in the center of a throng of schoolchildren, singing and playing her guitar. Her garden is lush and overflowing and her house is full of animals, including a large dog, several cats, and a chicken that has free range of the furniture. She has enormous patience for children and animals, but not much for certain adult frailties, and sometimes—as in the conversation about freezing children—she snaps in exasperation.

I had remarked on how often this image, or one like it, seemed to crop up in my conversations with parents. Eleanor felt there was something "anti-life" in this impulse, and I could understand why. Even when comically expressed, a parent's desire for stasis does tend to carry an edge of violence. "Why don't we just shellac her now?" my husband used to ask me when Ariel was small. And once the father of a sixteen-year-old boy confessed to me, "Sometimes I have this fantasy: I creep into his room at night, and I glue all his stuffed animals to him. That way, when he wakes up in the morning, he'll be too embarrassed to ever leave me."

Still, there is something in the impulse that even as it wishes to go against the nature of things, seems to me utterly natural. For the intensity of parental attachment and the fact that this attachment is to a being who is in a continual state of radical transformation—a state that never stops from the moment of conception until the child grows up and leaves home, never stops—parenthood is among the most powerful of all possible initiations into the relentlessly fleeting nature of time. As a child, I never understood why grown-ups carried on so much about "How you've grown!" I have no trouble understanding now. For to experience how quickly, and in what feels like the briefest parenthesis in an adult's life, a child goes from speck of flesh to an upright, fully conscious being is dizzying. It is dizzying in a strangely sobering way, because it forces us to see our own lives *as* this parenthesis, *as* the brief background interval from which the young emerge and take off into the future. No wonder that parents feel impelled to solidify and fetishize certain emblems of childhood: to bronze the baby's shoes, to put a lock of hair under glass, to think longingly of substances that bind and preserve, like glue and shellac. . . .

Yet, simultaneously, parenthood is an initiation into a radically different experience of time—an experience not of time's hyper-fleeting linearity, but of its fluid, recursive, even circular, quality. This experience begins early; already, caring for her first baby, a mother opens her mouth and hears voices, looks in the mirror and sees faces. She finds gestures coming out of herself that she didn't even know were there. It's as though these voices, faces, and gestures had been latent in a gland that had stored them up and was now secreting them from an ancient reservoir of intonations, melodies, ways of soothing, teasing, scolding. I didn't even know I remembered the words to "Slide down my rain barrel"—my mother's favorite childhood song from the 1930's—until one spring afternoon when I found myself, with stroller and umbrella, singing them to Ariel.

Remembering, reliving, repetition, return; the little word "re" is deeply embedded in the experience of parenting. It meant very little to me as a child to have my great-great-aunts exclaim over how much I resembled their sister Esther, who had died long before I was born. But now I think of how amazing it must feel to be in your seventies and encounter in the face of a young niece in California the face of your favorite sister, born in Russia, whom you lost some thirty years ago.

This retroactive understanding, my belated empathy for my aunts' amazement, is itself a feature of fluid familial time. Looking at photographs of her mother as a young woman, a friend of mine exclaimed, "My bossy mother! Look at how unsure of herself she was!" Sometimes, out of the blue, there is a sudden, and more forgiving, revision of a past experience. When a friend of mine was a little boy, his Uncle Louie always used to accuse him of stealing his cigarettes. Only a few years ago, my friend—who is now fifty—woke up one morning with the realization that his uncle had been teasing! A grudge of forty years dissolved in a single moment.

Sometimes, alas, the backward look is deeply disillusioning, and the grudge retroactive—but this, too, is a kind of time-travel. A woman realizes that the reason she had so many medical emergencies as a child and grew to think of herself as an invalid was that her mother was having an affair with the pediatrician, which necessitated his urgent house calls. A man looks back and suddenly sees the "nice ladies" that his father always invited to his childhood birthday parties in a different light—a light in which he includes his mother who, in her complicity, always urged him to be "nice" to the "nice ladies."

At other times, the very disillusionment, if not too drastic or acute, can itself turn into a form of empathy. When I was young, I thought that to be an adult meant to be completely flush with what one was—a mother, a teacher, a bus driver, a nurse. Self-doubt, insecurity, the longing to be something other, something different from oneself: these, I thought, were the province of the young. Now I can look back and realize that an adult whom I took so be so firmly rooted in her role was actually struggling—just as my friends and I struggle now. It's as though when I look back, I catch a forest of great spreading oaks quavering like poplars. And suddenly I understand in a different way the cutting remark, the pained glance, the dismissive gesture I've remembered all these years.

There's a poem by Philip Levine I've always loved, "The Secret of

Their Voices," in which the poet takes himself back to an ordinary morning from his childhood in Detroit.[28] He reenters the room in which his parents rise and get themselves ready for the day's work at the automobile factory. As if for the first time realizing what it must have meant to bear the double burden of work and parenting, he asks:

> If they left,
> whose hand cupped
> my forehead when I lay
> in fever? Who moaned,
> help me, help me?
> Who lay full length beside me, belted and all,
> and let his tears
> pour over my hands . . . ?

The poem ends with the exclamation, "Tell me! Tell me! I would have helped!" And what has always struck me about this line is the urgency with which it expresses an empathy that can come only *when it is too late*. For by the time the child is capable of having such an insight, he has long since left that room where the father woke and pulled on his socks and the mother sang to herself "Roses are blooming in Picardee . . ." as they dressed in preparation for the day's work.

But *is* it "too late"? Perhaps in the intensity of the grown son's longing, in the urgency of his desire to help, there is, in fact, something that *is* helped, something that *is* healed. Perhaps the eros that exists between parents and children really does overflow what we normally take to be the boundaries of time.

My friends who've lost a parent have let me know just how it is that the relationship continues to unfold even after the parent's death—not simply as a gathering of memories, but as a relationship capable of flaring into presence. My mother one day found herself compelled to make a certain kind of cake, a yellow cake with chocolate frosting, and not until she had sat down and devoured half of it (an unusual behavior for my mother, who's not at all given to bingeing), did she realize:

September twenty-fourth. It was her mother's birthday, and she had made her mother's favorite cake. She told me that it had suddenly seemed like a marvelous joke that they were sharing together and that—no less than a pregnant woman—she had felt herself, quite literally, to be *eating for two.*

There are also the dreams that have the quality of visitations and that actually further the relationship between parent and child. In these dreams, it is very much as if something new had transpired, as if there had finally been the talk that one needed to have, or as if the letter one needed to receive had finally arrived—sometimes long after a parent has died. My friend Kathryn's father had never accepted or encouraged her love for music, which he regarded as an impractical waste. Some months after his death, he came to her in a dream. She was in a canoe in the middle of the lake at their summer cottage, and he got into another canoe, paddled out alongside her and handed her a golden flute. She put the flute to her lips, and a most beautiful music came pouring out, sending waves of sound rippling over the lake. Her father beamed at her.

The writer Barbara Baer told me that she had been far way in New Zealand when her mother died very suddenly, before Barbara had a chance to say good-bye to her. What added immeasurably to Barbara's grief was that in the last hours before she left for New Zealand, she had rushed around "wasting time with insignificant errands" when she might have been sitting and talking with her mother. On Christmas day, she had tried to call her mother from New Zealand, but the call never got through and her mother died not long afterward. Some time after her mother's death, Barbara had a dream in which her mother appeared, stood next to her and told her *It's all right.* In the dream, her mother was forty—the age that Barbara herself was at the time—which Barbara knew, even in the dream, was "impossible." Impossible—and yet this simultaneity must have been part of what was so comforting about the dream. Not only was the mother restored to her younger, more robust self, but she emerged as a kind of twin, as a double presence of Barbara herself, rather than only and always as a grieved absence. Barbara told me, "I felt so completely visited by that dream. And the pain I had about not having properly said good-bye, not having been with her, vanished. That was ten years ago, and I never had another dream like that. It was so vivid that for days afterward, I really didn't even live in my own skin."

Permission. Forgiveness. These are two qualities that parents and children bestow upon one another, even after death.

In his book *The Politics of the Family*, the psychoanalyst R.D. Laing describes a patient of his as being "a sort of mausoleum, a haunted graveyard in which the ghosts of several generations still walked. . . ."[29] I remember that when I first encountered that description, it made me profoundly uncomfortable—as though a young man's body, as though all of our bodies, housed portions of the dead. But now I see it in a different way. I think not so much of the carcasses, the fossilized remains of familial patterns, but rather, of knots of suffering. Knots of suffering, passed—not intentionally, but for the most part, out of deep unconsciousness—from one generation to the next. And if this suffering is not dead but alive, not inert but an active ingredient, then perhaps it is not such a leap to imagine that it can be acted upon, it can be changed, diminished, healed.

When I was eighteen, a monk from Thailand came to my college and, wrapped in his saffron robe in a cold dormitory basement in Ohio, taught a small group of us how to meditate. I have followed the practice ever since, and sometimes as I sit cross-legged on my cushion, I feel that my grandfather is with me, though he has been dead for thirty-seven years and while alive, would never have been seen in such a posture.

Having been desperately poor as a child, my grandfather vowed that when he grew up, he would become rich. It was a goal that he eventually attained, and by the time I was born, he and my grandmother lived in a large house and were surrounded by many beautiful objects. I own the copy of the *Tao Te Ching* that my grandfather was reading in the last months of his life, and it is full of his underlinings. Wherever there is a reference to wealth not bringing happiness, his pencil strokes are particularly strong and emphatic. Knowing how weak he was in his final illness, it makes me sad to see the energy contained in those strokes, to think that with the last sparks of his life, he was repudiating his life's goal. And yet, as I sit cross-legged on my cushion, following a practice whose roots include the *Tao Te Ching*, there is a way in which I can sometimes feel a movement in two directions of time. It's as though a kind of gravitational pull from my grandfather's life moves through my own practice, while at the same time, there is something that flows backward and helps to soften his self-repudiation, to further something that he was unable to further for himself.

Do such notions seem elaborate or superstitious? There are simpler examples. Sometimes I look at my thirteen-year-old daughter and all of a sudden I can feel in a certain spot on my cheek the damp warmth of the moment when they first handed her to me in the hospital and I put my cheek against her cheek. As my mother wrote to me recently, along with a sketch she had done of me as a teenager holding my baby sister, "I think our children are the only people whose many selves, from infancy onward, we love simultaneously throughout their lives." (And now suddenly, writing this, I remember the day when my sister, at six, asked my mother, "Where did we live before I was born?" Folding her own not-yet-existing self into the "we," she had no doubts about the fullness of time.)

Sometimes the two kinds of moments—the awareness of impermanence and the sense of continuity—are themselves simultaneous. Recently, my friend Annie was eating in a restaurant with her husband and two young children. It was Valentine's Day, twenty-eight years and a day since her father's death. Annie was sixteen when, on a family skiing trip, her father collapsed and died on the slopes. On this anniversary of his death, Annie hadn't spoken to her children about the grandfather they had never met, but her heart was heavy with his absence. Suddenly her daughter Millie did something she had never done before. "Look at me, I can wiggle my ears—like your father did!" she said. Indeed, it was one of the things that Annie's father used to do—but she and the children hadn't talked about it in ages. Even if this story is "only" about the remarkable attunement of a sensitive child to her mother, it seems to me nonetheless a small miracle of boundary loss. The dead grandfather wiggles the granddaughter's ears, the granddaughter reaches inside her mother's heart and names her sorrow.

Inside and outside; loss and gain; birth and death; past, present, and future: these are inextricably linked in the weaving of one generation to another. A friend told me that not long ago, she was in the shower when she found herself weeping uncontrollably. Her oldest daughter is seventeen now, and soon will be leaving home. *Who will love her as I have?* was the question pounding in my friend's heart as the water poured down on her. And then the answer came, from deep inside her: *her* daughter.

8

THE HARDEST THING

AT THE TOP of the mountain, Abraham lifted the knife and was ready to plunge it into his young son's throat, as God had commanded him. But in the next-to-last moment, a voice from heaven called out, "Abraham! Abraham! Lay not thine hand upon the lad," for now what further proof was needed of Abraham's obedience? Just then a ram appeared in the thicket nearby. Abraham slit the animal's throat and offered it in sacrifice on the pile of wood that he had prepared for the burning of Isaac.[30]

Is it possible to imagine anything more difficult for a parent than what was asked of Abraham? To be compelled to kill one's own child, to look into those eyes as they register the ultimate betrayal: it takes us to the threshold of what we can bear to imagine. Yet the Danish philosopher Søren Kierkegaard believed that for himself there would be something even harder: not to sacrifice his child, but—having been forced to such as edge—to fully take him back again. "What Abraham found easiest," he wrote, "I would have found hard: namely, to be joyful again with Isaac. . . ."[31]

As horrific as the act of sacrifice would be, it invites a raw, elemental response: a plunge into profound, unadulterated despair. But to be joyful again requires something far more complex, an immense expansiveness and flexibility, the most passionate "Yes" to life. Why? When we put ourselves in Abraham's shoes, isn't it easy to imagine that his trust in the basic moral order of the universe, his sense of what can happen, or what one can be asked to bear, would have been so violated by the experience on the mountain that he would never again be able to partake of the same innocent happiness in his son that he once had? Would anyone be shocked to learn that, in the wake of his terrible trial, he remained forever bitter, suspicious, vigilant, forever looking over his shoulder, expecting the shadow of danger to darken his home?

Abraham's situation—even with its Biblical quality of rock-hard extremity—speaks to us in our present condition. For almost any day of the week, we could pick up the newspaper and read of some terrible crime against a child that violates our sense of what is possible, endurable. Yet Kierkegaard saw it as Abraham's task *to take Isaac back*—in the fullest sense. To delight in him, to hope for him and imagine a future, to share with him the goodness of life: the plants, the animals, sunlight, honey, breezes.

The hardest thing for us, in the wake of what we have too often witnessed, is—while keeping our children safe from harm—to experience the full measure of delight in them. To gaze at them while they sleep: on their backs with limbs flung like the petals of an open flower or curled on their sides like an inner ear. To tickle them. To toss them in the air; to soap their slippery wet skin, delighting in the smell of them, and pat them dry; to fold them into our arms when they cry; to comfort them, at night when they are afraid, with the sleeping warmth of our own bodies. This is the joy that is hard to take back, without the constant pressure of that harsh, accusing gaze—but that we can take back, trusting in the pliant, self-correcting process of attunement to lead us, again and again, to the "just right."

Between the two extremes of the molested child and the withered child, we make our way. Tickling them, we listen when they call "Stop." Twirling them in the air, we gauge when their shrieks contain more fear than thrill. Patting them dry, we learn the places, unique to each child, where they don't like to be touched. Sheltering them in our arms when they cry, we remember how little their tears mean, and how much—and we let them push us away when they have had enough.

This is the middle way of the eros of parenthood. It is the way to a love that must not be abused, and that must be freed from the withering gaze. For this is what lies at the very root of human health and happiness: the love of someone in skin.

NOTES

INTRODUCTION: *The Eros of Parenthood*

1. By "natural," I mean that there is a strong, biologically supported tendency in human beings to be attracted, and become attached, to their offspring. As doctors T. Berry Brazelton and Bertrand G. Cramer write in *The Earliest Relationship*, "The baby's appearance stimulates parenting responses. The soft, rounded face; the fuzzy, fine hair and delicate skin with an incredibly soft feel; the short limbs and relatively long torso; the beautifully molded tiny hands reaching helplessly out— all of these are markers of 'babyishness.' We know now that there is a program in adults of many species that makes them want to reach out and take care of any small, helpless member of their own species with certain specific physical characteristics." Reading, Mass.: Addison-Wesley Publishing, Co., 1990, p. 47.

2. Anthropologist Meredith Small writes, "Studies of premature babies, and how best to care for them, have demonstrated that physical proximity and skin contact are essential for healthy infant development. In one experiment, premature babies were stroked and massaged on their bodies and heads for fifteen minutes four times a day. The babies became calm, showed healthy skin-color changes, and enjoyed quieter sleep than did a control group of other premature babies. And at four months of age, the stroked babies had also made greater strides in their neurological development, mental development, and reflexes than the others. In another study with a similar protocol, physically stimulated premature babies took in more formula and gained more weight than did those under standard nursing care. *Our Babies Ourselves: How Biology and Culture Shape the Way We Parent*. New York: Anchor Books, 1998, p. 36.

Commenting on similar research, Diane Ackerman writes, "The touched infants in these studies and others cried less, had better temperaments, and so were more appealing to their parents, which is important because the 7 percent of babies born prematurely figure disproportionately among those who are victims of child abuse. Children who are difficult to raise get abused more often. And people who aren't touched much as children don't touch much as adults, so the cycle continues." *A Natural History of the Senses*. New York: Random House, 1990, p. 73.

3. Ashley Montagu. *Touching: The Human Significance of the Skin*. New York: Harper & Row, 1978, p. 169.

4. Diane Ackerman. *A Natural History of Love*. New York: Vintage Books, 1995, pp. 163–4.

5. Judith Newark. "Mother's Story Sounds Kafkaesque." *St. Louis Post Dispatch*, Feb. 17, 1992, p. 4D.

6. Sigmund Freud. *Three Essays on the Theory of Sexuality*. London: Imago, 1949, p. 60.

7. As with the words "natural" and "necessary," I do not use "human" merely rhetorically. As Meredith Small has written, "How we primates nurse, carry, and protect our infants, and the fact that we extend the parenting period longer than any other animal is striking: intensive and extensive parenting is, in fact, one of the distinguishing facts of us primates, and a major mark of the human species in particular." Op. cit., p. 14.

II. *Someone In Skin*

1. Jack Kornfield. *A Path With Heart*. New York: Bantam Books, 1993, p. 334.

2. Brandt F. Steele, M.D., referring to the work of psychiatrist L.W. Sandler, writes, "He describes how the infant works on a contingency basis, giving signals and getting responses. ('If I do *a*, then *b* happens.') In an ideal mother-infant relationship, the interaction proceeds harmoniously: The baby's physiologic metabolic state is registered in the brain as "hunger discomfort" and, in turn, stimulates neuronal impulses to motor areas that instigate crying and random muscular activity. The empathic mother recognizes the baby's crying and motor activity as a sign of hunger, offers her breast, and coos and talks to her baby, holding him close, while he sucks until satisfied. He relaxes, his physiological equilibrium is restored, and he is psychologically comforted. The mother is also pleased by seeing her baby's positive response to her ministrations." "Psychodynamic and Biological Factors in Child Maltreatment." In Helfer, Mary Edna (Ed.), et al. *The Battered Child*. Chicago: The University of Chicago Press, 1997, p. 76.

3. According to pediatrician T. Berry Brazelton, "We are convinced that in a 'good' interaction, mother and baby synchronize with each other from the very beginning, and that the pathways may be set up in intrauterine life ready to be entrained, especially by the mothers, immediately after birth." Quoted in Small, Meredith. Op. cit., p. 39.

4. Daniel Goleman. *Emotional Intelligence*. New York: Bantam Books, 1997, pp. 116–117.

5. Ibid., p. 100.

6. Jessica Benjamin. *The Bonds of Love*. New York: Pantheon Books, 1998, p. 29.

7. Jessica Benjamin writes that a parent "has to accept that she cannot make a perfect world for her child (where he gets everything he wants)—and this is the blow to her own narcissism. The self-obliteration of the permissive parent who cannot face this blow does not bring happiness to the child who gets everything he demands. The parent has ceased to function as an other who sets a boundary to the child's will, and the child experiences this as an abandonment; the parent co-opts all the child's intentions by agreement, pushing him back into an illusory oneness where he has no agency of his own." Op. cit., p. 35.

8. D. W. Winnicott. Quoted in Meredith Small, *Our Babies Ourselves*. New York: Anchor Books, 1998, p. 34.

9. Technically speaking, the human infant is "secondarily altricial" which, as Meredith Small explains, means that "we had precocially adapted ancestors and then, for some reason, evolved some altricial traits that now overlay that basic pattern." Op. cit., p. 6.

10. Meredith Small. Op.cit., pp. 128–129.

11. Ashley Montagu. *Growing Young*. New York: McGraw Hill, 1981, p. 91.

12. Emmy Payne. *Katy No Pocket*. Boston: Houghton Mifflin, 1944.

13. Meredith Small. Op. cit., pp. 215–216.

14. Stendhal. *Love*. Middlesex, England: Penguin, 1975, pp. 39–40.

15. In one particularly charming study, "infants less than a day old were placed in plastic seats, and each was given a fake nipple that was wired to a tape recorder, and a pair of headphones was set on each baby's ears. If the baby sucked on the nipple for a certain length of time, the voice of the baby's mother reading a Dr. Seuss story came through the headphones; but if the baby sucked for only a short period, another woman read the story. Babies quickly learned how the system worked and they chose to call up their mothers' voices over those of the other females, and listened to those particular voices for longer periods. This was true despite the fact that these newborns were nursery babies and had so far spent very little time with their mothers." Meredith Small. Op. cit., p. 36.

As for the sense of smell, Brazelton and Cramer report that "Seven-day-old babies can reliably distinguish the odor of their mother's breast pads from those of other lactating mothers . . ." Op. cit., p. 60.

And Jessica Benjamin writes of the new mother, "she would not be surprised to hear that rigorous experiments show that her baby can already distinguish her from other people, that newborns already prefer the sight, sound, and smell of their mothers." Op. cit., p. 13.

16. "It appears that the old wives' tale that breast-feeding makes for fewer children has genuine validity. Before artificial feeding, in the hunter-gatherer world of our ancestors, the interbirth interval was probably around four years . . . It evolved that way to allow mothers to invest heavily, and for longer periods, in one off-spring at a time." Meredith Small. Op. cit., p. 201.

17. Ibid., pp. 180–181.

18. Ibid., p. 181.

19. Ibid., p. 186.

20. Brandt F. Steele. "Psychodynamic and Biological Factors in Child Maltreatment." In Mary Edna Helfer (Ed.), et al. *The Battered Child.* Chicago: Univ. of Chicago Press, 1997, p. 75.

21. Sarah Blaffer Hrdy. *Mother Nature.* New York: Pantheon, 1999, p. 116.

22. A. A. Milne. *When We Were Very Young.* New York: Penguin, 1992, p. 33.

23. D.W. Winnicott. *Talking to Parents.* Reading, Mass: Addison-Wesley, 1933, p. 74.

24. Ibid., p. 74.

25. Diane Ackerman. *A Natural History of the Senses,* p. 78.

26. Sarah Blaffer Hrdy. Op. cit., p. 139.

27. Jean-Paul Sartre. *Being and Nothingness.* New York: Washington Square Press, 1956, p. 76.

28. Matthew 26:41; Romans 7:19.

29. John 3:8.

30. Kathleen Strassen Berger. *The Developing Person.* New York: Worth Publishers, 1991, p. 236.

31. Milan Kundera. *Life Is Elsewhere.* New York: Penguin, 1986, p. 12.

32. Meredith Small. Op. cit., p. 118.

33. I read this in a magazine circa 1987, but have not been able to trace the source.

34. Mircea Eliade, ed. *The Encyclopedia of Religion.* New York: MacMillan, 1987. V. 7, p. 226.

35. Sarah Blaffer Hrdy. Op. cit., p. 97.

II. A Nest of Dreams

1. Iona Opie and Moira Tatem. *A Dictionary of Superstitions*. Oxford: Oxford University Press, 1989, p. 290.

2. Sherab Chodzin Kohn. *The Awakened One: A Life of the Buddha*. Boston: Shambhala, 1994, p. 3.

3. Luke 1: 31–32.

4. T. Berry Brazelton, and Bertrand G. Cramer. *The Earliest Relationship*. Reading, Mass.: Addison-Wesley Publishing Co., 1990, p. 24.

5. Sherab Chodzin Kohn. Op. cit., p. 3.

6. Crockett Johnson. *Harold and the Purple Crayon*. New York: Harper & Row, 1955.

7. Brazelton and Cramer, Op. cit., p. 23.

8. Bronislaw Malinowski. *Sex and Repression in Savage Society*. London: Routledge & Kegan, 1949.

9. Penny Wolfson. An unpublished memoir.

10. Lawrence Wright. "Double Mystery." *The New Yorker*. August 7, 1995, p. 44ff.

11. Anthony Mercantante. *World Mythology and Legend*. New York: Oxford University Press, 1988, p. 625.

12. Peter Carey. *Oscar and Lucinda*. New York: Vintage Books, 1997, p. 31.

13. Ibid., p. 28.

14. Jane Hamilton. *A Map of the World*. New York: Anchor Books, 1995, p. 268.

15. Stéphane Mallarmé. "La Brise marine," (1864). In *Stéphane Mallarmé: Selected Poetry and Prose*, Mary Ann Caws, Ed. New York: New Directions, 1982, p. 16.

III. Scissors and Buds

1. Lloyd De Mause, Ed. *The History of Childhood*. New York: Peter Bedrick Books, 1974, p. 38.

2. Bertolt Brecht. *The Caucasian Chalk Circle*. New York: Grove Press, 1966.

3. Adam Phillips. *Monogamy*. New York: Pantheon Books, 1996, p. 38.

4. Ibid., p. 75

5. Ibid., p. 113.

6. Penelope Leach. *Your Growing Child.* New York: Alfred A. Knopf, 1997, p. 47.

7. Adam Phillips. Op. cit., p. 113

8. Milan Kundera. Op. cit., pp.12–13.

9. Mahler et al. *The Psychological Birth of the Human Infant.* New York: Basic Books, 1975, pp. 76–108.

10. Iris Murdoch. *The Sacred and Profane Love Machine.* New York: Viking Press, 1974, p. 13.

11. Mark Epstein. *Going to Pieces Without Falling Apart.* New York: Bantam Books, 1998, p. 18.

12. Milan Kundera. Op. cit., p. 13.

13. Ibid., p. 11.

14. Bruce Lincoln in *The Encyclopedia of Religion*, Eliade Mircea, Ed. V.7, p. 236.

15. Ruth Benedict. *Patterns of Culture.* Boston: Houghton Mifflin Co., 1989, p. 26.

16. Jacob and Wilhelm Grimm. *Fairy Tales.* Cleveland and New York: The World Publishing Co., 1947, pp. 286–290.

17. Marcel Proust. *Selected Letters, 1880–1903.*The University of Chicago Press, 1983.

18. Ingri D'Aulaires and Edgar Parin. *Book of Greek Myths.* Garden City, N.Y.: Doubleday & Co., 1962, pp. 58–63.

19. Eavan Boland. "The Blossom." *The New Yorker,* July 6, 1998.

20. D. W. Winnicott. *Talking to Parents.* Reading, Mass.: Addison-Wesley Publishing Co., 1993, p. 115.

IV. *The Tears of Eros**

1. As "far away as health": from Sylvia Plath's poem "Tulips" in *Naked Poetry*, Eds., Stephen Berg and Robert Mezey. Indianapolis and New York: 1969, p. 314.

2. Gary Snyder. "The Bath," in *Contemporary American Poetry*, A. Poulin, Jr, Ed. Boston: Houghton Mifflin, 1980, pp. 477–9.

---

*The title "The Tears of Eros" is borrowed from the work of Georges Batailles. See Georges Batailles. *Les Larmes d'Eros.* Paris: Jean-Jacques Pauvert, 1961.

3. Brandt Steele. Op cit., p. 84.

4. In his book *Child Sexual Abuse*, David Finkelhor provides a very thorough discussion of the factors that contribute to child sexual abuse. Using the model of "Four Preconditions" (p. 68) in her book *The Developing Person* (p. 499), Kathleen Strassen Berger synthesizes Finkelhor's model in this very concise chart:

Preconditions for Sexual Abuse of Children

1. *Adults must have sexual feelings about children.* Such feelings are encouraged by: childhood sexual experiences; exposure to child pornography; exposure to advertising that sexualizes children; male sex-role socialization that devalues nurturance and encourages sexual aggression; "successful" adult sexual experiences with children.

2. *Adults must overcome internal inhibitions against abuse.* These inhibitions are weakened by: cultural values that accept sexual interest in children; low impulse control; alcohol; stress; low self-esteem; fear of, or frustration with, sexual relationships with adults; values that emphasize father's unquestioned authority.

3. *Adults must overcome external inhibitions to committing sexual abuse.* These inhibitions are minimized by: an absent, sick, or powerless mother; a mother who is neglectful, unaware of her children's need for protection; crowded living conditions or sleeping together; opportunities to be alone with the child; social isolation—family members have few friends; geographical isolation—family has few nearby neighbors.

4. *Adults must overcome the child's resistance.* Overcoming this barrier is easier if the child is: emotionally deprived; socially isolated; acquainted with the adult; fond of the adult; vulnerable to incentives offered by the adult; ignorant of what is happening; sexually repressed and sexually curious; weak and frightened of physical force.

Finkelhor concludes his discussion of this model with the following observation: "One thing this model should do is remind us that sexual abuse is a complex phenomenon. Factors at a number of different levels, regarding a number of individuals, come into play in determining its occurrence. Keeping such a model in mind should keep us from being seduced by simple explanations." Op. cit., p. 68.

5. In *The Developing Person*, Kathleen Strassen Berger provides a cogent discussion regarding the difficulties of quantifying the incidence of sexual abuse, which I quote in full:

"As is the case with other forms of child maltreatment, precise data on sexual abuse are hard to come by because abuse is variously defined and its occurrence is, clearly, underreported. For example, some reporting agencies include only cases in which the child has been physically penetrated; most developmentalists, on the other hand, believe that 'sexual abuse' is the appropriate label for any act in which an adult uses a child or adolescent for his or her own sexual needs, whether it be through some form of intercourse or a less serious act, such as intentional touching of clothed breasts or genitals. Nevertheless, no matter how it is defined, sexual abuse is far more common than most people believe. As Kempe and Kempe (1984) explain:

The lowest estimates based on official reports suggest that . . . the number of women who experienced some form of childhood sexual abuse is well over 4 percent, or at least 4 million women in the United States . . . . These estimates are far below the actual incidence in both sexes, since most cases of sexual victimization are never reported to anyone.

Much higher estimates have resulted when adults were asked, confidentially, if they themselves had ever been sexually abused before they were adults. In one study of college students in New England, for example, 1 in every 5 (19.2 percent) women and 1 in every 12 (8.6 percent) men acknowledged that they had been abused before age 17. (Abuse in this study included the entire spectrum of sexual exploitation, from fondling and exhibitionism to rape [Finkelhor, 1979]). The actual rates may be even higher than that, for many adults are reluctant to admit, even to themselves, that they were sexually abused as children. Memories of parents manually examining the child's genitals with great concern, or kissing the child's body in a prolonged, erotic manner, or intruding on the adolescent's privacy during bathing or dressing are likely to stir feelings of confusion and guilt, and thus not be recognized as indications of abuse—particularly by abused males who have been taught by the culture that men cannot be sexual victims. (Hunter, 1990, p. 496)."

6. Kempe and Kempe report, "Longstanding in-house sexual abuse with a loved person and/or relative is particularly damaging for the preschool child and for the young adolescent: at these two important times both need to fulfill their sexual development in an orderly and sequential way which this misfortune totally disturbs. As a result, these victims have a much higher incidence of poor sexual adjustment and difficulties in sexual identity and preference. As teens, they are likely to run away from an intolerable situation, become pregnant, get involved in delinquency such as theft and substance abuse (both alcohol and other drugs), engage in teenage prostitution and, as has been the experience for some of our clients, make a significant number of attempts at suicide. Some have, indeed, killed themselves." In Berger, Op. cit., p. 498.

The prospect is not always so grim, however. As summarized by Berger: "The psychological effects of sexual abuse depend largely on the extent and duration of the abuse, and on the reaction of other people—family as well as authorities—once the abuse is known. If the abuse is a single, nonviolent incident, and a trusted caregiver believes and reassures the victim, taking steps to make certain the incident does not happen again, the psychological damage may last only a few days. . . . Even with abuse that is more serious, children and adolescents can be quite resilient if they are cared for with sensitivity, confidentiality, and respect." Ibid.

7. As summarized in Berger: "In the public's mind, the typical case of sexual abuse involves a stranger who lures a small child away from a public place such as a playground and then forces the child to participate in some type of sex act. This,

however, is the least common form of sexual abuse. In fact, relatives and family friends are the perpetrators in more than 75 percent of all cases of sexual abuse; physical force is used in only about 5 to 10 percent of all instances, and young children are the victims less often than young adolescents are." Berger, Op. cit., p. 495.

8. Gail Ryan. "The Sexual Abuser." In Helfer et al., *The Battered Child*, p. 341.

9. Finkelhor reports, "The data collected from a variety of studies seem to support clearly the presumption that most sexual offenses against children are perpetrated by males." Op. cit., p. 177.

10. Gail Ryan. Op. cit., p. 341.

11. By "emotional intelligence" I refer to the concept made popular by Daniel Goleman in his book of that title. As he presents it, emotional intelligence is many-faceted, and among its most important facets is empathy, the ability to gauge what others are feeling and to act responsively. Op.cit.

12. Jane Lazarre. *The Mother Knot*. London: Virago, 1987, p. ix.

13. Quoted in Rozsika Parker. *Mother Love, Mother Hate: The Power of Maternal Ambivalence*. New York.: Basic Books, 1995, p. 4.

14. Ibid., p. 6.

15. Ibid., p. 7.

16. Brandt Steele. Op. cit., p. 95.

17. Rozsika Parker. Op. cit., p. 261.

18. Ibid., p. 265.

19. Ibid., pp. 264–5.

20. Ibid., p. 267.

21. Brandt Steele. Op. cit., p. 90.

22. David Finkelhor. Op. cit., p. 44.

23. Gail Ryan. Op. cit., p. 336.

24. Alice Miller. *Thou Shalt Not Be Aware: Society's Betrayal of the Child*. New York: Farrar, Straus, Giroux, 1984. *For Your Own Good*. Toronto: Collins Publishers, 1983.

25. David L. Rosenhan and Martin E. P. Seligman, *Abnormal Psychology*. New York and London: W.W. Norton and Co., 1989.

26. David Finkelhor. Op. cit., p. 26.

27. Ibid., p. 25.

28. The quote in full reads, "It is possible that girls most bombarded with sexual pro-hibitions and punishments have the hardest time developing realistic standards about what constitutes danger. Blanket taboos often incite rebelliousness, and such girls may discard all the warnings they receive from their mothers about sex, including ones about sexual victimization. Moreover, if mothers have repressed all the healthier ways of satisfying sexual curiosity, these daughters may be more vul-nerable to an adult or authority figure who appears to give them permission and opportunity to explore sex, albeit in the process of being exploited." Finkelhor concludes, "Whatever the precise mechanism, it is clear from this finding that it is not sexually lax, but sexually severe, families that foster a high risk for sexual exploitation." Ibid., pp. 26–7.

29. Ann Patchett. *The Magician's Assistant.* New York: Harcourt Brace, 1997, p. 295.

30. Rozsika Parker, Op. cit., p. 214.

31. Ibid.

32. Brazelton and Cramer. Op. cit., p. 179

33. "The person most likely to abduct a child is not a stranger but the divorced parent who has lost custody of the child. According to a report entitled 'Missing, Abducted, Runaway, and Thrownaway Children in America' issued by the U.S. Department of Justice in May 1990, in 1988 there were 354,100 'broad scope' fam-ily abductions (both serious and minor incidents) compared to 3,200 to 4,600 non-family abductions. Of this latter figure, only 200 to 300 were defined as 'stereotypical kidnappings,' i.e., longterm, long-distance, or fatal episodes." David Laskin. *Parents' Book of Child Safety.* New York: Ballantine, 1991, p. 234.

34. Sally Mann. *Immediate Family.* New York: Aperture, 1992.

35. Rozsika Parker. Op. cit., p. 267.

V. *Goldilocks's Joy*

1. Milan Kundera. Op. Cit., p. 62.

2. Theodore Roethke. "The Waking." *The Norton Introduction to Literature.* New York: W. W. Norton & Co., 1986, p. 855.

3. According to the American Academy of Pediatrics: "Up to the age of 5 or 6 years, masturbation is quite common. Young children are very curious about their bodies and find masturbation pleasurable and comforting. Youngsters are also curious about the differences between girls and boys, and thus in the pre-school and

kindergarten years they may occasionally explore each other's bodies, including their genitals.

From age 6 on, the incidence of masturbation in public tends to subside, largely because children's social awareness increases and social mores assume greater import. Masturbation in private will continue to some extent and remains natural.

Excessive or public masturbation may indicate a more serious psychological or personal problem. It could be a sign that the child is stressed or overly preoccupied with sexual thoughts, fantasies, and urges or is not receiving adequate attention at home. Sometimes masturbation is a means of providing himself with personal comfort when he is feeling overwhelmed. Masturbation could even be a tip-off to sexual abuse. Children who are being sexually abused may become overly preoccupied with their sexuality, suggesting the need for further investigation." *The American Academy of Pediatrics: The Complete and Authoritative Guide: Caring for Your School-Age Child, Ages 5-12.* Ed., Edward L. Schor, M.D., New York: Bantam, 1999, p. 71.

4. The classic work on this subject is Philippe Aries's *Centuries of Childhood: A Social History of Family Life.* New York: Vintage Books, 1962.

James Kincaid takes up the theme of childhood innocence in his book *Erotic Innocence: the Culture of Child Molesting.* Durham, N.C., and London: Duke Univ. Press, 1998.

5. *Frontline.* "Prisoners of Silence." Dec. 27, 1994. Show #1202V.

6. Philippe Aries. Op. cit., p. 100.

7. In his book *The Sexual Life of Children,* Floyd M. Martinson writes: "In communities where parents speak openly about sex and place no taboos on physical contact, exploration of each other's bodies and actual intercourse take place between children as young as five or six years of age. Sexual life begins in earnest among Trobriand Island children at six to eight years for girls and ten to twelve years for boys. Sex play includes masturbation, oral stimulation of the genitals of the same and opposite sex, and heterosexual copulation. At any time a couple may retire to the bush, the bachelors' hut, an isolated yam house, or any convenient place and there engage in prolonged sexual play. Among the Ila-speaking peoples of Africa, this is regarded as a time of preparation for adult life and mature sexual functioning. It is reported that there are no virgins among these people after the age of ten. The Lapcha of India believe that girls will not mature without the benefit of sexual intercourse. Early sex play for boys and girls in that society characteristically involves many forms of mutual masturbation and usually ends in attempted copulation. By the time they are eleven or twelve years old, most girls regularly engage in sexual intercourse." Westport, Conn., and London: Bergin & Garvey, c. 1994., p. 53.

8. Penelope Leach. Op. cit., p. 335.

9. Ibid., p. 336.

10. Francesco Alberoni. *Il Primo Amore* (First Love). Milan: Rizzoli, 1997, p. 52. As of this writing, the book is not yet available in English. I am grateful to my mother, Jean Romano, for having first brought this book to my attention and translated long passages of it.

11. Ibid., p. 32.

12. Andrew Richter. From an unfinished novel, *Victor Gets Back*. Permission to use this passage, which was sent to me by Peter Levitt, was kindly granted by the author's widow.

13. According to Martinson, "Kinsey et al. (1948) reported that orgasm is not rare among children, both boys and girls, and has been observed in boys of every age from five months on and in an infant girl of four months." In *The Sexual Life of Children*. Westport, Connecticut and London: Bergin and Garvey, 1994, p.23.

14. Andrew Samuels. *The Plural Psyche*. Quoted in Rozsika Parker, Op. cit., p. 265.

15. The point here would seem to be that within a particular culture, there can be something that is experienced as "natural modesty" and that it is quite different from a sense of shame that seems to be imposed from without.

16. Brassard and Hardy. Op. cit., p. 399.

17. David Finkelhor. Op. cit., p. 79.

18. Andre Dubus. "A Father's Story," in *GOD: Stories*. Ed., C. Michael Curtis. Boston: Houghton Mifflin, 1998, p. 45.

19. Jonathan Slavin. "The Innocence of Sexuality." Forthcoming in *Psychoanalytic Quarterly*.

20. Ibid.

VI: *Conclusion*

1. The words "because I am your grandmother" acquired more resonance for me when I came upon Clarissa Pinkola Estes' discussion of "La Mariposa," the Butterfly Woman who is an important figure among the desert tribes of northern Mexico and the American Southwest. Describing the ritual Butterfly dance, Estes writes: "The butterfly dancer must be old because she represents the soul that is old. She is wide of thigh and broad of rump because she carries much. Her gray hair certifies that she need no longer observe taboos about touching others. She is allowed to touch everyone: boys, babies, men, women, children, girl children, the old, the ill, and the dead. The Butterfly Woman can touch everyone. It is her privilege to touch all, at last. This is her power. Hers is the body of La Mariposa, the butterfly." *Women Who Run With the Wolves*. New York: Ballantine Books, 1995, p. 210.

2. From an interview with artist Louise Bourgeois. Reprinted in *Harpers*, Sept. 1998, p. 34.

3. I have not been able to find the source of this quote, which I copied down in a notebook while studying the work of Dogen in a Soto Zen monastery in Northern California in 1978. It is possible that I wrote it down during a lecture.

4. *Herald Tribune*. August 21, 1999, p. 3A.

5. David Finkelhor. Op. cit., p. 31.

6. Ibid., p. 13. Kathleen Strassen Berger writes, "One researcher finds that incest is rare in families in which the fathers were involved in infant caregiving: presumably these fathers see their children in protective and nurturant ways, which makes sexual feelings unlikely and inhibition against them high." Op. cit., p. 500.

7. Robin Karr-Morse and Meredith S. Wiley. *Ghosts from the Nursery*. New York: The Atlantic Monthly Press, 1997, p. 235.

8. *USA Weekend*. February 6–8, 1999, p. 22.

9. Jonathan Slavin. Op. cit.

10. Joseph Bobrow, Ph.D., in conversation.

11. Ruth S. Kempe in *The Battered Child*, p. 543.

12. Brandt F. Steele. Op. cit., p. 74.

13. Robin Karr-Morse and Meredith S. Wiley, Op. cit., p. 184.

14. Marla R. Brassard and David B. Hardy. Op. cit., p. 399.

15. Ibid., p. 398.

16. David Finkelhor writes, "One large class of risk factors is anything that makes a child feel emotionally insecure, needy, or unsupported . . . A child who feels needy will be more vulnerable to the ploys of a potential abuser: the offers of attention, affection, or bribes. A child who feel unsupported will not have someone to turn to about the abuse or will be more afraid to tell. Children who are emotionally abused, who are disabled or disadvantaged, are all at risk for these reasons. Several of the factors we found associated with abuse . . . having few friends, not receiving physical affection from a father, not being close to a mother, or having her be punitive—fall into this category. They all erode a child's ability to resist" Op. cit., p. 61.

17. Marla R. Brassard and David B. Hardy. Op. cit., p. 398.

18. Robin Karr-Morse and Meredith S. Wiley. Op. cit., p. 184.

19. Ibid., p. 269.

20. There is a growing body of research that confirms the intimate relation between biology and emotion in human development. As Karr-Morse and Wiley write, "Perhaps the most disturbing implication from the research on the brain's adaptation to chronic fear and anger is the growing evidence that it may be altering the course of human evolution. Not only can the changes in hormone levels be permanent in an individual's lifetime, the altered chemical profile may actually be encoded in the genes and passed on to new generations, which may become successively more aggressive." Op. cit., p. 169.

21. *The New Yorker*, cartoon by Robert Mankoff. August 4, 1997, p. 25.

22. Gail Ryan. Op. cit., p. 332.

23. James Wright, "The Blessing." In *Contemporary American Poetry*. Ed., A Poulin Jr. Boston: Houghton Mifflin, 1981.

24. Desmond Morris. *The Human Animal*. New York: Crown Publishers, Inc., 1994, p. 130.

25. Diane Ackerman. *A Natural History of Love*, p. 162.

26. Russell Schweickart. Quoted in *Sunbeams: A Book of Quotations*. Ed., Sy Safransky. Berkeley: North Atlantic Books, 1990, p. 85.

27. Virginia Woolf. *A Writer's Diary*. New York: Harcourt Brace Jovanovich, 1981, p. 96.

28. Philip Levine. "The Secret of Their Voices." *The Names of the Lost*. New York: Atheneum, 1978, pp. 10–11.

29. R.D. Laing. *The Politics of the Family*. New York: Vintage Books, 1972. p. TK

30. Genesis 22.

31. Søren Kierkegaard. *Fear and Trembling* and *The Sickness Unto Death*. Princeton, N.J.: Princeton University Press, 1974, p. 46.

BIBLIOGRAPHY

Ackerman, Diane. *A Natural History of Love*. New York: Vintage Books, 1995. *A Natural History of the Senses*. New York: Random House, 1990.

Alberoni, Francesco. *Il Primo Amore*. Milan: Rizzoli, 1997.

Aries, Philippe. *Centuries of Childhood: A Social History of Family Life*. New York: Vintage Books, 1962.

Bataille, Georges. *The Tears of Eros*. San Francisco: City Lights Books, 1989.

Benedict, Ruth. *Patterns of Culture*. Boston: Houghton Mifflin Co., 1989.

Benjamin, Jessica. *The Bonds of Love*. New York: Pantheon Books, 1998.

Berger, Kathleen Strassen. *The Developing Person*. New York: Worth Publishers, 1991.

Blaffer Hrdy, Sarah. *Mother Nature*. New York: Pantheon, 1999.

Boland, Eaven. "The Blossom." *The New Yorker*. July 6, 1998.

Brassard, Marla R. and Hardy, David B. "Psychological Maltreatment." *The Battered Child*. Ed., Mary Edna Heifer et al. Chicago: University of Chicago Press, 1997.

Brazelton, T. Berry and Cramer, Bertrand G. *The Earliest Relationship*. Reading, Mass.: Addison-Wesley Publishing Co., 1990.

Brecht, Bertolt. *The Caucasian Chalk Circle*. New York: Grove Press, 1966.

Carey, Peter. *Oscar and Lucinda*. New York: Vintage Books, 1997.

D'Aulaires, Ingri and Edgar Parin. *Book of Greek Myths*. Garden City, New York: Doubleday & Co., 1962.

De Mause, Lloyd, Ed. *The History of Childhood*. New York: Peter Bedrick Books, 1974.

Dubus, Andre. "A Father's Story." *GOD: Stories*. Ed., C. Michael Curtis. Boston: Houghton Mifflin, 1998.

Eliade, Mircea. *The Encyclopedia of Religion*. New York: MacMillan, 1987.

Epstein, Mark. *Going to Pieces Without Falling Apart*. New York: Bantam Books, 1998.

Estes, Clarissa Pinkola. *Women Who Run With the Wolves*. New York: Ballantine Books, 1995.

Finkelhor, David. *Child Sexual Abuse: New Theory and Research*. New York: Free Press, 1984.

Goleman, Daniel. *Emotional Intelligence*. New York: Bantam Books, 1997.

Grimm, Jacob and Wilhelm. *Fairy Tales*. Cleveland and New York: The World Publishing Co., 1947.

Hamilton, Jane. *A Map of the World*. New York: Anchor Books, 1995.

Johnson, Crockett. *Harold and the Purple Crayon*. New York: Harper & Row, 1955.

Karr-Morse, Robin and Meredith S. Wiley. *Ghosts from the Nursery*. New York: The Atlantic Monthly Press, 1997.

Kierkegaard, Søren. *Fear and Trembling* and *The Sickness Unto Death*. Princeton, N.J.: Princeton University Press, 1974.

Kincaid, James. *Erotic Innocence. The Culture of Child Molesting*. Durham, N.C., and London: Duke University Press, 1988.

Kohn, Sherab Chodzin. *The Awakened One: A Life of the Buddha*. Boston: Shambhala, 1994.

Kornfield, Jack. *A Path With Heart*. New York: Bantam Books, 1993.

Kundera, Milan. *Life Is Elsewhere*. New York: Penguin Books, 1986.

Laing, R.D. *The Politics of the Family*. New York: Vintage Books, 1972.

Laskin, David. *Parents' Book of Child Safety*. New York: Ballantine, 1991.

Lazarre, Jane. *The Mother Knot*. London: Virago, 1987.

Leach, Penelope. *Your Growing Child*. New York: Alfred A. Knopf, 1991.

Levine, Philip. "The Secret of Their Voices." *The Names of the Lost*. New York: Atheneum, 1978.

Mahler, et al. *The Psychological Birth of the Human Infant*. New York: Basic Books, 1975.

Malinowski, Bronislaw. *Sex and Repression in Savage Society*. London: Routledge & Kegan, 1949.

Mallarmé, Stéphane. "*La Brise Marine*."

Mann, Sally. *Immediate Family*. New York: Aperture, 1992.

Martinson, Floyd M. *The Sexual Life of Children*. Westport, Connecticut, and London: Bergin & Garvey, 1994.

Mercantante, Anthony S. *World Mythology and Legend*. New York: Oxford Univ. Press, 1998.

Miller, Alice. *For Your Own Good*. Toronto: Collins Publishers, 1983. *Thou Shalt Not Be Aware. Society's Betrayal of the Child*. New York: Farrar, Straus, Giroux, 1984.

Milne, A.A. *When We Were Very Young*. New York: Penguin, 1992.

Montagu, Ashley. *Touching: The Human Significance of the Skin*. New York: Harper & Row, 1978. *Growing Young*. N.Y.: McGraw-Hill, 1981.

Morris, Desmond. *The Human Animal*. New York: Crown Publishers, Inc., 1994.

Murdoch, Iris. *The Sacred and Profane Love Machine*. New York: Viking Press, 1974.

Opie, Iona and Tatem, Moira. *A Dictionary of Superstitions*. Oxford, England: Oxford University Press, 1989.

Parker, Rozsika. *Mother Love, Mother Hate: The Power of Maternal Ambivalence*. New York: Basic Books, 1995.

Patchett, Ann. *The Magician's Assistant*. New York: Harcourt Brace, 1997.

Payne, Emmy. *Katy No Pocket*. Boston: Houghton Mifflin, 1944.

Phillips, Adam. *Monogamy*. New York: Pantheon Books, 1996.

Plath, Sylvia. "Tulips." *Naked Poetry*. Eds., Stephen Berg and Robert Mezey. Indianapolis and New York: 1969.

Proust, Marcel. *Selected Letters, 1880–1903*. Chicago: The University of Chicago Press, 1983.

Roethke, Theodore. "The Waking." *The Norton Introduction to Literature*. New York: W. W. Norton & Co., 1986.

Rosenhan, David L., and Martin E. P. Seligman. *Abnormal Psychology*. New York and London: W. W. Norton & Co., 1989.

Ryan, Gail. "The Sexual Abuser." *The Battered Child*. Eds., Mary Edna Helfer et al., Chicago and London: The University of Chicago Press, 1997.

Sartre, Jean-Paul. *Being and Nothingness*. New York: Washington Square Press, 1956.

Schor, Edward L., M.D., Ed.-in-chief, The American Academy of Pediatrics. *The Complete and Authoritative Guide: Caring for Your School-Age Child, Ages 5-12*. New York: Bantam, 1999.

Slavin, Jonathan. "The Innocence of Sexuality." Forthcoming in *Psychoanalytic Quarterly*.

Small, Meredith. *Our Babies Ourselves: How Biology and Culture Shape the Way We Parent*. New York: Anchor Books, 1998.

Snyder, Gary. "The Bath." *Contemporary American Poetry*. Ed., A. Poulin, Jr. Boston: Houghton Mifflin, 1980.

Steele, Brandt F., M.D. "Psychodynamic and Biological Factors in Child Maltreatment." In *The Battered Child*. Mary Edna Helfer, Ed., et al. Chicago and London: The University of Chicago Press, 1997.

Stendhal. *Love*. Middlesex, England: Penguin, 1975.

Winnicott, D. W. *Talking to Parents*. Reading, Mass.: Addison-Wesley, 1933.

Wolfson, Penny. An unpublished memoir.

Wright, James. "The Blessing." In *Contemporary American Poetry*. Ed., A. Poulin Jr. Boston: Houghton Mifflin, 1981.

Woolf, Virginia. *A Writer's Diary*. New York: Harcourt Brace Jovanovich, 1981.

ABOUT THE AUTHOR

NOELLE OXENHANDLER has been a longtime contributor to *The New Yorker* and is the author of *A Grief Out of Season*. A regular guest teacher in the graduate writing program at Sarah Lawrence College in New York, she makes her home in northern California, where she runs a private writing workshop. She is the mother of a daughter.